W9-BSL-340

Pamela Smith's

The Good Life

A Healthy Cookbook

CREATION HOUSE
BOOKS ABOUT SPIRIT-LED LIVING
ORLANDO, FLORIDA

Printed in the United States of America
Library of Congress Catalog Card Number: 95-068315
International Standard Book Number: 0-88419-400-0

Creation House
Strang Communications Company
600 Rinehart Road
Lake Mary, FL 32746
Phone: (407) 333-3132
Fax: (407) 333-7100

Meal pictured on cover: Chicken Marco (pg. 105)

Cover design: Monica Nagy
Interior design: Beth Thomas
Typography: Barbara Dycus
Photography: Debi Harbin

Special thanks and love to my terrific daughters, Nicole and Danielle; to Larry, my husband and friend; and to my incredible mom, Mae Martin. They are the four happiest people in my world since *The Good Life* is complete and we can get back to living it! Thanks for cheering, loving and helping a slightly frayed, but never-forgetting-her-family lady. I love you immensely.

To Jenny Phillips, who knows all and loves unconditionally. I can never fully express how much I love and appreciate you and how thankful I am to have a "sister."

To Kent, Lynn, Rebecca and Sam Shoemaker, our forever friends, with whom we've certainly experienced and enjoyed the good life. Thank you for good times and love.

To Dan, Ken and Pat, Shelby and Betty, and Wayne and Sherry, the unswerving Martin family, who have given me an undergirding of love, help and support that can never be appreciated enough. I love you so very much.

To Carolyn Coats, who never hesitates to help and never ceases to care. I have an emotional, heartfelt need to say, "Thanks — you're incredible!"

To Marco Barbitta, who always keeps me in line (and reminds me he taught me everything I know about food). Stay well, stay happy and stay in touch!

To Deborah, Barb, Ginger, Christina, Tom, Robin, Leyna, Rob and the entire terrific Creation House staff; to Mark, Beth and Monica of Strang Communications for their awesome design work; and, of course, to Debbie — you've gone the extra mile in making this book very special and full of impact. Your patience, diligence and desire for excellence go far beyond the written word.

To all of Danielle and Nicole's friends (Laurie, Mary, Sarah, Karin, Kristie, Josh and others) who have been a terrific taste-test team for many of these recipes. I love the smiles and hugs for "Mrs. Smith."

To Blaine and all of my other special friends at the New Business Division, Darden Restaurants, who gave me a burst of culinary creativity and a whole new view of the Caribbean.

To Lina Del Bondio, who loves my stories and my food, and loves telling people, "You don't have to eat everything on your plate. Sometimes it's there just to look pretty."

Beef Tip Skewers (pg. 121)

CONTENTS

THYME

Good Living, Good Cooking

THE FOUNDATION

Do you ever feel as if there's a conspiracy to keep you confused about good eating for good health? If so, you're not alone! Daily newspapers, popular magazines, radio and TV talk shows all promote a wide range of opinions and theories. It seems almost impossible to separate fact from fiction.

How can I have more energy? How do I lose weight and keep it off? How do I keep my cholesterol and blood pressure in check? How can I take charge of the stresses of life — or my hormones? These are the questions many of us ask about nutritious eating.

But today's fad diet designers cannot answer these questions. Instead, we need to consider how our bodies were designed to be fed and fueled.

Our problem is not just that we're eating unhealthy food or even that we're eating too much. It's that most of us push our bodies through the day, living on fumes rather than fuel. When we finally eat, it's too much too late.

In my book *Food for Life* I introduced you to seven secrets for staying fit and fueled that, if used, will help your body work right. On the following page you will find a chart listing these seven secrets. I developed this list to help my clients embrace a strategy of fulfilled and effective living — to teach them to "fuel the power." It's based on meeting the body's needs with the right fuel at the right time in the right balance.

Unlike diets you may have followed in the past, I put emphasis on *eating* rather than *avoiding* food: what to eat (rather than what to avoid), when to eat and why you should be eating it.

You can count the calories and nutrients taken in, but what really matters is which calories are burned and which nutrients are used. Our stressful nineties lifestyles have slowed our metabolic rates to a snail's pace, resulting in fats being stored rather than burned for energy. The body's cocooning effect of storing energy is the result of constant stress demands and not nearly enough energy supply to meet the body's needs. The body was designed to slow itself down as a protective response to such energy deficits. Erratic eating patterns keep our metabolisms stuck in low gear, storing away every meal as if it were our last.

Regardless of the number of calories consumed in a meal, the body can use only a small amount of energy, protein and nutrients quickly. The rest is thrown off as waste or stored as fat. We Americans typically go for long periods

THE SEVEN SECRETS FOR STAYING FIT, FUELED AND FREE

1. **Eating Is Better Than Starving**
   - Eat Early
   - Eat Often
   - Eat Balanced
   - Eat Lean
2. Water Is the Beverage of Champions
3. Variety Is the Spice of Life
4. Stress Is a Stretch That Makes You Snap or Makes You Strong!
5. Exercise Is Vital to Well-Being
6. Rest Is the Key to Recharging
7. The Good Life Is an Inside-Out Job

without eating and then try to make up for it with large meals. This lopsided way of eating robs the body of vital nutrients. We not only go wrong in how much we eat or what we eat, but we also overeat at the wrong times. The vast majority of us get three-fourths of our calories after six o'clock in the evening — again, too much, too late.

To get our bodies working with us and for us, we need to *eat early, eat often, eat balanced* and *eat lean*. In the following pages I explain each of these four key concepts in detail.

1. Eat Early

Your mother was right — you do need breakfast! Breakfast calories are like a smart investment: The return is greater than the initial deposit.

We don't save calories by skipping breakfast. On the contrary, because breakfast starts up our metabolisms for the new day, it helps ensure that the rest of the day's calories are burned more efficiently — as energy — rather than stored as fat. Breakfast also increases our ability to concentrate and keeps our appetites under control.

Our bodies respond differently to small meals than big meals. After a big meal, the body puts out an excess of insulin, which is a fat storage hormone. Extra insulin prevents fat cells from releasing fatty acid into the bloodstream where it can be picked up by other tissues and burned for energy. In other words, excess insulin released at large meals causes fat to be stored in the body rather than used for energy.

Eating smaller meals more often is a lot like throwing logs on our slow-burning metabolic fires, helping them burn better and brighter. It all starts with breakfast. We must "break the fast" with breakfast to rev up the body. If you miss breakfast, you'll be running with no fuel for sixteen to eighteen hours, the time since your last meal — probably dinner the night before. You drag through the day tired, irritable, unmotivated and unable to concentrate. Who wants to have a day like that?

Remember that breakfast does not have to be a time-robber — it is actually a time-giver. Because a smart breakfast stabilizes your blood chemistries, you will have more energy and alertness, and will even be able to think more clearly.

Breakfast makes you more productive and effective, helping you do what you do quickly, with fewer mistakes. How's that for a wise time investment?

You may not feel hungry in the morning. If that's the case, you simply need to wake up your natural appetite with a balanced breakfast. Breakfast will neutralize the body's blood sugars and stomach acids and get you out of that early morning slowed-down state.

Do you complain that eating breakfast *makes* you feel hungry throughout the day? It should. Not only does starving in the morning slow your metabolism, but the result is the use of your own tissue for energy. This deprivation releases waste products into your system that temporarily depress your appetite and give you a feeling of fullness. You can continue to starve without feeling hungry for hours. Sadly, this backfires later in the day.

The reason you get hungry so soon after you have eaten breakfast is that you have taken yourself out of the starved mode and lifted up your blood sugars. What goes up *will* come down. Even with a correctly balanced breakfast your blood sugar will crest and fall within three hours or so. (That's the time to have a power snack!)

If you have early morning appointments or an on-the-go family with little time for breakfast, eat breakfast on the run if you must. It can be a meal as simple as toast with melted cheese, fruited yogurt with a muffin, or whole grain cereal and fruit with skim milk. Even a turkey sandwich or slice of pizza will do. The key is to eat and eat soon — within a half hour after getting up from your night's sleep.

Plan a breakfast plate that is balanced. A balanced breakfast supplies adequate carbohydrates and protein — you can't live well on the fumes from a piece of toast or a cup of coffee.

Serve three different foods at breakfast: a quick energy-starting simple carbohydrate (fruit or juice), a long-lasting complex carbohydrate (grains, cereal, bread or muffins) and a power-building protein (dairy, eggs or meats). Again, don't be concerned if the meals are not made up of traditional choices. There is nothing wrong with pizza for breakfast or cereal for dinner! Just remember, the best breakfast foods are the ones that you will eat.

Try some of the "grab and go" breakfasts beginning on page 50. They are designed to stoke up your metabolism and start your day with boundless energy to meet the demands placed upon you. They make breakfast time-efficient and delicious!

2. Eat Often

Once you start with breakfast, eating mini-meals often throughout the day, about every two-and-a-half to three hours, will keep your metabolism and energy burning high and your appetite in better control. This power snacking also stabilizes insulin to low levels in the bloodstream — meaning less fat will be stored and more energy and more fat will be burned. That's good news!

Once you start power snacking, your body will reward you with higher energy and metabolism levels.

Many of us have grown up with a three-square-meals mentality, thinking snacks are harmful. Yet the truth about snacking is this: Wisely chosen snacks are a necessary part of a healthy diet, not a special treat or an afterthought.

One of the biggest health mistakes you can make is to starve throughout the day, saving up calories for the evening. This throws off your metabolism and sets you up for binge-like eating.

Above all else, remember your body was created to survive. It reads long hours without food as starvation and will slow your metabolic rate to preserve your valuable muscle mass. Then it plays a trick on itself and turns first to the muscle mass for energy and last to your fat stores!

Several small meals deposit less fat than one or two large meals, even if you eat the same amount of the same foods. And smaller, more frequent meals will create more energy, leaner bodies and better blood chemistries. Power snacking prevents plummeting blood sugars that leave you grouchy and craving sweets.

I plan my day to include three meals and three to four snacks (one mid-morning; one or two mid-afternoon, depending on the lateness of the dinner hour; and one bedtime snack). By planning to eat the right foods at the right times, you gain freedom from the constant battle that can rage between your appetite and your eating, lack of eating or compulsive overeating. Wise snacking through the day will keep an out-of-control appetite at bay!

Stock your kitchen with healthful and wise snack combos. Keep your snacks ready by placing one portion in a zip-top bag in your refrigerator or pantry. Tuck them into your briefcase or purse to take with you when you go to work.

Because healthy snacking is such a necessary part of a healthy diet, don't waste it on the typical snack foods that are low in essential nutrients yet loaded with salt, sugar, fat and calories. If only soda, chips, cookies and candy are available, that's what you will reach for. Wise Solomon seemed to know this, writing with inspiration: "He who is full loathes honey, but to the hungry even what is bitter tastes sweet" (Proverbs 27:7). No need to set these foods up as "forbidden fruit" — just focus on foods that bless your body.

POWER SNACK CHOICES

Baked Tostitos or Guiltless Gourmet tortilla chips with 1/3 cup fat-free bean dip and salsa

1/2 sandwich on whole grain kaiser roll or whole wheat bread, made with:
turkey and mozzarella (with light mayo and touch of mustard)
ham and fat-free cheese (with light mayo and touch of mustard)

1/2 cinnamon raisin bagel with light cream cheese and all-fruit spread

Whole grain cereal with skim milk

Date Cheese Spread (pg. 53) and whole grain crackers

Charlie's Lunch Kit or small pop-top can of tuna with whole grain crackers

Harvest Crisps crackers or Raisin Squares cereal with Laughing Cow Light cheese wedge or low-fat string cheese

Health Valley graham crackers or Quaker Banana Nut rice cakes with 2 Tbsp. natural peanut butter

Crispbread crackers with sliced turkey and Dijon mustard

Light popcorn with 2 Tbsp. fresh grated Parmesan cheese

Stonyfield Farm yogurt or plain, nonfat yogurt mixed with all-fruit spread

12 grapes or 10 fresh strawberries with low-fat string cheese or Armenian cheese

Gazpacho in cups with low-fat string cheese

Fruit shake (skim milk blended with frozen fruit and vanilla)

Low-fat cheese tortellini salad in vinaigrette with carrots and celery

Dill tortilla rolls: tortilla with fat-free cream cheese, lemon juice, fresh dill and creole seasoning

Trail mix (1 cup unsalted, dry-roasted peanuts; 1 cup unsalted, dry-roasted, shelled sunflower seeds; and 2 cups raisins) — make in abundance and bag into 1/4 cup portions

Homemade low-fat bran muffin and skim milk

Watch out for many of the fat-free foods that are becoming such a booming business. Many companies pander to the American sweet tooth and load them with sugar.

It is more nutritious to eat fresh fruit than fat-free (but probably sugar-laden) cupcakes. We need to learn to make good food choices. Manufactured foods, such as fat-free baked goods, just cultivate our taste for sweets. It makes no sense to trade a diet moderate in fat for one higher in sugar.

3. Eat Balanced

Balance is more than a wide variety of foods displayed on a pretty plate; it's giving our bodies the right foods at the right times. This means a balance of carbohydrates and proteins at every meal and snack.

These nutrients have two different yet equally vital functions. Carbohydrates are 100 percent pure energy — they are your body's fuel, designed to burn fast, clean and purely. Proteins, however, are your body's building blocks. They are designed to build lean body tissues, strengthen immunities, balance fluids and boost the metabolism.

The healthy goal is to choose carbohydrates in the most whole form possible and thus benefit from both their nutrients and fiber. This means eating whole grains when you can, such as brown rice, oats and 100 percent whole grain breads, crackers, cereals and pastas. Eat fruits and vegetables well-washed with their skins on, and choose the fruit rather than the fruit juice.

In addition, choose power-building proteins in the lowest-fat form that you can, and prepare them with the lowest-fat cooking methods possible. As much as you need carbohydrates to burn and proteins to build, it's fat that makes you fat! Yet it isn't worth sacrificing your protein intake to cut back on fat. Protein is too vital to skip. Just shift to proteins that are lean or, in the case of dairy products, that are made from skim milk.

On this page and the next I have included charts for power proteins and energy-giving carbohydrates. Be sure to include foods from these sources with every meal and snack.

Good life eating is based on this essential balance. In the recipes in this book, you'll see a breakdown of complex carbohydrates and simple carbohydrates for each meal. You'll also see a strong emphasis on variety — the time-tested answer to the "How do I keep healthy?" question.

No one food is perfect; no one food contains all the nutrients we need. But be sure to provide whole grain, low-fat meals that are full of a variety of brightly colored fruits and vegetables. The bright coloring is a sign of the nutritional content of a vegetable or fruit. Generally the more vivid the coloring, the more essential nutrients it holds. That deep orange or red coloring in carrots, sweet potatoes, cantaloupes, apricots, peaches and strawberries signals their vitamin A content. Dark green, leafy vegetables such as greens, spinach, romaine lettuce, brussels sprouts and broccoli are loaded with vitamin A as well as folic acid. Vitamin C is found in more than just citrus; it is also power-packed into strawberries, cantaloupes, tomatoes, green peppers and broccoli. You may not be able to tell a book by its cover, but you *can* tell the power of a fruit or veggie by its color!

Your health doesn't depend on a single food or a single meal. Healthy variety occurs when you make good food choices over a period of time. Because there is no one food you must have to survive, substitution is your best strategy. Mixing and matching foods for healthy variety over a period of one to two days is the name of the game.

4. Eat Lean

Most people today can tell you that fat is the

POWER PROTEINS

Each serving equals 1 ounce of protein (7 grams)

- nonfat milk or nonfat plain yogurt . . . . .4 oz.
- low-fat cheeses .1 oz. (or 1/4 cup grated)
- 1 percent low-fat or nonfat cottage cheese or part-skim or fat-free ricotta . . . . . . .1/4 cup
- eggs (particularly use egg whites) 1
- fish . . . . .1 oz. (or 1/4 cup flaked fish)
- seafood (crab, lobster) . . . . .1/4 cup
- seafood (clams, shrimp, oysters or scallops) 5
- turkey, cornish hens . . . . .1 oz. (or 1/4 cup chopped)
- chicken . . . . .1 oz. (or 1/4 cup chopped)
- beef, pork, lamb, veal (lean, trimmed) . . .1 oz.
- legumes . . . . .1/4 cup (black beans, garbanzo beans, Great Northern beans, kidney beans, lentils, navy beans, peanuts, red beans, split peas, soybeans and soy products such as tofu and soy milk)

  Although a plant food, legumes contain valuable protein if eaten with a grain — corn, wheat, rice, oats — or a seed — pumpkin, sunflower, sesame.
- natural peanut butter . . . . .2 Tbsp.

nutritional bad guy of the nineties. It's hard to pick up a magazine or newspaper without reading something about the wisdom of cutting the fat from our diets. But the truth is, it can seem like a pretty tall order; deciding to eat less fat seems simple, but it isn't.

I was raised on fried chicken, mashed potatoes and gravy, and green beans cooked in bacon grease. Maybe you were too. Embracing a lifestyle of better eating and better living meant a lot more to me than cutting out candy bars; it meant finding ways to enjoy flavorful foods without grease. I was thankful that God made eating a pleasurable experience, and I was not about to accept a life filled with dry, tasteless food that resembled cardboard. Even though I envisioned changes, I still had to establish new ways of shopping, cooking and dining out. Today I hear constant pleas for help from frustrated and overwhelmed people who are seeking to do the same thing. It has convinced me that the story about fat has become a version of "The Good, the Bad...and the Very Confusing!"

The most up-to-date research continues to point to fat as paving the road to obesity and disease, simply telling us that *fat makes us fat* and

ENERGY-GIVING CARBOHYDRATES

SIMPLE CARBOHYDRATES
(Fruits and Nonstarchy Vegetables)

All fruits and fruit juices

apples, apricots, bananas, berries, cherries, dates, grapefruit, grapes, kiwis, lemons, limes, melons, nectarines, oranges, peaches, pears, pineapples, plums, raisins

(Generally one serving of simple carbohydrate is obtained from 1/2 cup fruit, 1/2 cup fruit juice or 1/8 cup dried fruit. This gives 10 grams of simple carbohydrate.)

Nonstarchy vegetables

asparagus, beets, broccoli, brussels sprouts, cabbage, carrots, cauliflower, celery, green beans, green leafy vegetables, kale, mushrooms, okra, onions, snow peas, sugar snap peas, summer squash, tomatoes and zucchini

(Generally one serving of simple carbohydrate is obtained from 1/2 cup cooked vegetables or 1 cup raw vegetables or juice. This gives 10 grams of simple carbohydrate.)

COMPLEX CARBOHYDRATES
(Grains and Starchy Vegetables)

Grains

The following amounts provide one serving of complex carbohydrate, giving 15 grams:

barley, bulgur, couscous, grits, kasha, millet or polenta, cooked ...... 1/2 cup
bread .... 1 slice
cereals .... 1 oz.
(1/4 cup of a concentrated cereal such as Grape-Nuts or granola, 1/2 to 3/4 cup flaked cereals and 1 cup puffed cereals)
crackers or mini-rice cakes 5
crispbread or rice cakes 2
oats, uncooked .... 1/3 cup
pasta or rice, cooked .... 1/2 cup
fat-free tortillas (flour or corn) 1
wheat germ .... 1/4 cup

Starchy vegetables

black-eyed peas, corn, green peas, lima beans, parsnips, potatoes (white and sweet), rutabagas, turnips and winter squash

(Generally one serving of complex carbohydrate is obtained from 1/2 cup cooked starchy vegetables, giving 15 grams.)

unhealthy. The excess fat calories we consume are converted and stored as fat more readily than those from other sources. Fat is a more concentrated source of calories (all fats contain twice as many calories as equal amounts of carbohydrates or proteins, about 9 calories per gram, or 120 calories per tablespoon). In healthy weight loss, trimming the fat is more important than trimming calories.

Of course, fatness or thinness is not the only issue involved in food choices. Even if you have been blessed with a metabolism that burns brightly, allowing you to maintain your weight easily, excess fat intake can cause problems. You may not see the problems on the scale or on your waistline, but you'll want to consider these vital facts about fat and your health: Excess fat intake increases your cholesterol levels and your risk of heart disease and stroke. It has been indicated in cancer and gallbladder disease. Excess fat intake, particularly saturated fat, has been shown to elevate blood pressure, regardless of weight, in addition to increasing the susceptibility to diabetes in those genetically inclined. It's no wonder that Leviticus 3:17 warns, "This is a lasting ordinance for the generations to come, wherever you live: You must not eat any fat." Wow!

If your cholesterol count is normal, your blood pressure low and your family tree free of cancer, heart disease, and diabetes, these facts may seem irrelevant to you. Changing to a low-fat lifestyle may not be your priority. But let me encourage you to make it one.

Being free from all risk factors is rare, but it is a blessing that can be enhanced with a healthy way of eating. Preventing the diseases of tomorrow is wonderful, but the reason to change is for today!

Eating a balanced diet low in fat, yet high in whole grains, fruits and vegetables, gives us higher levels of energy and alertness, better stress management and even improved memory and sleep. These are the reasons I prescribe a low-fat eating plan for even my thinnest athletes.

These facts point to a less-is-more lifestyle choice: *Less* fat in our diet means *more* wellness and protection from disease and weight struggles. Of course, entering this low-fat lifestyle can be tricky when it is estimated that today's American takes in approximately 40 percent of his daily calories from fat. Chances are good that you may be eating more than you even realize. A typical adult eats the fat equivalent of one stick of butter a day!

The first line of defense in fighting any battle is to identify your enemies. In the war against excess fat, the enemy's hideouts are meats, poultry, dairy products and nuts, along with butter and oil toppings. Fruits, vegetables and grains have little or no fat, as long as they are not fattened up with butters and sauces. Like any worthy goal, reducing your personal fat intake requires some effort and commitment — to learn new ways to season foods without fat, to order more healthfully at restaurants and to discover positive snack foods. Focus on good foods that are well-prepared, and your desires will shift back to how you were created. High-fat foods will have less and less taste appeal as you begin to eat foods that give you energy, better digestion and a sense of well-being.

HOW MUCH IS ENOUGH?

Experts recommend limiting fat intake to between 25 and 30 percent of total calorie limit. Moderately active women need approximately 2,000 calories daily for maintaining weight; moderately active men need 2,500 calories. For weight loss goals, a good daily limit for women is 1,200 calories; for men, 1,500 calories. To determine the 25 percent fat allowance, use this formula:

25 percent x 1,200 calories = 300 calories
300 calories ÷ 9 calories per gram of fat =
33 grams maximum fat suggested each day.

Daily Calories	Grams of Fat per Day
1,200 calories	33 grams
1,500 calories	42 grams
1,800 calories	50 grams
2,000 calories	56 grams
2,500 calories	69 grams

Be assured that the benefits far exceed the effort. It's exciting to learn that everyday foods are full of potent healing ingredients that boost energy and help you feel and look better. With the creativity and innovation available today, tasty foods that are good for you are popping up everywhere!

Don't Accept Life Imprisonment

Changing your eating habits does not have to become duty or bondage. Choosing to eat the right foods at the right times actually is a step toward freedom! Rather than binding you, eating well makes you free — free from overeating, dieting and a life void of energy and vitality.

Yet it's not uncommon to think that if food tastes good, it's bad for you; and if it's good for you, it's going to taste and look like cardboard. That's what I call a prison built of rice cakes.

Do you feel that the choice to eat nutritiously is dooming you to a tasteless dungeon? Do you think that if food tastes like plastic, it must be nutritious; and if it's flavorful, it can't possibly be good for you?

If your answer is yes to these questions, and these thoughts mirror your attitudes about nutrition, you have lots of company. In a 1990 Gallup Poll survey, 56 percent of adults said they no longer found eating pleasurable because of their worries about fats, cholesterol and calories. Nearly half said they thought the foods they liked were not good for them.

The survey revealed a tremendous amount of guilt, but not much action: 36 percent said they felt guilty when they ate the foods they liked, knowing they were not good for them — but they ate them anyway.

Another study, completed by the National Restaurant Association in 1993, established that 87 percent of Americans clearly believed in a link between nutrition and disease, yet only 37 percent were willing to put their actions where their beliefs were. The rest report that, when dining out, they are most apt to order what they like, even if it's unhealthy.

This is no surprise to me — I hear it everyday. People feel guilty about eating food that is unhealthy and "bad," yet the biggest nutritional mistake people make is *not* eating good food. They are not getting the right foods in the right balance at the right times. People eat sporadically and erraticly until, driven by hunger and low blood sugars, they reach for the very foods they are striving to avoid.

There's only one path to healthy eating — having the right perspective. Eating well is not denying yourself — it's giving yourself a precious gift. It's not focusing on which foods to avoid but instead looking at the fresh, flavorful and fun foods that bless the body with energy, better moods and better bodies.

We have to defeat the lie that says food that's good for us is boring and tasteless.

Consider this: Food was created to nourish and energize us, allowing us to thrive. Food has the power to repair and restore our bodies in the wear-and-tear lives we lead.

Our bodies have been fashioned to use food in a rewarding way — to help us stay healthier, feel better and live longer. And remember that God created this process of eating food for life to be a pleasurable experience. Food is an ally, not an enemy to be feared.

Time Is Short. Taste and Beauty Are Everything. Health Is a Must

Food, along with the sharing of food, sustains human relationships. It's an extraordinarily important part of the family structure, and it's the common denominator that brings people together in the house.

For food to be enjoyable, it needs to taste great; if it doesn't taste good, it has limited power to satisfy.

But let's face it: Time is short. We are often mentally and emotionally exhausted from the thousand and one demands of living life in the nineties. On weeknights especially, spending less time in the kitchen becomes a clear necessity if we are to spend more time enjoying our food, friends and family. Too often, in our catch-as-catch-can way of doing things, something is compromised: taste, health or the entire satisfaction and fulfillment of making and enjoying a home-cooked meal.

Today's supermarkets carry a wide range of healthy foods that have opened the door to much more interesting meals that can be made in quick order. I have chosen my recipes in this book for ease, speed and flavor; I have chosen my meals and presentations for fun and enjoyment.

My menus are built around fundamental, healthy-eating guidelines — those outlined in my books *Eat Well – Live Well* and *Food for Life*.

With that said, I don't banish all butter, oil and other types of fat from my recipes. Instead I use small amounts of the highest possible quality, adding them at just the right moment to maximize the flavor.

When planning meals, consider what tastes good and looks good together, such as the color and texture contrasts. Pair something hard with something soft, something crisp with something creamy, something round with something angular, something white with something colorful. A plate with everything soft and creamy will be as unappealing as a plate of all brown foods. Be creative with bright colors and textures that let the dish look fresh and alive!

The art of cooking doesn't start or stop at the stove. It begins with planning meals and shopping for food, and carries through to the presentation.

The recipes and meals you'll find here are designed for beauty as you serve them. The good life of eating is more than just a nutritionally balanced plate; it's also a beautiful plate — one that gives pleasure to the eye as well as the palate.

Let your plate be your own canvas for a work of art. Notice how colors of food accent each other and compel you to eat and enjoy.

Garnishing Tips

One of the truest adages about food is, "You eat with your eyes first." A simple touch of garnish can turn a dull dish into a wonderful one. Garnishes add eye appeal and beauty to almost any food.

A general rule of thumb about garnishes is that they should be edible and, when possible, an ingredient that's in the dish. For example, a simple tomato wedge will add a uniqueness and beauty to a plate just because of its color and shape. If fresh cilantro is included, mince some extra to use as a garnish or arrange a whole sprig of cilantro on the dish. It doesn't take much effort to create a garnish while you're preparing the food.

Lots of specialized garnishing tools are available, but you'll create the most beautiful food with just a knife and some imagination.

- Always garnish food at the last minute to keep it looking fresh and inviting.
- Before garnishing dishes that have been standing or refrigerated, give them a gentle stir bringing the dressing, juices or marinade to the surface. This gives the food an inviting sheen.
- Easy garnishes include:
  - julienned vegetables
  - whole leaves or sprigs of herbs
  - finely minced peppers or herbs thrown confetti style onto the plate
  - fresh grated cheese
  - thin rings of red onion or peppers
  - slices of lemons, limes, pineapples or oranges
  - snipped chives or scallion greens
  - quartered cherry or plum tomatoes
  - crisp celery leaves
  - dollops of fat-free sour cream dusted with paprika or red pepper
- Give fresh herb leaves pizzazz by dipping them into cold water, shaking off the excess, then dipping leaf edges in paprika.
- Make a fruit or vegetable twist by taking a thin, round slice of orange, lemon or cucumber; make one cut from the center to the edge; then twist the slice in opposite directions into a spiral or *S* shape so the round will stand upright when placed on the dish.
- Make scallion brushes by trimming the root end of a scallion; then, using a sharp, pointed knife, slash both ends thin at one-eighth-inch intervals. Leave an inch uncut in the center of the scallion. Place in a bowl of ice water, and the slashed tips will curl within fifteen minutes.

- Fan out fruits and vegetables by cutting them lengthwise into thin slices with a sharp, pointed knife. Cut to within one-fourth inch of the stem end. Use your fingers to fan out the fruit or vegetable.
- Make a chiffonade of greens to garnish rice, vegetables or meat by stacking the leaves of greens such as romaine, green or red leaf lettuce, or spinach; roll them into a cigar shape; then thinly slice crosswise. The resulting "ribbons" of green make a garnish that's both flavorful and colorful.
- Make a radish rose by using a sharp knife to cut thin petals of the red peel vertically around the radish from the tip down almost to the stem end. Put radishes in a bowl of ice water, cover and refrigerate for an hour, or until petals pull away from the center portion.

How the Menus and Recipes Work

On the following pages are menus that incorporate all of my principles for great food and great health. Each menu is made up of separate recipes that have been designed to form a pleasing whole of contrasting tastes, textures and colors.

Each recipe grouping is arbitrary, influenced by such factors as market availability and personal food preferences. Use my menus as points of departure. Reorganize as you wish, taking a recipe from one menu and adding it to another, or substitute ingredients if you are missing one. You can use the foods you have on hand to create something new and personally yours.

Planning Your Plate

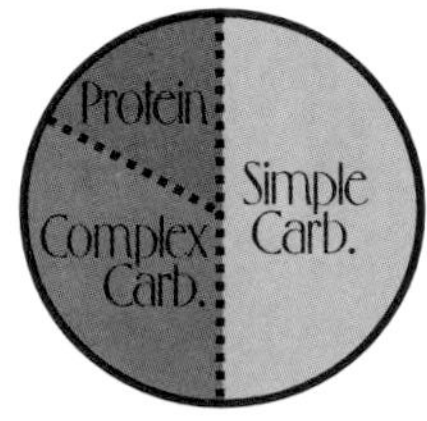

The breakfast, lunch and dinner sections of *The Good Life* have been designed using a whole meal approach. Rather than ten chicken recipes, five beef recipes and so on, I show you how to serve up complete meals that give taste, beauty in presentation and nutritional balance.

Each meal begins with the "Planning Your Plate" chart shown above. This chart is your reminder that every meal is designed with balance in mind. If the plate is directly under a single recipe name, then that recipe makes a complete meal by itself. If the plate is at the top of a page with several recipes on it, then all the recipes on that page are needed to make the complete meal.

The "Planning Your Plate" chart is followed by a breakdown of the meal's source of protein, complex carbohydrate and simple carbohydrate. Sometimes the recipe for that nutrient source will be included for you; at other times it will be an easy add-on source of nutrition, like a simple glass of skim milk.

The plate shows that a healthy meal will consist of larger amounts of carbohydrates and smaller amounts of protein than you may have eaten in the past. The U.S. Department of Agriculture used just such an eating pattern as a model for the Food Guide Pyramid, which you have probably seen on everything from cereal boxes to textbooks. Generally, a single serving of a lunch or dinner main dish will give a maximum of three to four ounces of protein, a far cry from the sixteen-ounce steaks we feasted on when we were growing up!

Protein should be part of the meal but not its focus. As critical as protein is to our wellness in building up the body, we need smaller amounts of it spread more evenly throughout the day, rather than a hunk of meat overloaded into one huge meal.

A Word About Nutritional Profile Charts

Per Serving: Calories	
Protein gr.	Carb. gr.
Fat gr.	Cal. from fat %
Chol. mg.	Sodium mg.

With the help of my computer I have analyzed each recipe in *The Good Life* for its nutritional value. Besides the calories and the carbohydrate, protein and fat grams, I have included information about sodium and cholesterol for those of you who are watching these numbers as well. The fat grams are also expressed in terms of the percentage of calories derived from fat in each particular dish. My meals are designed to give less than 25 percent of the calories from fat, with the average dish yielding 17 percent. Individual recipes that may be higher in percentage of fat calories are paired with those having low or no fat to balance the whole meal properly.

The nutrient values listed are as accurate as possible and are based on certain assumptions:

- All nutrient breakdowns are listed per serving.
- All meats are trimmed of all visible fat and skin before cooking.
- When a range is given for an ingredient (for example, one to two teaspoons), the lesser amount is calculated.
- When an option is given for ingredients, the first option is calculated.
- A large percentage of calories from alcohol evaporates in cooking, and this is reflected in the profiles.
- When a marinade is used, only the amount absorbed into the food is calculated.
- Garnishes and optional ingredients are not calculated.

Please also note that the analysis is for the recipe ingredients only. Many times you will see a dotted line underneath the ingredients followed by a note that says, "Serve with..." This note may tell you that Strawberry Sauce, Black Bean and Corn Salsa or some other dish is to be served with that meal, though the complete recipe is not shown. The "serve with" items will *not* be included in the nutritional analysis for that recipe. You may look up the nutritional analysis for the sauce or salsa on the page where their complete recipes are shown.

I have used these profiles to plan balanced meals that give appropriate levels of nutrients. Portion sizes may need to be adjusted to fit caloric needs according to your own individual meal plan. Calorie requirements will vary according to your age, size, weight, level of activity and even stress levels. So don't get caught up in counting every calorie you eat. Instead, focus on eating great foods, prepared in great ways, that are great for you.

What About Salt?

Although salt is certainly not the number one nutritional evil, it is nonetheless a concern. The main problem is how much we use of it — way, way too much! Actually, the average American consumes more than eight times his or her daily requirement — about fifteen pounds per year. This is the sodium equivalent of two to four teaspoons of salt a day.

Hypertension, fluid retention and kidney dysfunction are just a few of the health problems those little white granules contribute to — and good reasons to *pass* on the salt!

In America today, approximately sixty million people have abnormally high blood pressure. This means that one out of five are predisposed to the condition. However, it's not possible to identify who is at risk, so it's wise to practice prevention and cut back on excess salt — even before a doctor tells you that you must. An ounce of prevention can be worth a pound of cure.

Salt is made up of 60 percent sodium and 40 percent chloride. In the human body, excess sodium becomes a troublemaker, creating a temporary buildup of fluids, making it harder for the heart to pump blood through the system and causing a rise in the blood pressure (hypertension). Other factors besides salt intake, such as heredity and obesity, can also contribute to hypertension. Unlike heredity, however, salt consumption is a factor *within* our control. Unfortunately, for the majority of Americans it is *out* of control.

Shaking the salt habit can be difficult because of our taste buds. They were designed to pick up the taste of salt in foods, but our high-salt diets have overdeveloped that desire. We weren't born loving salt — but by being given salted foods, we began to prefer them. The good news is that this conditioned taste is reversible: As you use less salt, your tastes will change so that you will enjoy foods more without so much salt. It takes only six weeks or so to see a big difference in salt desire.

Salt does play a big part in food's enjoyment; it serves as a catalyst for flavor, enhancing the taste of ingredients. The key to making the good-for-you cutback is to learn to prepare foods in ways that naturally enhance the flavor so they need less salt to taste good. You'll notice *The Good Life* recipes use herbs and spices which allow you to reduce the amount of salt drastically.

WATCH OUT FOR HIGH-SODIUM FOODS

- any food pickled or brine-cured, including sauerkraut, pickles and olives
- any food salt-cured or smoked, including most ham, bacon and sausage
- any cold cut, including bologna, hot dogs, pastrami and salami
- convenience foods, such as canned vegetables, soups and frozen meals

What About Additives and Preservatives?

Serving hot dogs and cold cuts is an easy trap to fall into and one to be avoided! Bacon, hot dogs, sausages and the like are all high in saturated fats and sodium, and they contain nitrites, which are linked to cancer, and other chemical additives. There are far better sources for protein than these. Consider the wonderful building proteins on page 11.

I advocate "real foods" rather than highly processed packaged foods. For example, real orange juice or frozen concentrate is a far superior choice to fortified orange-flavored drink.

Think "Mother Nature" when you shop. Your grocery store is crammed full of healthful foods; you don't have to shop at a health food store to get them.

What About Cholesterol?

You need cholesterol for many body functions. It's necessary for hormone production, digestion, even efficient operation of the brain — but you don't have to eat it to have it. Your body makes plenty, often too much, all on its own. The liver produces cholesterol, and those with a genetic tendency toward heart disease may have a liver that produces too much and a body that metabolizes too little.

Dangerous levels of cholesterol come from eating too much of the kind of cholesterol that comes from animal products such as meat, chicken, eggs, milk, cheese and butter. More commonly, cholesterol levels in the blood rise from eating a diet high in saturated fats, which can convert to a bad form of cholesterol — LDL cholesterol.

When at a high level in the bloodstream, LDL cholesterol tends to deposit in the walls of the blood vessels, especially those in the heart, leading to arteriosclerosis or "hardening of the arteries." The "good" form of cholesterol (HDL) has just the opposite effect: It protects the body by pulling the bad cholesterol, like a magnet, from the bloodstream.

What About Artificial Sweeteners?

As you become aware (and possibly alarmed) about your intake of sugar, you may be tempted to use sugar substitutes as a replacement. Be careful not to do this. There are no absolutes in the safety of chemicals — saccharin, aspartame or any new one to come along. The long term effects of their use will not be known for years. As bad as sugar may be, and whatever the health hazards associated with its overuse, at least it's not a chemical. It has been used for centuries. The best wisdom to use is, "When in doubt, leave it out."

We don't eat desserts on a regular basis at our house, preferring to end our meals with fresh fruits, God's natural provision for our sweet tooth. I have included dessert recipes here, however, to complete certain menus and make them special for festive events.

But you won't find elaborate desserts in this book. Quick tricks with fresh fruits, frozen yogurts and fresh fruit sauces give you the opportunity for a fun and flavorful end to any meal.

TIPS FOR AVOIDING THE CHOLESTEROL TRAP

- **Eat breakfast; follow with power snacks**

  Eat small amounts of food, evenly distributed throughout the day. Starving through the day results in a metabolism that is more apt to store cholesterol than clear it from the body.

- **Eat high-fiber foods**

  Include brown rice, legumes, oat bran and barley in your diet. Foods high in pectin, such as strawberries and bananas, slow the absorption of cholesterol into the bloodstream.

- **Eat more fish**

  Fish contains wonderfully healthy EPA oils that lower total cholesterol and triglycerides while increasing the levels of good HDL cholesterol.

- **Eat onions and garlic**

  These appear to raise HDL cholesterol levels dramatically, along with lowering the LDL cholesterol levels.

- **Eat very little fat**

  The fat you eat should be monounsaturated oils, such as olive and canola oils. Avoid saturated animal and hydrogenated vegetable fats and the highly saturated coconut and palm oils.

- **Exercise aerobically**

  Best results come from an hour of aerobic exercise every other day.

- **Lose body fat**

  A lower body-fat percentage will help control cholesterol and triglyceride levels.

- **If you smoke, stop**

  Each cigarette you smoke raises your cholesterol level.

What About Caffeine?

As hard as it is to imagine, caffeine, a relatively mild stimulant, is among the world's most widely used and addictive drugs. And like any drug, there is a downside to caffeine. Because it's a central nervous system stimulant, even small amounts of it can cause side effects such as restlessness, disturbed sleep, stomach irritation and diarrhea. It can cause irritability, anxiety and mood disturbances.

The amount required to cause these effects is 250 mg. — about two mugs of coffee or three large glasses of tea. That adds up quickly, especially when you consider all of the other hidden sources of caffeine. Along with coffee and tea, caffeine is found in chocolate, sodas and some decongestants and aspirins.

Generally, the cola beverages have the highest levels of caffeine, but read all labels, since some of the fruit-flavored sodas contain caffeine as well. Some, such as Mountain Dew and Dr. Pepper, contain as much caffeine as coffee and tea. In the body of a 60-pound child, one of these sodas is the equivalent to the caffeine in four cups of coffee for a 175-pound man. Of course, the major problem with soda is not the caffeine; it's the artificial flavors, artificial colorings and the incredibly high concentration of sugar! Most sodas contain ten to twelve teaspoons of sugar per can; the diet sodas simply replace the sugar with chemicals.

Recipe Makeovers

Most of the recipes in the pages ahead have been my favorites, many passed on to me by friends (often chefs) and family. Some have been developed, others "made over" with health in mind. You will discover an endless array of cooking tricks — part art, part science — to turn unhealthy, full-of-fat dishes into tasty, nutritious ones. I have used them all in *The Good Life* meals, and you'll start to use them too.

Basically, I use three methods to reduce the amount of fat, calories and other detrimental substances in a recipe.

- I reduce the amount of high-fat, high-salt ingredients and look for ways to enhance flavor, texture and nutritive value.

- I replace a high-fat, high-salt ingredient with a different one that is lower in fat and sodium and higher in flavor.
- I use a cooking method that reduces fat yet enhances moisture and flavor.

Following are some of the specific ingredient substitutions and cooking techniques I used in creating the recipes in this book. You may want to use them on some of your own time-tested favorites.

Tips for Low-Fat Substitutions

- Use skim milk, nonfat plain yogurt, skim-milk cheese, low-fat or nonfat cottage cheese and light cream cheese instead of the higher-fat dairy products.
- Eat more fish and white meats and fewer red meats. If you eat red meats, buy lean and trim well, before and after cooking — and cook in a way that diminishes fat, such as grilling or broiling on a rack.
- Remove skin from poultry *before* cooking; you will cut the fat by 50 percent!
- Use cooking sprays and nonstick skillets that enable you to brown meats without grease. Sauté ingredients in stocks and broths rather than fats and oils.
- Adapt a recipe that says to baste with butter by basting with tomato or lemon juice, white wine Worcestershire or stock.
- Use monounsaturated oils such as canola or olive oil for salads or cooking. You can cut the amount called for in a recipe by two-thirds without sacrificing quality. For example, a recipe calling for three tablespoons of oil may be cut to one tablespoon. Depending on the recipe, the oil may be

SUPER SUBSTITUTE SAVINGS

INSTEAD OF	USE	AND SAVE
1 cup whole milk	1 cup skim milk	10 gr. fat, 90 calories
1 cup heavy cream	1 cup evaporated skim milk	87 gr. fat, 783 calories
1 cup sour cream	1 cup fat-free sour cream	48 gr. fat, 432 calories
8 ounces cream cheese	8 ounces light cream cheese	39 gr. fat, 351 calories
2 ounces oil	cooking spray	60 gr. fat, 540 calories
1 ounce oil	1 teaspoon oil	25 gr. fat, 225 calories
1 pint mayonnaise	1 pint plain nonfat yogurt	352 gr. fat, 3,168 calories
6 whole eggs	12 egg whites	36 gr. fat, 324 calories, 1,644 mg. cholesterol
1 pint sour cream	1 pint plain nonfat yogurt or nonfat sour cream	89 gr. fat, 803 calories
4 ounces cheddar cheese	4 ounces reduced-fat cheddar cheese	25 gr. fat, 225 calories
8 ounces cream cheese	8 ounces fat-free cream cheese	79 gr. fat, 711 calories
1 pound ground beef (80 percent lean)	1 pound ground turkey breast	91 gr. fat, 819 calories

cut out altogether if cooking spray is used. Ideally, no more than one teaspoon of oil per serving should be used.

- Substitute nonfat plain yogurt, nonfat sour cream or blended-till-smooth low-fat cottage cheese or skim milk ricotta in recipes calling for sour cream or mayonnaise. These products also make a great topping for baked potatoes, especially sprinkled with chives or grated Parmesan.
- Purchase tuna packed in water rather than oil; solid white tastes better.
- Use avocados and olives sparingly. Although vegetables, they are concentrated sources of fat. For example, five olives contain 50 calories of fat, and half an avocado gives you 180 calories of fat.
- Use legumes (dried beans and peas) as a main dish or a meat substitute; they make a high-nutrition, low-fat meal.
- Use egg whites or egg substitute in place of whole eggs (two egg whites = one egg). Egg whites are pure protein, and egg yolks are pure fat and cholesterol.
- Skim the fat from soup stocks, meat drippings and sauces. Refrigerate and remove the hardened surface layer of fat before reheating.
- Rarely, if ever, eat organ meats such as liver, sweetbreads and brains. They are loaded with cholesterol.
- Use only natural peanut butter and even this in small amounts. Avoid commercial peanut butter at all costs. Commercial peanut butter is not much more than shortening and sugar. Fresh-ground natural peanut butter still contains fat, but it is a good source of protein. If you have trouble switching from the commercial type, begin by mixing it half and half with natural. Gradually increase the proportion of the natural until you have abandoned the commercial.
- Use small amounts of added fats. Butter may be your best choice. If you use margarine, the soft, squeeze-type corn oil is best, then tub margarine, then stick. The firmer the margarine, the more saturated it is because of the hydrogenation process.
- Use fat-free cheeses. Though they do not melt as smoothly as fattier versions, you can overcome this by finely shredding the cheese or mixing it with a reduced-fat version. Two great blends are three parts fat-free mozzarella blended with one part Parmesan, or three parts fat-free sharp cheddar blended with one part part-skim mozzarella.
- Replace one-quarter to one-half of the ground meat or poultry in a casserole or meat sauce with cooked brown rice, couscous or cooked beans.
- Use pureed cooked vegetables, such as carrots, potatoes or peppers, to thicken soups and stews instead of creams, egg yolks or roux.
- Use small amounts of fattier foods that pack a powerful flavor punch: feta cheese, Parmesan, coconut, toasted nuts, and turkey bacon or sausage made from turkey. You can always cut the quantity called for by 50 percent.
- Beat egg whites until soft peaks form before folding them into baked goods; this increases the volume and tenderness.

Light Cooking Techniques

Second only to buying the best fresh foods to take advantage of their natural flavors is selecting the cooking method that best retains the natural moisture in foods. This reduces or eliminates the need for fats, oils and rich sauces.

Grilling and Broiling

Not just for weekends, grilling is an ideal cooking method, allowing foods to pick up extra flavor and to be cooked with a minimum of added fats.

When grilled over hot coals or broiled on a rack in the oven, meat, fish and poultry lose extra fat as it drips away. Remove as much fat as possible before cooking by skinning chicken and trimming all visible fat from meat; this prevents the fat from cooking into your food. Coat the broiler or grill rack with cooking spray to prevent sticking, and place the trimmed fat from steaks on the grill separately to allow better smoking and flavoring of the meat.

Marinating first is a key for flavorful grilling. Lemon juice, wine, vinegar and plain yogurt are good main ingredients for low-fat marinades. Combine with fruit juices, herbs or spices for taste. Baste frequently to keep food moist during grilling. Remember that marinades give moisture and tenderness, not fat, to the meat.

If grilling fish, choose firm-textured fish fillets or steaks which are about one-inch thick rather than thinner ones (thinner foods dry out on the grill). If frozen, the fish should be thawed first. Basting with marinade while broiling will keep the fish moist. Particularly good for grilling are snapper, sea bass, grouper, salmon, tuna and swordfish. Oysters and clams are also excellent for roasting on the grill. To roast unshucked oysters or clams, wash shells thoroughly; place on grill rack about four inches from hot coals; roast for ten to fifteen minutes or until shells begin to open; serve in shells.

Parchment Cooking

By encasing the food in parchment paper, aluminum foil, cooking bags or wax paper, evaporation is greatly reduced, and the food stays naturally moist and flavorful. Natural casings that may be used are lettuce leaves, cabbage leaves and corn husks.

Special microwave cooking bags are available at most supermarkets, usually in the foil or plastic wrap section. They're great for microwaving fish or chicken.

Poaching

To poach means to immerse a food in a simmering liquid. Poaching is generally reserved for fruits, eggs, poultry and fish, but lamb and veal can be poached with delicious results.

When poaching on top of the stove, the pan should be filled with a small amount of almost simmering liquid, with the food placed in the liquid. The pan should be covered so steam doesn't escape; the steam keeps the food moist.

For oven poaching the food is placed in a small amount of liquid, covered with foil and roasted.

Always allow food to cool in the liquid. This permits the flavor to be absorbed. When poached, foods stay tender, moist and low in fats.

Some good liquids to use in poaching are chicken stock, fruit juices, lemon juice, tomato juice and wine.

Following is a general time table for poaching foods:

- Boneless breast of chicken — fifteen minutes
- Breast of chicken (with bone) — twenty-five minutes
- Fish fillets — ten to twelve minutes (until flakes with fork)
- Fruits — eight to ten minutes

Sautéeing and Stir-Frying

Sautéeing and stir-frying are both methods of light cooking with a minimum amount of oil. Vegetables keep their flavor, have a nice texture and retain those important water-soluble vitamins. By using nonstick cookware or a regular skillet coated with cooking spray, vegetables and meats can be cooked quickly, often with no fat added.

Cooking sprays allow high-heat searing and cooking without sticking. A cooking spray will "grease" the pan while adding only a minimal amount of fat. By keeping a can of this in your kitchen, you will be able to add only as much additional oil as the flavor of a dish requires and not a drop more. You won't achieve perfect browning of the foods, but you will have fine results as long as you cook at a moderate temperature.

Nonstick pans are sold everywhere, and some are much better than others. As with every other piece of equipment you buy, high quality will pay for itself in the long run. The major quality differences will not be in the nonstick coating but in the thickness and sturdiness of the pans. Be sure that your nonstick pan is as heavy as possible.

In most recipes calling for foods to be sautéed, the fat can be drastically reduced or omitted. Some foods, such as green pepper and celery, will dry out if cooked with cooking spray alone, so I always use a small amount (no more than two teaspoons) of oil when sautéeing them. You may also sauté them in a half cup chicken or vegetable stock, stirring frequently to prevent burning. This adds a nice flavor to the vegetables.

Foods such as mushrooms, onions, meat, fish and poultry release some liquids as they cook and can easily be sautéed in cooking spray or a nonstick skillet without oil. Meats can also be browned in this way without using any fat.

Slice vegetables thin for sautéeing and stir-frying. Meat, fish and poultry should be cut into small, even pieces. Heat the pan, add a little oil, toss in the food and shake; toss or stir the food for even browning. Cook only until the vegetables are crisp tender.

Sautéeing and stir-frying in a minimum of olive or canola oil will also allow vegetables to be flavorful with a nice texture and not lose water-soluble vitamins.

Steaming

Steaming is an ideal method of cooking vegetables since it provides good retention of vitamins as well as taste. Vegetables will be more flavorful and nutritious if they are not cooked in a big pot of boiling water until limp and mushy. Steaming provides a healthy and tasty alternative.

Place vegetables in a steaming basket (inexpensive and easily purchased at any grocery store) above a small amount of water (keep one-fourth inch below the bottom of the steamer) and cover. Bring to a boil and continue to boil on medium heat until vegetables are crisp tender. Placing a garlic clove or a sliced onion in the steaming water will help to flavor the vegetables without fat or calories.

Be careful: Steam burns! Remove the cover slowly, with the opening away from you.

Boiling

If you are boiling vegetables in a traditional fashion, use these principles: 1) cook over high heat, 2) use a small amount of stock or water and 3) cook for a short period of time.

Microwaving

Microwaving is a great way to cook vegetables to retain nutrients and flavor, but you must be sure not to overcook. The best foods for microwave cooking are those high in moisture and low in fat, such as fish, poultry, vegetables and fruits. The foods that do not microwave well are those high in fat and low in moisture, such as beef, pork and lamb.

Getting Started

One last point to remember: It's your day-to-day eating that counts most for health and wellness — not what you eat at a ball game or on your birthday. One day, even a week, of less-than-great eating will not send your body head-first into disease or nutrient deficiency.

What *is* important is getting started with the energy and excitement of a new way of eating! It's progress, not perfection, that counts. You may start with eating breakfast, perhaps for the first time since you were five years old. Or you may start packing a more interesting lunch that's healthier too. It may be one fabulous dinner a week or elements of health sprinkled throughout your life.

Whatever you choose as your first step, the rewards of better eating come quickly: terrific energy, resistance to infection, good moods, superior concentration, alertness and even a better memory!

Get cooking — and get living — the good life!

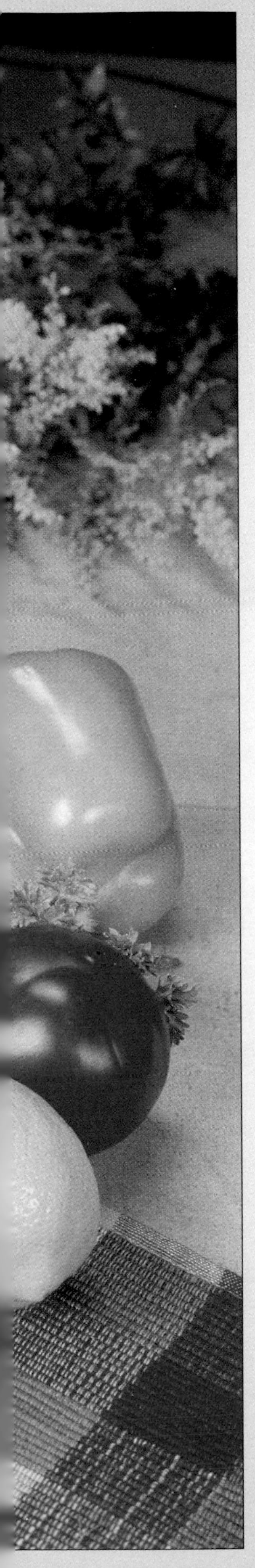

The Well-Stocked Kitchen

TIPS AND RECIPES

If you struggle to eat well, you are more than likely among the nutrient-deficient majority — and you aren't getting what it takes to live fit and fueled. Here's the bottom line: We will only eat well and cook well if we fill our pantries with the right foods. Unhealthy food traps can be avoided if they are out of sight and out of mind — then they will be out of mouth. Rethinking your food supply is a major step toward making healthy habits. Eating well is much simpler if nutritious foods are kept within reach.

A well-stocked kitchen makes the difference between efficiently putting together healthy flavorful foods versus a meal-time-blues headache or a fast-food nightmare.

Human nature dictates that if the right choice is not available, you'll most likely reach for the wrong choice — or not eat at all. Both set you up for disaster later in your day.

Take a long look at what's in your grocery cart. If it's a grease trap loaded with butter, bacon and Twinkies, chances are you're not going to be producing slim fixings on the home front. Now is a good time to strengthen and streamline your food shopping, your fridge and, thereby, your body. Whether you grocery shop frequently or only do necessary flybys, whether you're a microwave fan or a gourmet great, here are some quick tips

The Well-Stocked Kitchen

TIPS AND RECIPES

Whole grain cereal choices:

- *All Bran With Extra Fiber*
- *Cheerios*
- *Familia Müesli Granola (no sugar added)*
- *Grape-Nuts*
- *Kashi*
- *Kellogg's Just Right*
- *Kellogg's Nutri-Grain (wheat, corn or almond raisin)*
- *Kellogg's Raisin Squares*
- *Nabisco Shredded Wheat*
- *Post Bran Flakes*
- *Ralston Muesli*

for adding a health advantage to your shopping cart.

Choosing Cereals and Breads

Whole grain is a must for fiber and nutrition. The word *whole* should be the first word of the ingredient list, such as "whole wheat, whole oats." Also check labels for hidden fats and hidden sugars; some cereals, like granola, are nutritional nightmares in a bowl. Remember the available variety of whole grain English muffins, bagels, pita breads and, of course, rice cakes.

Buying the Basics

Stock up on whole wheat or artichoke pastas and brown rice. Incorporate barley, oats, cracked wheat and cornmeal into recipes. Include dried or canned beans, split peas, lentils and chickpeas.

Daring Dairy

Although they get a bad rap these days, dairy foods are a treasure chest of protein, calcium and other body-building nutrients. But they can also be loaded with fat, so look for lower-fat variations on favorites: skim milk, buttermilk, nonfat yogurt, skim milk ricotta, pot or farmer's cheese, part-skim mozzarella and skim milk cottage cheese. Check the labels to be sure they fit your nutrition standards of having fewer than three grams of fat per hundred-calorie serving.

Doing the Deli

Select sliced turkey or chicken, lean ham and low-fat cheeses instead of the usual lunch meats. Limit use of high-fat, high-sodium processed sausages and meats, hot dogs, bacon and salami.

Fending Against Fats and Oils

Limit use of butter, margarines and cream cheese. Select reduced-fat or light mayonnaises and salad dressings. Do not use polyunsaturated oils, but instead use olive or canola oil in small amounts. All of these choices should be used sparingly. Remember that it's the fat that makes you unhealthy, fat and slows you down!

Making Meat Choices

All cuts should be lean and trimmed of visible fat. Choose the following: beef — round, loin, sirloin and extra lean ground beef; lamb — leg, arm, loin, rib; pork — tenderloin, leg, shoulder; turkey or chicken — skinless; fish and shellfish — fresh, just delivered.

Water, Water Everywhere

Stock up on bottled waters to replace sugary sodas, which offer zero nutrition and lots of calories. Try sparkling mineral waters (add a splash of fruit juice for flavor).

Picking Produce

Fruits and vegetables are no-fat, no-cholesterol beauties with fiber that help in stabilizing the body — providing for lower cholesterol levels, boosted immunities against sicknesses, lovelier skin, nails and hair, higher energy levels and less body aches and pains. Keep enough on hand so that you can always make a salad. Buy the freshest — and the most colorful — produce possible for top nutrition. Generally, the more vivid the coloring of the pulp, the more essential nutrients it holds.

Wonderfully fresh fruits and vegetables are a particular passion of mine. For the sweetest produce, choose what is in season — a good price and abundant supply will tell you a fruit or vegetable is at its peak. Ask at your grocery store or farmer's market which are freshest buying days and where the vegetables are grown; search for locally grown and in-season fruits and vegetables. Out-of-season produce is more expensive and often imported. If it is imported, it may be only spot-checked for pesticide residues. (Use the fruit and vegetable guides on pages 28 through 31 when getting ready to purchase fruit or vegetables.)

When fresh is not possible, frozen is the next choice; avoid vegetables that are prepared with butters or sauces, and fruits that are packed with sugar. (Freezing foods doesn't destroy their nutrients and quality as readily as canning does.)

Take advantage of your grocer's pre-cut, pre-chopped vegetables and fruits. They are available in the produce area or may be purchased by the pound from the salad bar.

The Nutritional Top 10

Ever wish the science of nutrition could be pared down to a simple checklist? Good news! No longer must you stand dazed in the produce aisle, racking your brain for information about which fruits and veggies are rich in beta-carotene (whatever that is).

Here's a shopping list to set you on a clear, no-brainer course: Simply toss these Top 10 foods into your grocery cart every week, make sure they get into your body, and you will have taken a giant step forward to good nutrition!

1. BROCCOLI. This is the best one-stop vegetable for beta-carotene, fiber and vitamins C and A. It also contains sulforaphane, which blocks cancer growth.
2. CHICKEN OR TURKEY. These low-fat meats are great choices for building the body. Cook them in lean, flavorful ways.
3. FISH. Buy salmon, tuna and swordfish. Valuable oils in fish provide protection against heart disease and other degenerative diseases such as arthritis.
4. LEGUMES. These high-fiber beauties are also high in protein and complex carbohydrates. Beans are loaded with phytochemicals and bioflavonoids that may help prevent cancer. They also lower LDL cholesterol levels in the blood, reducing heart disease risk.
5. ORANGES. Fresh, whole citrus is a great source of vitamin C (oranges have the most). More than thirty studies have shown that vitamin C helps the body fight cancers. Oranges, along with mangoes, are also rich in bioflavonoids, which capture energy from the sun and become powerful boosters to our immune systems.
6. SWEET POTATOES. One of these (or two carrots) every other day provides enough beta-carotene to protect against a host of diseases.
7. SKIM OR LOW-FAT DAIRY PRODUCTS. Milk, cheeses and yogurts are loaded with calcium and magnesium that keep blood pressure stable and bones strong. They're also excellent, low-fat sources of protein in convenient packaging.
8. SPINACH. This provides a bumper crop of vitamins A and C, and folic acid. It includes a bit of magnesium too, which helps control cancer, reduces the risk of stroke and heart disease, and may prevent osteoporosis.
9. STRAWBERRIES AND TOMATOES. These two foods are rich in substances that stimulate immune functions and slow degenerative diseases.
10. WHOLE GRAINS. Found in breads, cereals, crackers, rice and pasta, grains have fibers that lower cholesterol and blood pressure, and may reduce the risk of colon cancer. Whole grains are loaded with B vitamins, calcium and magnesium, and vitamin E. These nutrients enhance the immune system and help prevent coronary artery disease.

Don't forget two other little powerhouses: garlic and chili peppers. Garlic lowers cholesterol and blood pressure and boosts immunity. It also contains chemicals that may destroy cancer cells. Go for the real stuff, though. The capsules may not leave the garlic aroma with you, but they don't give you the health benefits either.

Chili peppers contain an antioxidant with many benefits. It boosts the immune system, protects against strokes and cancer-causing substances, lowers cholesterol and may even affect your mood by stimulating the release of endorphins!

Start with the freshest of ingredients and your end product will reflect the quality. Handpick what you eat and be selective.

(Continued on page 34.)

A GUIDE TO SWEET AND WONDERFUL FRUIT

Fruit	Description	Serving Size
Apples	Should be firm and crisp without a watery, soft give. *Excellent for eating:* Braeburn, Red and Golden Delicious, Elstar, Fuji, Granny Smith, McIntosh, Jonathan, Winesap. *Excellent for cooking:* Golden Delicious, Rome Beauty, Cortland, Granny Smith, McIntosh (never Red Delicious as they are too dry). *Hint:* Drizzling cut apples with lemon juice will prevent browning.	1 small apple
Apricots	Should be fat and golden. Easiest to find in dried form. Very high in potassium and vitamin A.	2 fresh or 4 dried halves
Avocados	Use sparingly since avocados are a source of fat. They are ripe when soft to the touch and skin is darkened.	1/8 whole or 2 Tbsp. mashed avocado
Bananas	Are considered ripe when covered with brown specks. Once ripe, refrigeration will keep them in excellent eating condition for another three to five days. (Skin may brown completely.) Bananas are very high in potassium. They are best for use as a sweetener when very brown and ripe. *Hint:* If using in fruit salad, top the salad with sliced bananas just before serving and sprinkle with lemon juice to prevent browning.	1/2 large or 1 small (6-inch) banana
Berries	Sweet packages of nutritional power. Berries should be firm when purchased; avoid stained containers.	1/2 cup
Cantaloupe	Very high in vitamins A and C; also potassium. The outside should be dull, creamy yellow when purchased, and the blossom end should be slightly soft when ripe. Look for pronounced lacy netting.	1/4 cantaloupe or 3/4 cup cubed
Coconut	Use sparingly since it is a source of fat. Most natural food stores have unsweetened flaked coconut. For fresher flavor, soak in small amount of milk before cooking.	2 Tbsp. unsweetened flaked coconut
Figs	Should be ripe (soft when squeezed) and plump; should smell sweet, not sour. Refrigerate.	1 medium fig
Grapefruit and oranges	Should be round, heavy for their size and thin-skinned.	1/2 grapefruit 1 medium orange 1/2 cup sections
Grapes	Choose a ripe bunch. Do not ripen off the vine. The point where the grape attaches to stem should be strong and fresh, and grapes should have a full color.	12 grapes

Fruit	Description	Serving Size
Honeydew	Should have a soft blossom end; skin should be slightly sticky.	1/8 honeydew
Kiwi	Should yield slightly to the touch.	1 kiwi
Mangoes	Should yield slightly to the touch but should not be soft.	1/3 whole or 1/3 cup diced
Nectarines, peaches and pears	Are ripe when slightly soft at stem end and yellowish rather than greenish. Peaches and nectarines should have a pink blush as well. To help with the ripening, place nectarines, peaches, pears or plums in a brown paper bag with a banana. As the banana ripens, it releases a natural gas that ripens the other fruit as if it were still on the tree.	1 medium fruit
Papaya	Should be mostly yellow, should yield slightly to pressure and have a pleasant aroma.	3/4 cup cubed
Pineapple	Is ripe when it has deep green leaves at the crown, heaviness for its size and a sweet aroma (not fermented or acidic). It should yield slightly when pressed with finger.	2 slices or 1/3 cup chunked or crushed
Plums	Should not be rock hard but plump and firm to the touch.	2 small plums
Watermelon	Should be purchased with a smooth surface, dullish sheen and a creamy yellow underside.	1 cup cubed melon

DRIED FRUIT

Fruit	Serving Size
Dried apple rings	1/2 ounce or 8 rings
Dried apricots	4 halves
Dates (unsweetened)	2 dates
Dried peaches, pears	1 fruit
Prunes	2 large prunes
Raisins	2 Tbsp. or 1 small box

A GUIDE TO VIBRANT VEGETABLES

Vegetable	Preparation	Minutes to Steam	Yield	Complementary Seasonings
Asparagus	remove tough ends before cooking; stand in boiling water	5 minutes uncovered, then 7 to 10 minutes covered	1 lb. raw = 2 cups cooked	chives, garlic, lemon juice, parsley
Green beans	wash and snap ends off	8 to 10 minutes until crisp tender	1 lb. raw = 3 cups cooked	basil, dill, garlic, lemon, parsley, rosemary
Beets	scrub well; do not peel	20 to 30 minutes until crisp tender	1 lb. raw = 3 cups cooked	basil, cloves, mint, tarragon
Broccoli	pare stalk of tough skin before cooking	8 to 20 minutes until crisp tender	1 bunch (2 lbs.) raw = 2 cups cooked	garlic, lemon juice, pimento, vinegar
Brussels sprouts	cut off stems and slash stem ends for quicker cooking	12 minutes	1 lb. raw = 3 cups cooked	chives, nutmeg
Cabbage	core and cut into wedges or quarters or shred	12 to 15 minutes for wedges; 5 minutes for shredded	1 lb. raw = 2 cups cooked	basil, caraway seeds, dill, poppy seeds, sage
Carrots	scrub thoroughly or pare; leave whole or slice	10 minutes	7 to 8 raw = 2 cups cooked	basil, ginger, mint, nutmeg, parsley
Cauliflower	core and remove outer leaves; leave whole or cut into florets	12 to 15 minutes	1 head (2 lbs.) raw = 3 cups cooked	basil, chives, nutmeg, rosemary, tarragon
Corn	remove husks; remove silk; wash	boil or steam for 8 minutes	1 small ear = 1/2 cup	celery seeds, chives, green pepper, pimento
Eggplant	peel and slice; salt slices and let stand 15 minutes; rinse well before use	better to grill 5 to 7 minutes or use in soups or casseroles	11 slices (1/2-inch thick) raw = 2 cups cooked	basil, oregano, parsley, tarragon, thyme
Greens	wash well; discard discolored leaves	8 to 9 minutes or until wilted	1 lb. raw = 1 1/2 to 2 cups cooked	basil, dill, oregano, onion, black pepper, vinegar
Mushrooms	wash gently or wipe with damp cloth; trim stem ends	sauté for 5 to 7 minutes or use raw or cooked in other dishes	10 mushrooms raw = 1 cup cooked	basil, chives, marjoram, parsley, thyme

Vegetable	Preparation	Minutes to Steam	Yield	Complementary Seasonings
Okra	wash and remove stem ends	use in mixtures for soups and stews	1 lb. raw = 2 cups cooked	basil, bay leaf, onion, parsley, thyme
Onions	remove outer, loosest layer of skin	sauté 3 to 4 minutes or bake at 400 degrees for 40 minutes	1 medium = $^1/_2$ cup chopped	dill, cloves, mint, parsley, tarragon
Parsnips	scrub well or pare; leave whole or slice	10 minutes	4 medium raw = 1 cup cooked	dill, parsley, sage
Peas	shell and wash	6 to 7 minutes	1 lb. raw = 1 cup cooked	basil, dill, mint, parsley, rosemary
Potatoes, white and sweet	scrub and remove any brown spots; do not peel	bake 1 hour; steam 15 to 20 minutes	3 medium raw = $2^1/_2$ cups cooked	white: dill, chives, parsley, rosemary sweet: chives, cinnamon, nutmeg
Spinach	wash thoroughly and remove stems; serve raw in salads	steam 4 to 5 minutes until wilted	1 lb. raw = $1^1/_2$ to 2 cups cooked	basil, chives, dill, garlic, lemon, vinegar
Squash, spaghetti	cut in half; remove seeds and place cut side down in small amount of water on a baking sheet	bake at 350 degrees for 45 minutes, until strands pull free with a fork	1 squash (2 lbs.) = 2 cups cooked	basil, oregano, parsley
Squash, summer	wash; trim off ends	steam or boil for 6 to 8 minutes	2 lbs. raw = 2 cups cooked	basil, oregano, parsley
Squash, winter	wash; cut in half and place cut side down on baking sheet, or peel and cut into small pieces to steam	bake at 350 degrees for 1 hour or steam pieces for 20 to 30 minutes	2 lbs. raw = 2 cups cooked	cinnamon, nutmeg, orange peel

Pam Smith's Good Life Grocery List

GRAINS AND BREADS
Brown rice: ❑ Instant
❑ Long-grain ❑ Short-grain
❑ Wild rice ❑ Arborio rice
❑ Cornmeal
❑ Couscous
Tortillas, flour: ❑ Mission
❑ Buena Vida Fat Free
❑ Whole wheat bagels
❑ 100% whole wheat bread *("whole" is the first word of the ingredients)*
❑ Whole wheat English muffins
❑ Whole wheat hamburger buns
Whole wheat or artichoke pasta:
❑ Angel hair ❑ Elbows
❑ Flat ❑ Lasagna ❑ Orzo
❑ Penne ❑ Spaghetti
❑ Rotini *(spirals)*
❑ Whole wheat pastry flour
❑ Whole wheat pita bread
❑ ________________
❑ ________________

CEREALS *(whole grain and less than 5 grams of added sugar)*:
❑ All Bran With Extra Fiber
❑ Cheerios
❑ Familia Müesli ❑ Granola
❑ Grape-Nuts
❑ Grits ❑ Kashi
❑ Kellogg's Just Right
❑ Kellogg's Low Fat Granola
❑ Kellogg's Nutri-Grain Almond Raisin
❑ Kellogg's Raisin Squares
❑ Nabisco Shredded Wheat
❑ Ralston Muesli
Oats: ❑ Old-fashioned
❑ Quick-cooking
❑ Post Bran Flakes
Puffed cereals: ❑ Rice ❑ Wheat
❑ Shredded Wheat 'N Bran
Unprocessed bran: ❑ Oat
❑ Wheat
❑ Wheatena
❑ ________________

CRACKERS
Crispbread: ❑ Kavli ❑ Wasa
❑ Crispy cakes
❑ Health Valley graham crackers
❑ Harvest Crisps 5-Grain *(not all whole grain, but good for variety)*
❑ Mr. Phipps
Rice Cakes: ❑ Plain
❑ Quaker Banana Nut
❑ Ry Krisp
❑ ________________
❑ ________________

DAIRY
❑ Butter ❑ Light butter
Cheese *(low-fat — fewer than 5 grams of fat per ounce)*:
Cheddar:
❑ Kraft Fat Free
❑ Kraft Natural Reduced Fat
❑ Cottage cheese *(1% or nonfat)*
Cream cheese:
❑ Philadelphia Light *(tub)*
❑ Philadelphia Free
❑ Farmer's
❑ Jarlsberg Lite
Mozzarella: ❑ Nonfat
❑ Part-skim
❑ String cheese
Nonrefrigerated:
❑ Laughing Cow Light
❑ Parmesan
Ricotta: ❑ Nonfat ❑ Skim milk
❑ Sun-Ni Armenian String
❑ Egg substitute
❑ Eggs
❑ Milk *(skim or 1%)*
❑ Nonfat sour cream
❑ Nonfat plain yogurt
❑ Stonyfield Farm yogurt
❑ ________________
❑ ________________

CANNED GOODS
Chicken broth: ❑ Swanson's Natural Goodness
❑ Evaporated skim milk
❑ Hearts of Palm
Soups: ❑ Healthy Choice
❑ Pritikin
Progresso: ❑ Hearty Black Bean
❑ Lentil
Tomatoes: ❑ Paste ❑ Sauce
❑ Stewed ❑ Whole
❑ ________________
❑ ________________
❑ ________________

CONDIMENTS
❑ Honey
Hot Pepper Sauce:
❑ Pickapeppa sauce
❑ Shriracha Chili Sauce
❑ Jamaican Hell Fire
❑ Tabasco
Mayonnaise: ❑ Light
❑ Miracle Whip Light
Mustard: ❑ Dijon ❑ Spicy hot
❑ Pepperoncini peppers
Salad Dressing:
❑ Bernstein's Reduced Calorie
❑ Good Seasons ❑ Kraft Free
❑ Jardine's Fat Free Garlic Vinaigrette
❑ Pritikin
❑ Soy sauce *(low-sodium)*
❑ Salsa or picante sauce
Spices and herbs: ❑ Allspice
❑ Basil ❑ Black pepper
❑ Cayenne ❑ Celery seed
❑ Chili powder ❑ Cinnamon
❑ Creole seasoning ❑ Curry
❑ Dill weed ❑ Five spice
❑ Garlic powder ❑ Ginger
❑ Mrs. Dash Original Blend
❑ Mrs. Dash Garlic and Herb Seasoning
❑ Mustard ❑ Nutmeg
❑ Oregano
❑ Onion powder
❑ Paprika ❑ Parsley
❑ Pepper, cracked
❑ Rosemary ❑ Saffron

❑ Salt ❑ Thyme
Fresh herbs: ❑ Basil
❑ Chives ❑ Cilantro ❑ Ginger
❑ Parsley ❑ Rosemary ❑ Thyme
❑ Vanilla extract
Vinegars: ❑ Balsamic ❑ Cider
❑ Red wine ❑ Rice wine
❑ Tarragon ❑ White wine
❑ White wine Worcestershire sauce
❑ ____________________

FRUITS
Fresh fruits: ❑ Apples ❑ Apricots
❑ Bananas ❑ Berries ❑ Cherries
❑ Dates *(unsweetened, pitted)*
❑ Grapefruit ❑ Grapes ❑ Kiwi
❑ Lemons ❑ Limes ❑ Mango
❑ Melon ❑ Nectarines
❑ Oranges ❑ Papaya ❑ Peaches
❑ Pears ❑ Pineapple ❑ Plantains
❑ Plums
Dried fruits: ❑ Apricots ❑ Peaches
❑ Pineapple
❑ Raisins (dark and golden)
❑ Mixed
❑ ____________________
❑ ____________________

VEGETABLES
❑ Asparagus ❑ Beets
❑ Bell peppers ❑ Broccoli
❑ Brussels sprouts ❑ Cabbage
❑ Carrots ❑ Cauliflower ❑ Celery
❑ Corn ❑ Cucumbers ❑ Eggplant
❑ Garlic ❑ Green beans ❑ Greens
❑ Hot peppers ❑ Kale
❑ Mushrooms ❑ Okra ❑ Onions
❑ Peas ❑ Red potatoes ❑ Radicchio
❑ Romaine lettuce
❑ Salad greens ❑ Shallots
❑ Simply Potatoes hash browns
❑ Spinach
❑ Squash *(yellow, crookneck)*
❑ Sugar snap peas *(frozen)*
❑ Sun-dried tomatoes
❑ Sweet potatoes ❑ Tomatoes
❑ White potatoes ❑ Zucchini
❑ ____________________
❑ ____________________

BEANS AND MEATS
Beans and peas: ❑ Black
❑ Chickpeas/garbanzo beans
❑ Cannelini ❑ Kidney ❑ Lentils
❑ Navy ❑ Pinto ❑ Split peas
❑ ____________________
Beef *(lean)*: ❑ Deli-sliced
❑ Ground round
❑ London broil
❑ Round steak
❑ ____________________
Fish and seafood: ❑ Clams
❑ Cod ❑ Grouper ❑ Mussels
❑ Salmon ❑ Scallops
❑ Shrimp ❑ Snapper
❑ Swordfish ❑ Tuna
❑ ____________________
Lamb: ❑ Leg ❑ Loin chops
Pork: ❑ Canadian bacon
❑ Center cut chops
❑ Tenderloin
Poultry:
Chicken: ❑ Boneless breasts
❑ Legs/Thighs
❑ Whole fryer
Turkey: ❑ Bacon ❑ Breast
❑ Ground ❑ Deli-Sliced
❑ Whole
❑ ____________________
Veal: ❑ Chops ❑ Cutlets
❑ Ground
Water-packed cans: ❑ Chicken
❑ Salmon ❑ Tuna
❑ Charlie's Lunch Kit
❑ ____________________
❑ ____________________

MISCELLANEOUS
All-fruit spreads and pourable fruit:
❑ Knudsen ❑ Polaner
❑ Smucker's Simply Fruit
❑ Welch's Totally Fruit
❑ Baking powder
❑ Baking soda
Bean dips: ❑ Jardine's
❑ Guiltless Gourmet
❑ Bread crumbs
Cooking oils: ❑ Canola ❑ Olive
❑ Cornstarch
Fruit Juices *(unsweetened)*:
❑ Apple ❑ Cranberry-apple
❑ White grape ❑ Orange
❑ Nonstick cooking spray
Nuts/seeds *(dry-roasted, unsalted)*:
❑ Peanuts ❑ Sunflower kernels
❑ Pecans ❑ Walnuts
Pasta Sauce: ❑ Pritikin
❑ Classico Tomato and Basil
❑ Ragú Chunky Gardenstyle
❑ Peanut butter *(natural)*
❑ Phyllo dough
Popcorn:
❑ Orville Redenbacher's Natural Light or Smart Pop microwave popcorn
❑ Plain kernels
❑ ____________________
Tortilla chips: ❑ Baked Tostitos
❑ Guiltless Gourmet
❑ Water *(spring or sparkling)*
Wine: ❑ Dealcoholized ❑ Red
❑ White
❑ ____________________
❑ ____________________
❑ ____________________
❑ ____________________
❑ ____________________
❑ ____________________
❑ ____________________
❑ ____________________
❑ ____________________
❑ ____________________
❑ ____________________
❑ ____________________
❑ ____________________
❑ ____________________
❑ ____________________
❑ ____________________
❑ ____________________
❑ ____________________
❑ ____________________
❑ ____________________
❑ ____________________
❑ ____________________
❑ ____________________
❑ ____________________
❑ ____________________
❑ ____________________
❑ ____________________
❑ ____________________
❑ ____________________
❑ ____________________
❑ ____________________
❑ ____________________
❑ ____________________

The Well-Stocked Kitchen

TIPS AND RECIPES

Prepare the following recipe for homemade creole seasoning, and store it in an airtight container, ready to add to your favorite recipe:

Homemade Creole Seasoning

2 1/2 Tbsp. paprika
2 Tbsp. garlic powder
1 Tbsp. salt
1 Tbsp. onion powder
1 Tbsp. dried oregano
1 Tbsp. dried thyme
1 Tbsp. red pepper
1 Tbsp. black pepper

Combine all ingredients in a small bowl; stir well. Store in an airtight container. Yield: about 2/3 cup (serving size: 1 tsp.)

1 tsp. gives 201 mg. sodium.

Special Grocery Items

A few of the ingredients used in *The Good Life* grocery list and recipes may be unfamiliar to you or may not be available at your local supermarket, depending on the region. Ask your grocer for help, or try a nearby health food store or ethnic specialty shop.

ARBORIO RICE: This Italian grain is a must for risotto because the high-starch kernels add creamy texture. Arborio is now found in most supermarket and health food stores.

ARUGULA: This aromatic green lends a special flavor to salads. It is sold in small bunches in the supermarket produce section or farmer's markets.

CANADIAN BACON: The lean eye meat of a pork loin, this low-fat breakfast meat is not just for breakfast. One to two tablespoons of finely chopped Canadian bacon added at the end of cooking any recipe calling for salt pork or bacon, will yield a delicious smoky presence with far less fat. Use it occasionally, and enjoy it!

CAPERS: These little packages of flavor pack a powerful punch — sour, bitter and salty all at the same time. You'll find them in the supermarket's condiment section pickled and packed in small jars. You'll use them sparingly because they are so highly salted, never more than 1 tablespoon in a serving. Always rinse capers before using. Don't despair using such a small amount; they last in the refrigerator for several weeks.

CILANTRO: The flat leaf of the coriander plant, this herb is also called Chinese parsley and fresh coriander. It's terrific in Mexican, Asian and Caribbean dishes, but if it's new to you, use it sparingly (start with just a teaspoon): too much and it can make the dish taste like soap! You'll find it looking like parsley in the produce department of the supermarket.

COUSCOUS: These tiny beads of ground wheat semolina resemble rice, but couscous is actually a type of pasta. Most couscous you find will be precooked; it requires only a 5-minute plumping in hot stock or water. Whole wheat couscous is available at health food stores.

CREOLE SEASONING: The blend of spices used in creole seasonings can add a sassy surprise to your favorite recipes for soups, meat dishes and salads. Make your own creole seasoning and keep it handy when you cook, or purchase in the spice aisle.

Tony Chachere's is my favorite!

EVAPORATED SKIM MILK: A terrific way to add richness and creaminess to a sauce without heavy cream. It has a cream-like flavor and is richer in texture than regular milk. You'll find it in the baking ingredients aisle of the supermarket with the shelf-stable milks such as Parmalat — another new milk that's great to keep on hand and to travel with.

EUROPEAN CUCUMBERS: You'll find these long, dark green cucumbers vacuum-seal wrapped in the produce department. Their claim to fame is that they are seedless and crisp — and don't bring on the indigestion of their "normal" cucumber cousins.

FISH SAUCE: This is an essential Asian ingredient and can be used in place of soy sauce. The better brands are really wonderful. Look for it packaged in glass, not plastic, from companies in Thailand.

FIVE SPICE: Chinese five spice powder is a blend of equal parts of cinnamon, cloves, fennel seed, star anise and Szechuan peppercorns. It has a pungent, slightly sweet licorice flavor and is used in Oriental cuisine.

FRUIT JUICES: 100 percent pure juices (no sugar added) make wonderful marinades, bringing out the flavor of foods such as poultry and seafood. In their concentrated form they are also natural sweeteners that can easily replace refined sugar.

SALAD GREENS: There are many exotic greens found in the salads of *The Good Life* — frizee, radicchio and arugula among them. Ask your produce grocer about their availability; they add much interest to a salad. If you don't have these, substitute red leaf lettuce along with romaine and green leaf lettuces.

HERBS: These are surprise packages of flavor — accenting and enhancing the flavor of whatever you serve. Whole leaves of basil, cilantro, thyme and rosemary are wonderful for garnish; a chopped mixture is great to throw into a dish while cooking and onto the whole plate confetti-style when serving.

You may also use dried herbs in cooking and save the fresh herbs for garnish where their full flavor can be enjoyed. Because dried herbs are so much stronger than fresh, use only one-third as much. (One tablespoon of fresh equals one teaspoon of dried.)

Finely chop and blend the following herbs: 1 bunch cilantro, 1 bunch basil, 1 bunch rosemary and 1 bunch thyme. You may store them in your refrigerator for several days. Add them as you prepare your favorite recipes.

To wash herbs, fill a pitcher with water, and hold herbs by the stem while swishing them in the water. Lay them on paper towels to dry.

ORZO: This tiny pasta resembles a soft, wonderful rice. Orzo cooks up in about five minutes and makes a delightful side dish.

PARMESAN CHEESE: Don't even bother with the pre-grated Parmesan cheese dust — it's not worth the fat calories. But do try a chunk of fresh Parmesan grated directly onto your meals right as you're serving. The world's best Parmesan, from the cows around Parma, Italy, is called parmigiano-reggiano. It is semisweet and slightly salty and has a dry crumbly texture. It is also made from skim milk, which helps lower its fat content.

HOT PEPPER SAUCE: My favorite pepper sauce is an Asian one called Shriracha Chili Sauce and another from Jamaica called Jamaican Hell Fire. I'm also very fond of Pickapeppa sauce. They are found in the condiment aisle of the supermarket or a specialty store. If you don't find either, Tabasco will do fine.

PEPPERCORNS: Green peppercorns are harvested early and are best when pickled in brine. They have a salty taste like a caper, a bite like a pepper and a somewhat nutty texture. Black peppercorns are dried, and are great when rough ground at the last moment. White pepper is good used in light-colored sauces and mashed potatoes.

PENNE: A common pasta, penne is named because of its pointed ends, reminiscent of the pointed end of a fountain pen.

PIZZA CRUSTS: Make your own pizza dough from scratch; but when time is short, try pleasant Boboli, available in thin crust rounds. Prepared pizza dough can also be found in the dairy case.

PORCINI MUSHROOMS: These wild mushrooms are also known as cèpes. Dried porcini are used widely in Italian cooking; they contribute a rich, woodsy flavor to dishes. Packages of dried porcini may be found in the specialty section of most supermarkets and in Italian markets.

PHYLLO DOUGH: With the help of cooking spray, this makes a terrific pie crust. Find it in the freezer section of your supermarket. See techniques for using on pages 159 and 165.

RADICCHIO: This red-leaf Italian chicory with a deep purple-red hue and a somewhat hot taste is readily available and adds great flavor to salads. Peak season is midwinter to spring. It's terrific in salads as an alternative to tomatoes or as an enhancement.

ROASTED PEPPERS: The homemade version of these are the best, but the jarred variety are a convenient alternative. The peppers are bottled with water in 7 1/2-ounce or larger jars and can usually be found alongside other Italian items in the supermarket.

SALSAS: These low-fat, flavorful toppings or dips can be purchased at the grocery store, either fresh at the deli area or jarred on the shelves. You can also make your own; it will stay fresh and high quality for four to five days. Try the recipes on pages 44 and 72.

STOCKS: These are flavor-packed liquids for almost all cooking in *The Good Life.* They are readily available in the soup section of supermarkets, in low-sodium and low-fat versions. You can "defat" even these canned stocks by

For skimming fat from stocks (and soups or other liquids), trim a piece of wax paper the same size as the container the stock is in.

Gently lay wax paper directly on top of the stock, being careful not to let any liquid spill over it. Refrigerate to chill.

When ready, simply peel up the wax paper and all hardened fat will stick to it.

refrigerating the can and skimming off the thin layer of fat after careful opening.

You can also make your own more flavorful, less expensive stocks and store them in the freezer until ready to use. (Freeze stocks in ice cube trays till frozen, then empty these quarter-cup cubes into a freezer zip-top bag.)

Stock recipes are found on page 37.

TOMATO BASIL SAUCE: This all-round, perfect-for-many-uses sauce may be purchased jarred (on the grocer's shelves) or made fresh. If you opt to keep the purchased variety on hand, look for one such as Classico, made from naturally fresh ingredients with less than two grams of fat per serving. You may also want to try the recipe on page 48; it freezes beautifully in small freezer zip-top bags for up to three months.

WASHED SALAD PACKS AND FRESH VEGETABLES: Fresh Express and TKO market bags of washed, attractive, ready-to-eat salads come in 10- to 12-ounce bags. Some produce sections also offer cut vegetables — broccoli, cauliflower, carrots, celery — sold both separately and in combinations. They make for quick salads, stir-frying and fresh veggie platters.

WHOLE WHEAT PASTRY FLOUR: Most easily found in the natural foods store, this flour is the best choice for muffins, pancakes or waffles because it is finely milled from a soft wheat. It will make your whole grain breads much lighter and less dense. Don't use for yeast breads, however, since this flour doesn't contain enough gluten for rising.

WINE: Wine is an excellent ingredient for adding flavor without caloric, fat or alcohol cost. Almost all of the alcohol evaporates during the cooking process. If you don't ordinarily have wine in your house when a recipe calls for it, buy wine splits (6.4 ounces or one-fourth of a standard wine bottle). Splits are easier to store and use up once opened.

WINE WITHOUT ALCOHOL: Because there are a number of people who choose not to use wine, even in cooking, you may want to substitute a good dealcoholized wine as an attractive ingredient.

These wines are distinguished by the fact that they are made from classic grapes, by classic methods, and only subjected to the removal of the alcohol by a system of reverse osmosis. There are several producers; ask your supermarket for the best-selling brands and availability.

Some examples of dealcoholized wines are Sutter Home Fré and Ariel. Some grocery stores stock these in the juice aisle rather than with the traditional wines.

When cooking with these wines, it's best to split the amount, adding half at the beginning of the cooking process and half to freshen at the end.

VINEGARS: The zip and flavor that can be added to recipes through balsamic, raspberry, rice, red wine and tarragon vinegars can't be stressed enough. Plus, they add virtually no calories.

Balsamic is an incredibly complex vinegar that's great in salads and for marinades and finishing vegetables. Balsamic is aged in barrels of oak, chestnut, mulberry and juniper, picking up the flavors of each. Some are very old and expensive — but go for the mid-priced variety that doesn't rely on a fancy label for status selling.

Rice wine vinegar is a wonderful mild vinegar that is perfect for vinaigrettes and Asian salads. Chinese is mildest; Japanese does fine.

Stock Recipes

The secret of setting a "good table" is organization, which means planning ahead. Even if you have only half an hour to get a meal on the table, you can make it a healthy, balanced one, prepared from scratch, if you get — or even keep — most of the ingredients ready ahead of time.

On the following pages you will find a grouping of stock recipes — dressings, spreads, sauces, salsas and such. Although most are used in recipes within *The Good Life,* you can mix and match them, creating your own special dish. Here is the beauty of this kind of fresh and flavorful cuisine: If you start with good ingredients and a little guidance, you can make up your own rules.

Homemade Stocks

Hearty Meat Stock

3 to 4 pounds chicken pieces (or beef or veal bones with meat on them)
6 black peppercorns
2 carrots, sliced
2 cloves garlic, minced
1 medium onion, chopped
1 stalk celery with leaves, sliced
1 bay leaf
2 Tbsp. chopped fresh parsley (or 1 Tbsp. dried)
1 tsp. salt

Cover chicken with water; add peppercorns. Simmer uncovered for 30 minutes. Add remaining ingredients. Cover and simmer for 2 additional hours (4 additional hours for beef or veal). Strain stock and remove chicken. Use deboned chicken in salads or recipes calling for cubed chicken.

Chill stock until the fat can be skimmed off easily. The stock is then ready to use, or it can be frozen for use later.

1 serving = 4 oz. or 1/2 cup.

Per Serving: 10 Calories	
Protein 1.8 gr.	Carb. less than 1 gr.
Fat less than 1 gr.	Cal. from fat 0%
Chol. 0 mg.	Sodium 120 mg.

Trimmings Stock

scrubbed vegetable tops, peelings and scraps
salt (or low-sodium soy sauce)
onions (or garlic) for flavoring as desired
herbs as desired (choose from bay leaves, rosemary, basil and others)

Load a heavy pot with scrubbed vegetable scraps. (These can be collected for up to a week and stored in the refrigerator in a plastic bag.) Cover the scraps with water; add a pinch of salt. Salt is optional but will draw nutrients into the stock. Add onions and your favorite herbs. Cover the pot and let simmer for 1 to 2 hours, stirring occasionally.

Let cool; strain and refrigerate or freeze. Stock will keep for 8 to 10 days in the refrigerator. Freeze the stock in either pint-sized containers or ice cube trays (store frozen cubes in plastic bags). One cube equals 1/4 cup stock.

1 serving = 4 oz. or 1/2 cup.

Per Serving: 4 Calories	
Protein 0 gr.	Carb. less than 1 gr.
Fat 0 gr.	Cal. from fat 0%
Chol. 0 mg.	Sodium 120 mg.

The Well-Stocked Kitchen

TIPS AND RECIPES

Always have stocks on hand for steaming vegetables, cooking pasta and rice, and making soups and sauces. They provide flavor in a light way.

Cook stocks in large quantities and chill to allow all the fat to rise to the surface. Skim off this fat, then freeze or refrigerate.

Hint: Everything can be used as scraps — seeds and cores of peppers, broccoli leaves and stalks, outer leaves of greens, onion slices, even cauliflower cores! Go light on vegetables from the cabbage family, however, since they provide a strong flavor.

Salad Dressings

It's easy to pick up a bottle of fat-free dressing at the store, but with scarcely more effort, you can whip up delicious homemade versions of your store-bought favorites.

Don't despair that these dressings seem to have such a high percentage of calories from fat — the calories are so low that even a gram of fat looks like a lot. When used in a recipe, the percentage normalizes.

These salad dressings rely on the mild flavors of wonderful vinegars, herbs and spices, and chicken stock. I often use skim milk cheeses to thicken these dressings, so precious little oil is added.

Honey-Orange Vinaigrette

1/2 cup orange juice
1 Tbsp. honey
1/2 cup balsamic vinegar
1/2 tsp. creole seasoning
1 tsp. Pickapeppa sauce (or hot pepper sauce)
juice of 1/2 lemon
1 Tbsp. chopped fresh herbs (cilantro, basil, rosemary, thyme)

Mix together all ingredients. Refrigerate. Makes 10 servings, 2 Tbsp. each.

Per Serving: 12 Calories	
Protein 0 gr.	Carb. 3 gr.
Fat 0 gr.	Cal. from fat 0%
Chol. 0 mg.	Sodium 53 mg.

Greek Vinaigrette

1/4 cup olive oil
1 1/4 cups rice wine vinegar
3/4 cup chicken stock (fat-free/low salt)
1/4 cup Dijon mustard
1/2 cup pepperoncini juice
1 Tbsp. minced garlic
1 Tbsp. minced shallots
1 tsp. creole seasoning
2 Tbsp. chopped fresh herbs (cilantro, basil, rosemary, thyme)
1 Tbsp. chopped fresh oregano (or 1 tsp. dried)

In a large bowl, whisk together all ingredients. Refrigerate.

Makes 25 servings, 2 Tbsp. each.

Per Serving: 21 Calories	
Protein 0 gr.	Carb. 1 gr.
Fat 2 gr.	Cal. from fat 66%
Chol. 0 mg.	Sodium 139 mg.

Herbal Vinaigrette

2 cups chicken stock (fat-free/low salt)
1/4 cup olive oil
1 cup balsamic vinegar
1 tsp. cornstarch
1 Tbsp. cold water
2 tsp. minced garlic
1/4 tsp. cracked black pepper
1 tsp. creole seasoning
1 Tbsp. chopped fresh thyme
1 Tbsp. chopped fresh parsley
1 Tbsp. chopped fresh basil
1 Tbsp. chopped fresh oregano
1 Tbsp. chopped fresh chives

Heat together chicken stock, olive oil and vinegar.

In a separate bowl, whisk cornstarch together with cold water. Add to stock mixture and let simmer for 1 minute to thicken.

Take off heat and cool. Add remaining ingredients and refrigerate.

Makes 25 servings, 2 Tbsp. each.

Per Serving: 21 Calories	
Protein 0 gr.	Carb. 1 gr.
Fat 2 gr.	Cal. from fat 66%
Chol. 0 mg.	Sodium 145 mg.

Citrus Vinaigrette

2 Tbsp. olive oil
2/3 cup rice wine vinegar
1/3 cup orange juice
1 Tbsp. Dijon mustard
1 tsp. honey
2 tsp. minced garlic
1 Tbsp. minced shallots
1/2 tsp. creole seasoning
2 Tbsp. chopped fresh cilantro

Mix all ingredients together. Refrigerate. Makes 12 servings, 2 Tbsp. each.

Per Serving: 30 Calories	
Protein 0 gr.	Carb. 3 gr.
Fat 2 gr.	Cal. from fat 62%
Chol. 0 mg.	Sodium 62 mg.

Green Goddess Dressing

1 cup nonfat cottage cheese
1/2 cup cider vinegar
2 stalks celery, diced
1/2 cup spinach leaves, washed and stemmed
1/3 cup fresh parsley
1/2 tsp. cracked black pepper
2 Tbsp. chopped fresh tarragon
1 Tbsp. lemon juice
2 scallions, sliced thin
1 tsp. Mrs. Dash seasoning
1/2 tsp. creole seasoning

Blend cottage cheese in blender or food processor until smooth. Add remaining ingredients and blend well. Refrigerate.

Makes 12 servings, 2 Tbsp. each.

Per Serving: 14 Calories	
Protein 2 gr.	Carb. 1.5 gr.
Fat 0 gr.	Cal. from fat 0 %
Chol. 1 mg.	Sodium 54 mg.

Cucumber Dill Dressing

6 oz. light cream cheese
1/3 cup farmer's cheese
1 cup skim milk
1 cup cucumbers, peeled, seeded and chopped
1 1/2 Tbsp. Dijon mustard
2 cloves garlic, minced
1/4 tsp. cracked black pepper
1 tsp. creole seasoning
1 Tbsp. olive oil
juice of 1 lemon
1/2 tsp. Tabasco
2 Tbsp. chopped fresh dill

Blend cheeses and skim milk in a blender. Add all other ingredients except the dill and blend until smooth. Stir in dill.

Makes 24 servings, 4 Tbsp. each.

Per Serving: 38 Calories	
Protein 1.5 gr.	Carb. 1 gr.
Fat 3 gr.	Cal. from fat 71%
Chol. 3 mg.	Sodium 34 mg.

The Well-Stocked Kitchen

TIPS AND RECIPES

You can make your own flavored vinegars easily and inexpensively.

To make Herb Vinegar: Start with a wine vinegar, cider vinegar or rice wine vinegar base, then add fresh herbs of your choosing, such as tarragon or basil. Whole garlic cloves may be added as well.

To make Fruit-Flavored Vinegar: Add top-quality berries such as raspberries to a wine vinegar, cider vinegar or rice wine vinegar base. Use 2 cups fruit for every 2 cups of vinegar. Let the mixture steep, covered, in a wide-mouthed jar for a week, then transfer all to a clean bottle and refrigerate. May use for 6 weeks.

Salad Dressings (continued)

Horseradish Dressing

3 Tbsp. grated fresh horseradish
16 oz. nonfat plain yogurt
2 Tbsp. minced shallots
1/4 tsp. white pepper
1/2 tsp. creole seasoning
1 tsp. Mrs. Dash seasoning
1 Tbsp. low-sodium soy sauce
2 Tbsp. rice wine vinegar
juice of 2 lemons
1/3 cup orange juice concentrate

Use fresh horseradish, if possible. Peel and grate very fine.

Whisk horseradish together with remaining ingredients. Chill.

Makes 25 servings, 2 Tbsp. each.

Per Serving: 14 Calories	
Protein 1 gr.	Carb. 2.5 gr.
Fat 0 gr.	Cal. from fat 0%
Chol. 0 mg.	Sodium 98 mg.

Fresh horseradish is found in your supermarket's produce section and can be stored, in airtight plastic bags for up to 3 weeks. Peel and cut out the fibrous core just before grating.

Bottled horseradish can be found in the refrigerated case of the supermarket. Once opened, it loses its flavor within 4 weeks. You can freeze it for longer use by spooning tablespoons onto a baking sheet and freezing till solid. Then transfer them to an airtight plastic bag for use over the next 6 months.

Peppercorn-Parmesan Dressing

1 cup nonfat buttermilk
1/4 cup grated Parmesan cheese
1/3 cup nonfat sour cream
1/4 cup light mayonnaise
2 Tbsp. lemon juice
2 tsp. cracked black pepper
1/4 tsp. salt

Combine all ingredients in a bowl; stir well with wire whisk. Cover and chill. Perfect served over mixed greens.

Makes 12 servings, 2 Tbsp. each.

Per Serving: 33 Calories	
Protein 1 gr.	Carb. 1 gr.
Fat 2 gr.	Cal. from fat 53%
Chol. 2 mg.	Sodium 100 mg.

Caesar Salad Dressing

2 tsp. spicy hot mustard
1 tsp. anchovy paste
1 clove garlic, minced
1/2 cup nonfat buttermilk
1/4 cup grated Parmesan cheese
2 Tbsp. white wine*
2 Tbsp. red wine vinegar
1/2 tsp. creole seasoning
1 Tbsp. chopped fresh parsley
1 Tbsp. lemon juice
1 Tbsp. olive oil
*** *or substitute dealcoholized wine or chicken stock (fat-free/low salt)***

Combine mustard, anchovy paste and garlic in a small bowl; stir well. Add remaining ingredients, stirring with a wire whisk until blended. Cover and chill. Try this over mixed greens.

Makes 8 servings, 2 Tbsp. each.

Per Serving: 39 Calories	
Protein 2 gr.	Carb. 1.5 gr.
Fat 2.5 gr.	Cal. from fat 58%
Chol. 2.5 mg.	Sodium 152 mg.

Roasted Garlic Dijon Vinaigrette

5 full heads garlic, roasted* and pureed
1 tsp. creole seasoning
1/2 cup rice wine vinegar
2 Tbsp. honey
1/2 cup Dijon mustard
1 tsp. cracked black pepper
1 tsp. Mrs. Dash Garlic and Herb Seasoning
1 cup chicken stock (fat-free/low salt)
1/4 cup olive oil

* To roast garlic, chop stems off garlic heads until the flesh of the cloves is visible. Place open ends down on very lightly oiled baking pan. Cover with aluminum foil and bake in 350-degree oven until soft, about 45 minutes to 1 hour. Remove from oven and allow to cool. Then squeeze out all the tender and flavorful flesh from the heads. Discard emptied heads.

Combine all ingredients except oil in food processor or blender. Blend together. While blending, slowly add oil and continue processing until oil is incorporated and dressing is well blended. Refrigerate.

Makes 25 servings, 2 Tbsp. each.

Per Serving: 36 Calories	
Protein 1 gr.	Carb. 3.5 gr.
Fat 2 gr.	Cal. from fat 58%
Chol. 0 mg.	Sodium 110 mg.

Dressing in a Hurry

1/2 cup balsamic or rice wine vinegar
1/3 cup chicken stock (fat-free/low salt)
1 pkg. dried Italian dressing mix
1 Tbsp. olive oil

Pour vinegar and chicken stock into shakable container with lid. Add dressing mix and olive oil. Shake well and refrigerate.

Makes 8 servings, 2 Tbsp. each.

Per Serving: 15 Calories	
Protein 0 gr.	Carb. 1 gr.
Fat 1.2 gr.	Cal. from fat 79%
Chol. 0 mg.	Sodium 320 mg.

Cumin-Dijon Dressing

3 Tbsp. lemon juice
1 Tbsp. olive oil
1 Tbsp. red wine vinegar
2 Tbsp. chicken stock (fat-free/low salt)
1 tsp. cumin
1 tsp. Dijon mustard
2 cloves garlic, minced
1/2 tsp. creole seasoning

Whisk ingredients together. This dressing can be used with salads and is a delicious addition to pita sandwiches.

Makes 4 servings, 2 Tbsp. each.

Per Serving: 31 Calories	
Protein 0 gr.	Carb. 0 gr.
Fat 3.4 gr.	Cal. from fat 98%
Chol. 0 mg.	Sodium 150 mg.

The Well-Stocked Kitchen

TIPS AND RECIPES

For an extra smooth vinaigrette, combine the ingredients and an ice cube in a screw-top jar and shake vigorously. Discard the ice cube once the dressing is mixed.

The Well-Stocked Kitchen

TIPS AND RECIPES

Marinades flavor and tenderize foods. Most marinades contain an acid ingredient (like lemon or lime juice, vinegar or wine) which tenderizes tough cuts of meat.

Always marinate food in a glass or plastic container, never metal. Allow the marinade to cover the food. Food can also be marinated in a large zip-top plastic bag. Turn the bag occasionally to distribute the marinade.

Unused marinade may be refrigerated for up to 2 weeks.

Used marinade must be frozen, then thawed for future use. Boil before using.

BBQ Sauces and Marinades

Balsamic Marinade

3 cups chicken stock (fat-free/low salt)
1/2 cup olive oil
2 cups balsamic vinegar
1 Tbsp. cornstarch
2 Tbsp. water
1 Tbsp. minced garlic
1 tsp. cracked black pepper
1 Tbsp. chopped fresh thyme
2 Tbsp. chopped fresh cilantro
1 Tbsp. chopped fresh basil
1/2 Tbsp. chopped fresh oregano
1/2 Tbsp. chopped chives
1 Tbsp. Pickapeppa sauce (or hot pepper sauce)
1/4 cup orange juice
juice of 1 lime
1 serrano or jalapeño pepper, seeded and diced
2 tsp. creole seasoning

Heat chicken stock, oil and vinegar. In a separate bowl, blend together the cornstarch and water. Add to the stock mixture. Gently boil for 1 minute to thicken.

Remove from heat and cool. Add remaining ingredients and refrigerate.

Use for marinating meats and vegetables. Marinating time can vary from 15 minutes to overnight.

Makes 50 servings, 2 Tbsp. each.

Per Serving: 21 Calories	
Protein 0 gr.	Carb. 1 gr.
Fat 2 gr.	Cal. from fat 85%
Chol. 0 mg.	Sodium 43 mg.

Citrus BBQ Sauce

2 cups KC Masterpiece BBQ Sauce (or your favorite BBQ sauce)
1 can (6 oz.) orange juice concentrate
1 tsp. creole seasoning
1 Tbsp. Jamaican jerk seasoning
juice of 1/2 lime

In a medium bowl, whisk together all ingredients. Refrigerate. Excellent on chicken, pork chops and turkey cutlets.

Makes 3 cups, 24 servings, 2 Tbsp. per serving.

Per Serving: 29 Calories	
Protein 0 gr.	Carb. 6 gr.
Fat less than 1 gr.	Cal. from fat 0%
Chol. 0 mg.	Sodium 205 mg.

European Marinade

1/2 cup lime or lemon juice
2 tsp. dried thyme
2 cloves garlic, minced
1 Tbsp. olive oil
1/2 tsp. salt
1/2 tsp. cracked black pepper

Combine all ingredients. Marinate skinned chicken, meat, fish or seafood for 3 to 4 hours or overnight. Grill.

Makes 1/2 cup, 4 servings, 2 Tbsp. per serving.

Per Serving: 26 Calories	
Protein 0 gr.	Carb. 2 gr.
Fat 2 gr.	Cal. from fat 69%
Chol. 0 mg.	Sodium 267 mg.

Jamaican Marinade

1/4 cup olive oil
2 Tbsp. Jamaican jerk seasoning
1/4 cup orange juice
2 Tbsp. low-sodium soy sauce
1/4 cup white vinegar
1 Tbsp. dark Jamaican rum (optional)
juice of 1 lime
1 Scotch bonnet or habanero pepper, seeded and minced
2 cloves garlic, minced
1/2 cup chopped white onions
2 green onions, chopped
1/2 tsp. creole seasoning

Slowly add the olive oil to the jerk seasoning, stirring with a wire whisk. Then add all remaining ingredients; stir. Refrigerate. Use to marinate chicken, pork and lean beef.

Makes 1 1/2 cups of marinade, about 12 servings, 2 Tbsp. per serving.

Per Serving: 47 Calories	
Protein 0 gr.	Carb. 1.5 gr.
Fat 4 gr.	Cal. from fat 83%
Chol. 0 mg.	Sodium 131 mg.

Tropical Marinade

1/3 cup unsweetened pineapple juice
1/3 cup low-sodium soy sauce
1/3 cup sherry or chicken stock (fat-free/low salt)
2 cloves garlic, minced
2 Tbsp. chopped fresh parsley (or 1 Tbsp. dried)
1/2 tsp. cracked black pepper

Combine all ingredients. Marinate skinned chicken, beef, fish or seafood for 3 to 4 hours or overnight. (The marinade adds no significant calories to the meat.) Grill.

Makes 1 cup, 8 servings, 2 Tbsp. per serving.

Per Serving: 9 Calories	
Protein 0 gr.	Carb. 2 gr.
Fat 0 gr.	Cal. from fat 0%
Chol. 0 mg.	Sodium 387 mg.

Oriental Sauce

1/4 cup chicken stock (fat-free/low salt)
2 Tbsp. dry sherry or dealcoholized wine
2 Tbsp. hoisin sauce
2 Tbsp. low-sodium soy sauce
1 1/2 tsp. minced ginger root
2 cloves garlic, minced
1 tsp. Shriracha Chili Sauce (or hot pepper sauce)

Mix together all ingredients and refrigerate. Use as either a marinade or BBQ sauce.

Makes 3/4 cup, 6 servings, 2 Tbsp. per serving.

Per Serving: 26 Calories	
Protein 0 gr.	Carb. 6 gr.
Fat 0 gr.	Cal. from fat 0
Chol. 0 mg.	Sodium 515 mg.

The undisputed hottest peppers in the world are those flaming-orange gems known as Scotch bonnets from Jamaica and habaneros from Mexico.

They are so similar that some say they're one and the same (but Jamaicans disagree).

Whichever you choose, a little goes a long way. Wear rubber gloves, and be careful not to get the oil on your skin or in your eyes. Removing the seeds and membranes will moderate the heat.

If you can't find the real thing, you can substitute fresh serrano peppers or dried habaneros.

Special Salsas

Pineapple Tomato Salsa

1 pineapple, diced
1 red bell pepper, cut into strips
2 plum tomatoes, diced
juice of 1 lime
1 Tbsp. chopped fresh cilantro
1/4 tsp. dried coriander seed
1 tsp. creole seasoning

Mix all ingredients. Refrigerate at least 1 hour to blend flavors. This salsa will keep in the refrigerator for 4 to 5 days. Serve with sandwiches or salads.

Makes 4 servings, 1/3 cup each.

Per Serving: 32 Calories	
Protein 0 gr.	Carb. 8 gr.
Fat 0 gr.	Cal. from fat 0%
Chol. 0 mg.	Sodium 268 mg.

Tropical Salsa

1 papaya, diced
1 ripe mango, diced
1/2 pineapple, diced
1 red bell pepper, cut into strips
1 tomato, diced
juice of 1 lemon
juice of 1 lime
1 Tbsp. chopped fresh cilantro
1 Tbsp. coconut rum (or 1 tsp. coconut extract)
1/4 tsp. dried coriander seed
1 tsp. creole seasoning

Mix all ingredients. Refrigerate to blend flavors. Serve as a sensational side for sandwiches or as a bed for grilled fish, poultry or beef.

Makes 8 servings, 1/3 cup each.

Per Serving: 40 Calories	
Protein 0 gr.	Carb. 10 gr.
Fat 0 gr.	Cal. from fat 0%
Chol. 0 mg.	Sodium 136 mg.

Black Bean and Corn Salsa

2 cups black beans, drained and rinsed
1 cup frozen corn kernels, thawed
2 plum tomatoes, diced
1/2 red onion, minced
1 serrano pepper, minced
1 Tbsp. chopped fresh cilantro
1 Tbsp. olive oil
4 cloves garlic, minced
juice of 2 limes
1 Tbsp. balsamic vinegar
1 tsp. cumin
2 tsp. hot pepper sauce
1 tsp. creole seasoning

In a large bowl, combine all ingredients and mix well. Allow to marinate at least one hour before serving.

Makes 10 servings, 1/3 cup each.

Per Serving: 79 Calories	
Protein 4 gr.	Carb. 13 gr.
Fat 1.5 gr.	Cal. from fat 17%
Chol. 0 mg.	Sodium 118 mg.

Choose lemons and limes with smooth, brightly colored skin — they should be firm, plump and heavy for their size. One medium lemon yields 3 Tbsp. juice (and 2 to 3 tsp. zest).

Buy lemons in peak season. Squeeze the juice and freeze it in ice cube trays. Once solid, turn them into heavy-weight plastic bags, seal tightly and freeze for up to 6 months.

Lemons at room temperature will yield more juice than refrigerated ones. Popping them into the microwave for 30 seconds on high will also release more juice. Cut them lengthwise for the best squeezing.

Sensational Spreads

Spicy Dijonnaise

1 cup light mayonnaise
1/2 cup nonfat plain yogurt
1 1/2 tsp. Pickapeppa sauce (or hot pepper sauce)
1 1/2 tsp. Sriracha chili sauce (or Tabasco sauce)
1/4 cup Dijon mustard
1/2 tsp. curry powder
1/2 tsp. creole seasoning
3 green onions, diced
1 Tbsp. chopped fresh cilantro
2 cloves garlic, minced
1/2 tsp. black pepper

Mix together mayonnaise, yogurt, sauces, mustard, curry and seasoning. Add onions, cilantro, garlic and pepper. Serve as a flavorful spread for sandwiches.

Makes 30 servings, 1 Tbsp. each.

Per Serving: 24 Calories	
Protein 0 gr.	Carb. 1 gr.
Fat 2 gr.	Cal. from fat 78%
Chol. 3 mg.	Sodium 49 mg.

Garlic Aioli

1 cup light mayonnaise
1/2 cup nonfat plain yogurt
1/2 tsp. creole seasoning
1 Tbsp. minced shallots
2 tsp. chopped fresh herbs (cilantro, basil, rosemary, thyme)
4 cloves garlic, minced
juice of 1/2 lemon

Mix together all ingredients. Great on turkey burgers, fish sandwiches or any special sandwich.

Makes 25 servings, 1 Tbsp. each.

Per Serving: 28 Calories	
Protein 0 gr.	Carb. 1 gr.
Fat 2.5 gr.	Cal. from fat 80%
Chol. 3 mg.	Sodium 25 mg.

Bean and Garlic Pesto

1 1/2 Tbsp. olive oil, divided
3 cloves garlic, left whole
2 cups white cannelini beans, rinsed and drained
1/4 cup lemon juice
2 Tbsp. chicken stock (fat-free/low salt)
1 Tbsp. chopped fresh parsley
1 tsp. hot pepper sauce
1/4 tsp. creole seasoning
1 tsp. chopped fresh rosemary
3 Tbsp. roasted red pepper, finely chopped (purchased)

In an ovenproof skillet over medium-high heat, warm 1/2 Tbsp. of the olive oil. Add garlic and sauté until lightly browned, 3 to 5 minutes. Leave garlic in skillet and bake in oven at 400 degrees until well-browned and softened, 15 to 20 minutes.

In a food processor or blender, puree the rest of the ingredients with roasted garlic and remaining 1 Tbsp. of oil.

This goes perfectly with vegetable baguettes, pocket pitas or any sensational sandwich. Also excellent with whole grain crackers as a protein snack.

Makes 10 servings, 1/4 cup each.

Per Serving: 68 Calories	
Protein 3 gr.	Carb. 10 gr.
Fat 2 gr.	Cal. from fat 28%
Chol. 0 mg.	Sodium 54 mg.

When it comes to mayo, don't get caught in the fat-free trap. If a product says "fat-free," you must ask, "Then, what is in it?" The best choice for mayonnaise is the reduced-fat or light variety; it is low in fat only because it's been whipped with added air and water. The fat-free choice is loaded with multiple sugars, chemicals and food dyes.

You can avoid a lot of mayo by focusing on Dijon mustard, salsa or aioli-type spread made with nonfat yogurt.

Crowd-Pleaser Dips for Chips

Black Bean Dip

2 cans (15 oz. each) black beans, drained and rinsed
4 Tbsp. finely chopped canned or fresh jalapeño peppers
2 Tbsp. red wine vinegar
2 tsp. chili powder (or to taste)
1/2 tsp. creole seasoning
1/4 tsp. cumin
1 Tbsp. minced onion
1 tsp. minced garlic
1 Tbsp. chopped fresh parsley

Place in blender the beans, peppers, vinegar, chili powder, seasoning and cumin. Blend until smooth. Transfer the mixture to a bowl.

Stir in the onion, garlic and parsley.

Makes 12 servings, 1/3 cup each.

Per Serving: 117 Calories	
Protein 8 gr.	Carb. 21 gr.
Fat 0 gr.	Cal. from fat 0%
Chol. 0 mg.	Sodium 68 mg.

Baked Tortilla Chips

Be sure to try the new baked tortilla chips — a tasty, crunchy alternative to the high-fat, fried versions. Generally, 25 chips or so give less than 1 gram of fat. They serve as great dippers for fat-free bean dips and salsas and are a way to add texture to salads.

You can also make your own baked chips. Lightly spray tortillas with cooking spray and season lightly to taste with salt, pepper and/or chili powder. Cut into 12 wedges and bake at 350 degrees until crisp.

Salmon Dip

5 oz. smoked salmon fillet
1 tsp. low-sodium soy sauce
juice of 1/2 lemon
1 tsp. lime juice
1 Tbsp. chopped fresh parsley (or 1 tsp. dried)
1 tsp. Worcestershire sauce
1/2 tsp. grated fresh wasabi or horseradish
1 tsp. minced ginger root
dash of Tabasco sauce
dash of cracked black pepper

Roughly chop salmon. Mix it with all ingredients. Very good with whole wheat toast points.

Makes 4 servings, 1/4 cup each.

Per Serving: 49 Calories	
Protein 8 gr.	Carb. 3 gr.
Fat less than 1 gr.	Cal. from fat 6%
Chol. 16 mg.	Sodium 97 mg.

Creamy Herb Dip

4 oz. light cream cheese, softened
1/4 cup nonfat sour cream
3 Tbsp. chopped fresh chives or scallions
1 Tbsp. chopped fresh dill
1/2 tsp. creole seasoning
1 tsp. Mrs. Dash seasoning
1 tsp. prepared horseradish

Stir cream cheese into sour cream until smooth. Mix in chives, dill, seasonings and horseradish. Spoon into a small bowl. Wonderful with fresh vegetables.

Makes 4 servings, 1/4 cup each.

Per Serving: 24 Calories	
Protein 4 gr.	Carb. 1.5 gr.
Fat 0 gr.	Cal. from fat 0%
Chol. 1 mg.	Sodium 147 mg.

Refreshing Relishes

White Bean Relish

3 cups cooked white beans, drained
juice of 1 lime
3/4 cup Herbal Vinaigrette (pg. 38)
1 tsp. creole seasoning
2 tsp. minced garlic
2 Tbsp. minced shallots
4 Tbsp. chopped fresh cilantro
3 Tbsp. each diced yellow, red and green bell peppers
1 plum tomato, seeded and diced

Mix all ingredients together with beans. Refrigerate.

Use as a sensational side for salads, sandwiches and grilled vegetables.

Makes 10 servings, 1/3 cup each.

Per Serving: 85 Calories	
Protein 5 gr.	Carb. 14 gr.
Fat 1 gr.	Cal. from fat 17%
Chol. 0 mg.	Sodium 108 mg.

Mango Chutney

1/2 ripe mango, cut in strips
1 Tbsp. hot mango chutney
1/2 red bell pepper, cut into strips
1/4 cup orange juice
juice of 1/2 lime
1 Tbsp. fresh coriander or cilantro
1/2 tsp. creole seasoning
1 Tbsp. low-sodium soy sauce

Mix all ingredients. Refrigerate to blend flavors.

Makes 6 servings, 1/4 cup each.

Per Serving: 25 Calories	
Protein 0 gr.	Carb. 6 gr.
Fat 0 gr.	Cal. from fat 0%
Chol. 0 mg.	Sodium 184 mg.

Papaya Ginger Relish

1 papaya, diced
1 Tbsp. ginger root, cut into fine strips
1 red bell pepper, cut into strips
1 serrano or Hungarian pepper, diced
juice of 1 lemon
1/2 cup orange juice
2 chives, cut in 1-inch lengths
1 tsp. creole seasoning

Mix all ingredients. Refrigerate to blend flavors. Super with grilled fish, seafood or chicken, or as a side dish for a sandwich.

Makes 6 servings, 1/3 cup each.

Per Serving: 32 Calories	
Protein 0 gr.	Carb. 8 gr.
Fat 0 gr.	Cal. from fat 0%
Chol. 0 mg.	Sodium 180 mg.

The Well-Stocked Kitchen

TIPS AND RECIPES

Choose mangoes and papayas with unblemished, yellow skin blushed with red. The larger the fruit, the higher the fruit-to-seed ratio. Ripe mangoes will yield to gentle pressure and have a tropical fragrance. Avoid those with shriveled or black-speckled skin.

Refrigerate ripe fruit in a plastic bag for up to 5 days. Place underripe fruit in a paper bag (pierce bag with tip of knife) with a banana at room temperature for 1 to 3 days. Green, rock-hard mangoes and papayas will probably never ripen.

The Well-Stocked Kitchen

TIPS AND RECIPES

Vegetable purees added to sauces and side dishes can be a clever way of coaxing finicky eaters to try a dreaded vegetable. Cook them, throw them in a blender, add some chicken stock and puree. You've just made a sauce for grilled meat. Try laying the meat on the sauce instead of putting the sauce on the meat.

Purees take well to advance preparation and gentle reheating over a double boiler or in a microwave. Keep them tightly wrapped in the refrigerator so they don't dry out.

Sauces

Tomato Basil Sauce

1 Tbsp. olive oil
2 white onions, diced medium
2 tsp. minced garlic
1/2 cup minced shallots
1 Tbsp. chopped fresh thyme
1 tsp. chopped fresh rosemary
1 Tbsp. chopped fresh oregano
2 Tbsp. chopped fresh basil
5 tomatoes, skinned, seeded and diced*
1 can (32 oz.) whole tomatoes
1 Tbsp. creole seasoning
1 Tbsp. Mrs. Dash Garlic and Herb Seasoning

* Tomatoes are easily skinned by immersing them in boiling water for 10 seconds. Remove with slotted spoon. Skins will "slip off."

Sauté onions, garlic, shallots and herbs in olive oil until onions are transparent, about 3 to 4 minutes.

Add fresh and canned tomatoes. Cook for 5 minutes at full heat. Lower heat and continue cooking until sauce has reduced by one-third.

Add seasonings. Cook for about 1 1/2 hours, stirring occasionally. Leave chunky; do not grind or blend.

This sauce may be made in large quantities and frozen (after cooling) in zip-top bags for later use. Microwave or place in refrigerator to thaw.

Makes 14 servings, 1/2 cup each.

Per Serving: 40 Calories	
Protein 1 gr.	Carb. 7 gr.
Fat 1 gr.	Cal. from fat 25%
Chol. 0 mg.	Sodium 240 mg.

Fire-Roasted Pepper Sauce

1 tsp. olive oil
1/2 red onion, diced
2 cloves garlic, minced
8 red bell peppers, fire-roasted*
8 pablano peppers, fire-roasted*
2 Tbsp. white wine Worcestershire sauce
2 cups chicken stock (fat-free/low salt)
1 Tbsp. creole seasoning

* To fire-roast peppers, slice peppers in half lengthwise, core and remove the seeds. Put the sliced peppers directly on the rack of a preheated broiler, cut side down. Broil for about 5 minutes, until the skin blisters. Transfer the roasted peppers to a tightly sealed plastic bag, close it and leave them for 10 to 15 minutes. When cool, the charred skin can be rubbed easily from the peppers and discarded.

Heat olive oil in saucepan. Add onion and garlic, and begin to sauté. Add peppers, Worcestershire sauce, chicken stock and seasoning. Cook until the sauce begins to reduce.

Perfect as a sauce for grilled fish, poultry or beef, or as a dipping sauce for sandwiches.

Makes 25 servings, 1/4 cup each.

Per Serving: 16 Calories	
Protein 0 gr.	Carb. 3 gr.
Fat less than 1 gr.	Cal. from fat 15%
Chol. 0 mg.	Sodium 142 mg.

Fruit Toppings

Apple Compote

3/4 cup water
1/4 cup honey
2 Granny Smith apples, peeled, cored and sliced
1 tsp. cornstarch
1/8 tsp. nutmeg
1/4 tsp. cinnamon

Combine water and honey in saucepan; add apples. Bring to boil, reduce heat and simmer until apples are tender. Remove apples from liquid.

Dissolve cornstarch in a portion of the liquid. Bring remaining liquid back to a boil and add cornstarch mixture. Cook another minute to thicken, then remove from heat. Add spices and stir. Gently fold in apples. Great over pancakes or frozen yogurt.

Makes 8 servings, 1/4 cup each.

Per Serving: 53 Calories	
Protein 0 gr.	Carb. 14 gr.
Fat 0 gr.	Cal. from fat 0%
Chol. 0 mg.	Sodium 1 mg.

Yogurt Fruit Sauce

4 cups nonfat plain yogurt
1 cup orange juice
1/2 cup honey
2 Tbsp. grated orange rind
2 Tbsp. grated lemon rind
1/2 Tbsp. nutmeg
fresh fruit, chopped

Whisk together yogurt, orange juice, honey, orange rind, lemon rind and nutmeg. Chill.

When serving, mix in 2 Tbsp. chopped fresh fruit per 1/4 cup serving of yogurt sauce. Wonderful with pancakes, waffles or french toast, or use as a dipping sauce for fruit.

Makes 25 servings, 1/4 cup each.

Per Serving: 46 Calories	
Protein 2 gr.	Carb. 9 gr.
Fat 0 gr.	Cal. from fat 0%
Chol. 0 mg.	Sodium 28 mg.

Strawberry Sauce

1 cup fresh strawberries
1/4 cup all-fruit strawberry spread

Puree strawberries in blender until smooth. Add fruit spread and mix well.

A delicious dessert sauce or topping for fresh fruit, pancakes or French toast.

Makes 4 servings, 1/4 cup each.

Per Serving: 35 Calories	
Protein 0 gr.	Carb. 8.5 gr.
Fat 0 gr.	Cal. from fat 0%
Chol. 0 mg.	Sodium 17 mg.

The Well-Stocked Kitchen

TIPS AND RECIPES

Fruit sauces can be more than sweet toppings, they can become the crowning touch to your presentation. Buy a ketchup-type squirt bottle and spoon the sauce into it (you may need to thin the sauce with unsweetened white grape juice). Then you can "paint" it on dishes with a plan or with a random, creative squeeze.

You can make a beautiful heart design by squeezing droplets of sauce on the plate, then quickly pulling a toothpick through the sauce. You can also blend sauces together, using the whiter yogurt sauce as the base, and adding drops of fruit sauce on top.

Breakfasts

TWENTY-TWO MEALS

Don't let busy mornings keep you from getting the fuel your body needs! Just as mom always said — breakfast really is vital for peak performance that lasts all day long. It's the perfect start to a day filled with boundless energy and well-being! Breakfast stokes the fire of your metabolism and gets it burning bright and strong. Eating breakfast even sets the stage for optimal moods and performance — even clearer thinking and memory!

The key for breakfast is to have it, to have it soon (within half an hour of arising) and to have it balanced. A balanced breakfast supplies adequate carbohydrates and protein.

Don't resort to the food industry's versions of "instant" breakfasts, like toaster fruit pies, granola bars (just candy with oats) and artificially flavored and colored powdered drink mixes. Instead of going for breakfast in the fast lane — and getting much more fat, calories and sodium than you've bargained for — grab and go with your own quick and easy breakfast. Your body will be grateful and will gladly return the favor by working for you rather than working against you.

When you grab coffee and toast, you're depriving your body of the simple carbohydrates and protein it needs to get started. American breakfast favorites focus on the complex carbohydrates (bagels, English muffins, pancakes, muffins and toast) but ignore the rest.

A power breakfast includes some breakfast add-ons. For simple carbohydrate add-ons, choose seasonal fresh fruit in the portion sizes shown on pages 28 and 29. In addition to eggs, Canadian bacon and low-fat cheese, there are extra-quick proteins you can choose such as skim milk, yogurt and nonfat cream cheese. Their nutritional analyses are as follows.

SKIM MILK: 80 calories per 1 cup serving, 8 gr. protein, 12 gr. carbohydrates, 0 gr. fat, 0% calories from fat, 4 mg. cholesterol, 125 mg. sodium.

NONFAT YOGURT: 120 calories per 1 cup serving, 13 gr. protein, 17 gr. carbohydrates, 0 gr. fat, 0% calories from fat, 4 mg. cholesterol, 174 mg. sodium.

NONFAT CREAM CHEESE: 20 calories per 2 Tbsp. serving, 3 gr. protein, 2 gr. carbohydrate, 0 gr. fat, 0% calories from fat, 15 mg. cholesterol, 150 mg. sodium.

The recipes on the following pages are just a few of the many ways you can get your morning — and your metabolism off to a terrific start. I take many of our traditional favorites and reduce the fat while powering up the flavor. I also introduce you to some treats you may not have tried before, including grits and a very special yogurt parfait.

Pictured: Bran and Apple Raisin Muffins (pgs. 52-53)

Muffins

Removing fat from muffins, quick breads and other baked goods often leaves them with a rubbery texture. Fortunately, you can overcome this by replacing the fat with fruit or pureed vegetables like pumpkin. The fruit's pectin prevents moisture loss during baking.

Lower-fat muffins will also retain their moisture better when baked in large 3-inch muffin cups.

You can bake enough of these high-fiber low-fat muffins for 2 weeks. Store in sealable plastic freezer bags and heat in microwave or toaster as needed.

Bran Muffins

skim milk or yogurt (protein)
muffin (complex carb.)
raisins (simple carb.)

1/4 cup unprocessed wheat bran
1/4 cup unprocessed oat bran
1/3 cup boiling water
1/2 cup milk
3 Tbsp. packed brown sugar
3 Tbsp. canola oil
3 Tbsp. honey
4 egg whites (or 1/2 cup egg substitute)
1 1/3 cups whole wheat pastry flour
2 tsp. baking powder
1 tsp. cinnamon
1/4 tsp. salt
1/2 cup raisins

Serve with 8 oz. yogurt or skim milk per serving.

Preheat oven to 400 degrees.

Spray the bottoms in a 12-well muffin tin with cooking spray or line with paper baking cups.

Mix brans and boiling water; set aside. In medium bowl, beat milk, brown sugar, oil, honey and egg whites. Add bran mixture, flour, baking powder, cinnamon and salt; stir until moistened (batter will be lumpy). Fold in raisins.

Divide batter evenly among muffin cups. Cups will be about two-thirds full. Bake 20 to 25 minutes or until golden brown. Immediately remove from pan. Makes 12 muffins.

Serve 1 muffin.

Per Serving: 138 Calories	
Protein 4 gr.	Carb. 24 gr.
Fat 3 gr.	Cal. from fat 23%
Chol. 0 mg.	Sodium 71 mg.

Pumpkin-Spice Muffins

cheese spread (protein)
muffin (complex carb.)
pumpkin, apricots (simple carb.)

2 cups whole wheat pastry flour
3 Tbsp. packed brown sugar
1 tsp. cinnamon
1 tsp. pumpkin pie spice
1/4 tsp. salt
1/2 tsp. baking soda
2 tsp. baking powder
2/3 cup canned pumpkin
1 cup evaporated skim milk
3 Tbsp. canola oil
2 Tbsp. honey
2 egg whites (or 1/4 cup egg substitute)

Serve with 2 Tbsp. Apricot Cheese Spread (pg. 53) per serving.

Preheat oven to 400 degrees.

Spray the bottoms in a 12-well muffin tin with cooking spray or line with paper baking cups.

Mix flour, sugar, spices, salt, baking soda and baking powder in a bowl. In another bowl whisk together pumpkin, evaporated milk, oil, honey and egg whites. Add pumpkin mixture to dry ingredients and stir until just moistened (batter will be lumpy).

Divide batter evenly among muffin cups. Cups will be about two-thirds full. Bake 20 to 25 minutes or until golden brown. Immediately remove from pan and place on wire rack to cool. Makes 12 muffins.

Serve 1 muffin warm or cooled.

Per Serving: 146 Calories	
Protein 5 gr.	Carb. 24 gr.
Fat 3 gr.	Cal. from fat 23%
Chol. 0 mg.	Sodium 80 mg.

Apple-Raisin Muffins

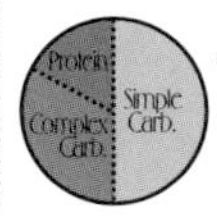

cheese spread, skim milk or yogurt (protein)
muffin (complex carb.)
raisins, apples (simple carb.)

2 large egg whites
1/3 cup maple syrup
3 Tbsp. unsweetened white grape juice
1 cup skim milk
1 Tbsp. vanilla extract
1 tsp. cinnamon
1 tsp. allspice
1/2 tsp. ground cloves
1/4 tsp. salt
1 1/2 cups rolled oats
1 cup whole wheat pastry flour
1 tsp. baking powder
1/4 cup pecans, chopped
1 cup peeled and chopped apples
1/4 cup golden raisins

Serve with your choice of Date Cheese Spread, Apricot Cheese Spread or 8 oz. yogurt or skim milk per serving.

Preheat oven to 350 degrees.

Spray the bottoms in a 12-well muffin tin with cooking spray or line with paper baking cups.

Put the egg whites in a large mixing bowl and whisk until frothy. Whisk in the syrup, juice and milk. Add the vanilla, spices and salt. Stir in the oats, flour and baking powder. Fold in the pecans, apples and raisins.

Divide batter evenly among muffin cups. Cups will be about two-thirds full. Bake for about 20 minutes or until the muffins are firm in the center.

Makes 12 muffins, 1 per serving.

Per Serving: 128 Calories	
Protein 4.5 gr.	Carb. 23 gr.
Fat 2.4 gr.	Cal. from fat 16%
Chol. 0 mg.	Sodium 94 mg.

Date Cheese Spread

2 pkgs. (8 oz. each) fat-free or light cream cheese
8 oz. unsweetened pitted dates, chopped
2 Tbsp. skim milk
1/2 cup walnuts, chopped

Process all ingredients in a food processor or blender until mixed evenly. Transfer to airtight container and store in refrigerator for up to 2 weeks.

Serving size: 3 Tbsp.

Per Serving: 64 Calories	
Protein 4 gr.	Carb. 12 gr.
Fat 1 gr.	Cal. from fat 14%
Chol. 15 mg.	Sodium 151 mg.

Apricot Cheese Spread

1 pkg. (8 oz.) fat-free cream cheese, softened
1/4 cup apricot all-fruit spread

In a bowl, blend cream cheese and all-fruit spread. Store in refrigerator for up to 4 weeks.

Makes about 1 1/4 cups, 2 Tbsp. per serving.

Per Serving: 40 Calories	
Protein 3 gr.	Carb. 7 gr.
Fat 0 gr.	Cal. from fat 0%
Chol. 15 mg.	Sodium 150 mg.

- *Substituting buttermilk or yogurt for milk in muffin batter will yield light, tender muffins; just add 1/2 tsp. baking soda for each cup of buttermilk or yogurt used.*
- *If a muffin recipe calls for whole eggs, separating them will make the muffin lighter. Mix the yolks with the other moist ingredients; beat the whites until stiff and fold them in after the rest of ingredients are combined.*
- *Stirring muffin batter too vigorously creates tough muffins. Stir the batter only until all the dry ingredients are moistened, leaving it lumpy.*

Great Granola and Cereal

Granola typically contains lots of fat from the oil, nuts and seeds, and is often loaded with sweeteners and honey. Why not try a great tasting, great-for-you alternative?

The health benefits of yogurt have long been touted. It's a good source of B vitamins, protein and calcium, and is much more digestible than fresh milk. It keeps the intestinal system populated with good bacteria (acidophilus and lactobacillus) and therefore healthy. Unfortunately, frozen yogurt doesn't have the same promise! Buy nonfat plain yogurt or fruit-flavored yogurt (sweetened with juice, preferably with no sugar added).

You may store yogurt in the refrigerator for up to 10 days after the carton date.

Good Life Granola

1/3 cup dried apricots
2/3 cup dried pears, peaches or apples
1/3 cup golden raisins
3 cups old-fashioned oats
1/3 cup pumpkin seeds, shelled
1/3 cup sunflower seed kernels
1 cup unsweetened coconut milk
1 cup unsweetened prune juice

Preheat oven to 350 degrees.

Dice fruits into 1/4-inch bits. Toss with oats and seeds. Set aside.

In a saucepan, combine the coconut milk and prune juice. Over low heat, reduce juices to 1 cup (1/2 their original volume). This should take about 20 to 25 minutes. Mix juices with oat mixture. Spread into a shallow pan. Bake for 15 to 20 minutes, stirring every 5 minutes, until golden brown. Break into pieces and cool uncovered. Store in an airtight container.

This granola may be used in many of my breakfast meals, or may be sprinkled over fruit or yogurt as a crunchy dessert.

Makes 8 cups, 1/2 cup per serving.

Per Serving: 145 Calories	
Protein 4.4 gr.	Carb. 30 gr.
Fat 4 gr.	Cal. from fat 23%
Chol. 0 mg.	Sodium 3 mg.

Granola Breakfast

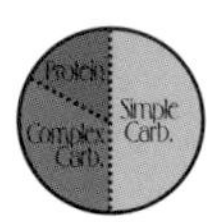

milk, seeds (protein)
oats (complex carb.)
fruits, juices (simple carb.)

1/2 cup Good Life Granola
2 sliced strawberries
1/4 banana, sliced
2 Tbsp. blueberries
3/4 cup skim milk or nonfat yogurt

Combine all in a bowl and enjoy.

Serves 1.

Per Serving: 247 Calories	
Protein 11 gr.	Carb. 43 gr.
Fat 4 gr.	Cal. from fat 14%
Chol. 3 mg.	Sodium 98 mg.

Whole Grain Cereal With Berries

skim milk (protein)
cereal (complex carb.)
strawberries (simple carb.)

1 oz. (about 3/4 cup) any whole grain cereal (list of cereals on pg. 26)
1/2 cup sliced strawberries
1 cup skim milk

Pour cereal into bowl. Top with sliced strawberries and skim milk.

Serves 1.

Per Serving: 227 Calories	
Protein 11 gr.	Carb. 45 gr.
Fat 1 gr.	Cal. from fat 4%
Chol. 4 mg.	Sodium 351 mg.

Cool Starts

Freshly Fruited Yogurt Parfait

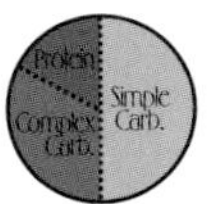

yogurt (protein)
granola (complex carb.)
fruit (simple carb.)

1/4 cup low-fat granola (purchased or Good Life Granola, pg. 54)
2 Tbsp. blueberries
4 strawberries, sliced
1/2 banana, sliced
1 cup nonfat plain yogurt
1 Tbsp. all-fruit spread

Crunch 1 Tbsp. of granola into the bottom of a parfait glass. Top with 2 sliced strawberries, 1 Tbsp. blueberries and half of the banana slices.

Mix the yogurt with the all-fruit spread; spoon half of yogurt mixture atop the fruit, then sprinkle with 2 Tbsp. granola. Top with the remaining strawberries, blueberries and bananas, and the rest of the yogurt mixture. Sprinkle with final 1 Tbsp. granola.

Other fresh seasonal berries may be used in place of strawberries and blueberries. Good choices are raspberries and blackberries.

Serves 1.

Per Serving: 246 Calories	
Protein 15 gr.	Carb. 41 gr.
Fat 2 gr.	Cal. from fat 7%
Chol. 4 mg.	Sodium 195 mg.

Fresh Fruit Shake

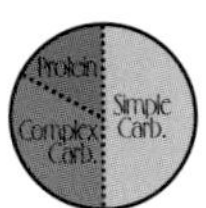

yogurt (protein)
bread (complex carb.)
fruit (simple carb.)

1/2 cup ice cubes
1/2 cup fresh berries
1/2 banana
1/2 cup orange juice
1 cup nonfat plain yogurt
2 tsp. honey
1 tsp. vanilla

Serve with 1 slice of toast or 1/2 of an English muffin.

Place ice into a blender, cover and crush. Add fruit and blend until smooth. Add remaining ingredients and blend until mixed well.

Serves 2.

Per Serving: 150 Calories	
Protein 7.5 gr.	Carb. 30 gr.
Fat less than 1 gr.	Cal. from fat 3%
Chol. 2 mg.	Sodium 88 mg.

- *Make your own "instant breakfast" by assembling fruit shake ingredients (except the ice cubes) in a blender before bed; cover and refrigerate. All you have to do the next morning is add crushed ice and push the blender button to create this delicious jump start to your day!*
- *Do your bananas ripen quicker than you can eat them? Freeze them whole and in their skin. (They'll turn black as molasses, but they'll be fine.) You can also freeze in-season ripe peaches or berries in zip-top freezer bags. These will make your fruit shake quick, easy and great!*

Freshly Fruited Yogurt Parfait

Cinnamon Raisin Oatmeal

A steaming bowl of apple-scented oatmeal perfectly spiced with cinnamon and raisins can warm you down to your toes — and supply you with wholesome fiber, essential nutrients and stick-to-the-ribs satisfaction. Oatmeal can be cooked quickly in the microwave or gently on the stove. Either will get your day started in a smart way!

Morning Warm-Ups

Cinnamon Raisin Oatmeal

skim milk (protein)
oats (complex carb.)
juice, raisins (simple carb.)

2/3 cup quick oatmeal
1 cup skim milk
1/2 cup unsweetened white grape juice or apple juice
2 Tbsp. raisins, dark or golden
1/2 tsp. cinnamon
1 tsp. vanilla extract

In a microwave-safe bowl, stir together oatmeal, skim milk and juice. Microwave on high, covered with plastic wrap and vented, for 4 minutes or until it reaches desired thickness. Stir in raisins, cinnamon and vanilla, and serve.

Serves 2.

Per Serving: 206 Calories	
Protein 9 gr.	Carb. 39 gr.
Fat 2 gr.	Cal. from fat 9%
Chol. 2 mg.	Sodium 65 mg.

Nicole's Cheesy Hash Browns

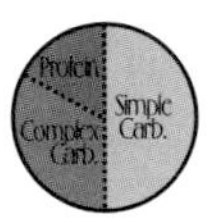

cheese (protein)
potatoes (complex carb.)
melon (simple carb.)

1 bag Simply Potatoes shredded hash browns
1 tsp. Mrs. Dash seasoning
1/2 tsp. creole seasoning
1 cup grated part-skim cheddar cheese
1 Tbsp. chopped fresh herbs (cilantro, basil, rosemary, thyme)

Serve with 1/4 melon, sliced, and 1 sliced strawberry per serving.

Spray nonstick skillet with cooking spray; heat. Empty hash browns into pan and add seasonings. Allow bottom of potatoes to brown lightly, then flip over in sections until all are browned and crisp. Sprinkle with chopped herbs. Top with grated cheese and let melt.

Serves 4.

Per Serving: 298 Calories	
Protein 10 gr.	Carb. 39 mg.
Fat 4.5 gr.	Cal. from fat 18%
Chol. 18 mg.	Sodium 282 mg.

There are two types of fibers: soluble and non-soluble. Soluble fibers are found in apples, dried beans, peanuts, barley and oat bran.

These fibers have been found to lower both triglycerides and cholesterol, and they help control blood sugars.

The nonsoluble fibers are found in wheat bran, whole grain breads, cereals, fruits and vegetables. They are an excellent means of controlling digestive challenges.

You need both soluble and nonsoluble fiber and lots of wonderful water to keep your body working at its best!

Skillet Breakfasts

Sweet Pepper Frittata

egg substitute, egg whites (protein)
potatoes (complex carb.)
oranges, vegetables (simple carb.)

Eggs have been given a bad rap and for somewhat of a good reason. It's true that one egg gives 71 percent of all the cholesterol the average person needs in one day. Yet up-to-date studies have shown that eggs are not the culprit. The highly saturated fat in other breakfast foods such as bacon, sausage and butter is the real enemy. It converts to the bad form of cholesterol in the body. Next time, hold the bacon!

4 small red-skinned potatoes, cut into quarters
1 tsp. olive oil
1/2 each red and yellow bell peppers, sliced thin lengthwise
1 small onion, diced
1 clove garlic, minced
1 tsp. Mrs. Dash seasoning
1/2 tsp. creole seasoning
1 tomato, seeded and chopped
1 cup egg substitute (or 4 large eggs)
4 large egg whites
1/4 cup grated Parmesan cheese

Serve with 3 oranges, cut into quarters.

Place potatoes in a microwavable bowl with 1/4 cup water; cover with plastic wrap and vent. Microwave on high for 5 to 6 minutes or until potatoes begin to get tender. Drain.

Preheat oven broiler. Spray a large, ovenproof nonstick skillet with cooking spray. Add olive oil and heat on the stove to medium-high heat. Add peppers, onion, garlic, seasonings and half of the tomato. Cook, stirring, until the onions are limp, about 4 minutes. Add the microwaved potatoes.

In a bowl whisk together the egg substitute, egg whites and Parmesan cheese, and pour into the skillet, gently stirring to distribute the vegetables. Cook over low heat until the underside is light golden, about 5 minutes.

Place the skillet under the broiler and broil until the top of the frittata is puffed and golden brown, 1 to 2 minutes. Loosen the frittata and slide onto a platter. Cut into 4 wedges and sprinkle with remaining tomatoes. Add 3 wedges of orange to each serving.

Makes 4 servings.

Per Serving: 167 Calories	
Protein 11 gr.	Carb. 25 gr.
Fat 2.5 gr.	Cal. from fat 14%
Chol. 4 mg.	Sodium 282 mg.

Huevos Rancheros

egg substitute, beans (protein)
tortilla, beans (complex carb.)
salsa, melon (simple carb.)

1 burrito-sized, fat-free flour tortilla
1/4 cup black beans, cooked and drained
1/4 cup chicken stock (fat-free/low salt)
1/4 tsp. creole seasoning, divided
1 tsp. Mrs. Dash seasoning, divided
1/2 cup egg substitute (or 2 large eggs)
1/4 cup tomato salsa (purchased)

Serve with 1/4 cantaloupe, sliced.

Spray tortilla with nonstick cooking spray. Place into heated nonstick skillet and grill until crisp. Set aside.

Spray skillet with cooking spray. Add black beans, chicken stock, 1/8 tsp. creole seasoning and 1/2 tsp. of Mrs. Dash; sauté until beans are easily mashed. Spread black bean mixture on tortilla.

Spray skillet with cooking spray again; add egg substitute and remaining seasonings. Scramble. Spoon on top of beans and top with salsa.

Serves 1.

Per Serving: 200 Calories	
Protein 14 gr.	Carb. 38 gr.
Fat 1 gr.	Cal. from fat 5%
Chol. 0 mg.	Sodium 599 mg.

Grits: A Southern Specialty

Cheese Grits Pie

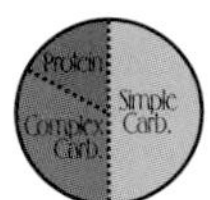

cheese, turkey bacon (protein)
grits (complex carb.)
strawberries (simple carb.)

3/4 cup grated Jarlsberg Lite cheese
4 cups cooked grits
2 Tbsp. chopped fresh parsley
1 tsp. Mrs. Dash seasoning
1 tsp. creole seasoning

Serve with 1 pt. strawberries, washed and hulled, and 8 slices turkey bacon, microwaved.

Mix cheese, grits, parsley and seasonings, and pour into a sheet pan sprayed with cooking spray. Refrigerate till firm; cut into 8 squares. In nonstick skillet sprayed with cooking spray, brown the squares over medium to medium-high heat until lightly browned and crisp. Place 2 squares on plate with 5 sliced strawberries and 2 slices turkey bacon.

Serves 4.

Per Serving: 286 Calories	
Protein 13.5 gr.	Carb. 40 gr.
Fat 8 gr.	Cal. from fat 25%
Chol. 32 mg.	Sodium 747 mg.

Get-Going Grits

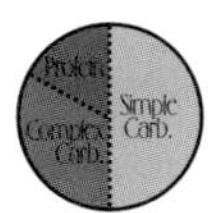

cheese (protein)
grits (complex carb.)
apple (simple carb.)

1 tsp. canola oil
2 Tbsp. minced onions
1 small green bell pepper, seeded and finely chopped
2 medium tomatoes, peeled and coarsely chopped
3 drops hot pepper sauce
3 cups water
1/2 tsp. creole seasoning
3/4 cup quick-cooking grits
1 1/2 cups grated part-skim sharp cheddar cheese

Serve with 1 apple per serving, cut into wedges.

Spray a medium-sized nonstick skillet with cooking spray. Add canola oil and heat over medium-high heat. Add onion and green pepper and sauté until tender. Stir in tomatoes and hot pepper sauce. Reduce heat and simmer uncovered 20 minutes or until thickened. Set aside.

Combine water and seasoning in medium saucepan; bring to a boil. Stir in grits. Cover, reduce heat and simmer 5 minutes or until thickened, stirring occasionally. Stir in grated cheese and remove from heat; stir in tomato mixture. Serve immediately with apple wedges.

Serves 6.

Per Serving: 232 Calories	
Protein 8 gr.	Carb. 40 gr.
Fat 5 gr.	Cal. from fat 20%
Chol. 13 mg.	Sodium 203 mg.

If you've never tried grits before, you're in for a treat. This Southern favorite will add a dash of variety to your breakfast menus.

You can prepare grits simply, according to the package directions, as a delicious side dish for eggs or lean meats. Or, try these cheese grits recipes and see why grits are called "Georgia ice cream"!

Omelettes

Egg White Omelette

egg whites (protein)
bran muffin (complex carb.)
berries, sauce (simple carb.)

3 egg whites
1 Tbsp. white wine*
2 tsp. chopped chives
1/2 tsp. Mrs. Dash seasoning
1/4 tsp. creole seasoning
2 strawberries, quartered
2 Tbsp. blueberries
2 Tbsp. Strawberry Sauce (pg. 49)
**** or substitute dealcoholized wine or chicken stock (fat-free/low salt)***

Serve with 1 warmed Bran Muffin (pg. 52).

Whip egg whites halfway stiff. Stir in wine, chives and seasonings. Spray a 12-inch nonstick skillet with cooking spray. Heat skillet on very low heat; add egg white mixture. Cook on very low heat until mixture stiffens on bottom. With spatula, carefully turn over like a pancake. Finish cooking, and fold to make an omelette.

Drizzle with strawberry sauce and fresh berries.

Serves 1.

Per Serving: 116 Calories	
Protein 11 gr.	Carb. 17 gr.
Fat less than 1 gr.	Cal. from fat 0%
Chol. 0 mg.	Sodium 467 mg.

Garden Omelette

egg substitute (protein)
English muffin (complex carb.)
strawberries, vegetables (simple carb.)

1/2 tomato, seeded and diced
2 medium mushrooms, diced
1/2 green onion, sliced
1/2 cup egg substitute (or 2 large eggs)
1 tsp. Mrs. Dash seasoning
1/4 tsp. creole seasoning

Serve with 1/2 English muffin, toasted, and 5 strawberries.

Spray a nonstick skillet with cooking spray. Heat on medium heat. Add tomato, mushroom and onion; quickly sauté until tender.

Whip egg substitute with seasonings, and pour into pan with vegetables. Cook both sides, folding to make an omelette.

Serves 1.

Per Serving: 188 Calories	
Protein 18 gr.	Carb. 26 gr.
Fat 1 gr.	Cal. from fat 5%
Chol. 0 mg.	Sodium 705 mg.

Cholesterol-free egg substitutes can be used in cooking and baking in many (though not all) of the same ways as regular eggs. Egg substitutes are egg whites mixed with beta-carotene for color. They also contain a touch of natural coagulant derived from seaweed. Vitamins and minerals are added to boost nutrition.

You can also replace whole eggs (although loaded with nutrients, they are also loaded with fat) with no-fat, no-cholesterol, pure protein egg whites. Just use 2 egg whites (1/4 cup) for one whole egg in cooking.

You can easily separate cold eggs by cracking them into a wire mesh strainer over a mixing bowl. The white will drip through the strainer's holes into the bowl and the yolk will remain in the strainer.

Cheese Delights

Fiesta Cheese Cloud

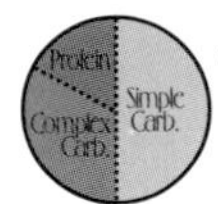

cheese, eggs, milk, bacon (protein)
bread (complex carb.)
strawberries (simple carb.)

12 slices whole wheat bread
½ lb. turkey bacon, chopped
2 Tbsp. grated red onion
2 cloves garlic, minced
8 oz. grated part-skim mozzarella/ part-skim cheddar cheese blend
1 cup egg substitute (or 4 eggs)
2½ cups skim milk
1 Tbsp. Dijon mustard
½ tsp. creole seasoning
1 tsp. Mrs. Dash seasoning
1 small can of green chilies, chopped

Serve with ½ cup sliced strawberries per serving.

Preheat oven to 325 degrees.

Trim crusts from bread cut in half into triangular shapes. Arrange 12 of the triangles in bottom of a 12 x 8-inch greased baking dish.

In a nonstick skillet, sauté bacon until crisp. Remove from pan and drain on paper towel. Add onion and garlic to pan, and sauté until transparent.

Sprinkle turkey bacon and half of grated cheese onto bread slices in pan, then top with sauté onion and garlic. Add remaining bread slices.

Beat eggs; add milk, mustard and seasonings; add chilies (with liquid). Pour liquid over casserole and let stand at room temperature for 1 hour (or even refrigerate overnight if more convenient). Bake 1 hour; serve immediately.

Serves 8.

Per Serving: 249 Calories	
Protein 22 gr.	Carb. 23 gr.
Fat 7 gr.	Cal. from fat 17%
Chol. 39 mg.	Sodium 545 mg.

Turkey Bacon and Cheese Biscuits

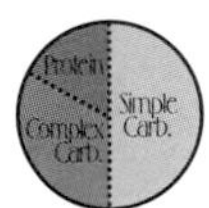

turkey bacon, cheese (protein)
biscuit (complex carb.)
cantaloupe (simple carb.)

1 can purchased low-fat biscuits
3 slices turkey bacon, halved
¾ cup grated part-skim cheddar/ fat-free mozzarella cheese blend

Serve with ¼ of a cantaloupe, sliced, per serving.

Bake biscuits according to package directions. While biscuits are baking, place turkey bacon slices on a paper towel-lined plate, and microwave for 3 minutes or until crisp. Or, brown and crisp bacon in a nonstick skillet.

When biscuits are done, slice each open partway, add ½ slice of bacon and sprinkle with 1 Tbsp. grated cheese. Put back into hot oven for 1 to 2 minutes or until cheese melts.

Makes 3 servings, 2 biscuits each.

Per Serving: 206 Calories	
Protein 11 gr.	Carb. 27 gr.
Fat 6 gr.	Cal. from fat 26%
Chol. 18 mg.	Sodium 415 mg.

Turkey bacon is a new product that serves well the occasional desire for this popular breakfast meat. It has less than half the fat of traditional bacon, yet contains more protein.

To microwave bacon, line a microwaveable rack or paper plate with a double layer of microwavable paper towels. Place strips side by side and cover with another paper towel. Six slices cooked on high will take about 3 to 4 minutes.

The sodium and nitrate content is still present in turkey bacon, so don't make this a daily treat!

Country French Toast

This breakfast can be a sunshiny start to your day — simple and quick to make, yet deliciously satisfying. The orange and vanilla flavorings are a perfect complement to yogurt sauce and berry topping — and any in-season fruit makes for a perfect garnish. Try tripling this recipe for future breakfasts — freeze individual slices in zip-top bags for a toast-'n-go breakfast.

Country French Toast

eggs, milk (protein)
bread (complex carb.)
fruit, fruit sauce (simple carb.)

1/4 cup orange juice
1/2 cup skim milk
4 egg whites, lightly beaten
2 tsp. vanilla
1 tsp. cinnamon
6 slices whole wheat bread
1 cup Yogurt Fruit Sauce (pg. 49)

Serve with 1/4 cup Strawberry Sauce (pg. 49) and 1/4 cup fresh berries per serving.

In a medium-sized dish, whisk together juice, milk, egg whites, vanilla and cinnamon. Add bread slices, one at a time, allowing to soak in egg mixture. Let sit for 4 to 5 minutes.

Spray a nonstick skillet or griddle with cooking spray. Heat. With spatula, gently lift bread slices onto heated surface and brown on both sides. When done, cut toast into triangles and place 3 triangles on each plate; top with 1/4 cup Yogurt Fruit Sauce, then drizzle plate with 2 Tbsp. Strawberry Sauce and garnish with berries.

Makes 4 servings, 1 1/2 slices of bread each.

Per Serving: 286 Calories	
Protein 13 gr.	Carb. 56 gr.
Fat 2 gr.	Cal. from fat 7%
Chol. 1.5 mg.	Sodium 416 mg.

Cinnamon Apple Puff Pancakes

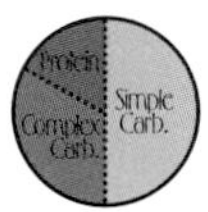

eggs (protein)
pancakes (complex carb.)
apples (simple carb.)

1 cup whole wheat pastry flour
1 tsp. baking powder
1/2 tsp. salt
1 1/2 cups egg substitute (or 5 eggs)
1 cup skim milk
2 tsp. canola oil
3 cups fresh apples, sliced
1 Tbsp. honey
juice of 1/2 lemon
1 tsp. ground cinnamon

Preheat oven to 425 degrees.

In a medium bowl, mix together flour, baking powder and salt. In another bowl, beat eggs with wire whisk; whisk in milk. Pour into dry ingredients and blend until moistened.

Coat a 12-inch ovenproof skillet with cooking spray. Spread oil over bottom of skillet and heat over medium heat until water droplets "dance" over bottom. Pour all batter into skillet and cook for 1 minute. Transfer skillet to oven and bake uncovered for 20 minutes until pancake is golden and puffy.

While pancake is baking, spray a nonstick skillet with cooking spray; heat. Add apples and quickly sauté with honey, lemon juice and cinnamon until tender and syrupy.

When pancake is done, remove from oven and spread with apples. Slice into 4 wedges to serve.

Makes 4 servings.

Per Serving: 231 Calories	
Protein 11 gr.	Carb. 42 gr.
Fat 3 gr.	Cal. from fat 10%
Chol. 1 mg.	Sodium 476 mg.

Whole wheat flour is a light brown flour that has the nutty taste of the grain. It has a higher fiber and nutritional content than all-purpose or bread flour because it's milled from the whole kernel and contains the germ.

Whole wheat pastry flour is the best choice for muffins, pancakes or waffles because it is more finely milled from a soft wheat. If not available, use a blend of unbleached white and regular whole wheat.

Pancakes

To make fluffy pancakes, only mix the ingredients together until moistened, yet still lumpy. Beating till smooth will make rubber tires!

Most pancake batters can be covered and refrigerated overnight to save precious morning time. If the batter thickens too much, add 1 to 2 Tbsp. skim milk. If it's more than a day old, add 1/4 tsp. more baking powder along with the cold milk.

Use 1/4-cup measure of batter to make a 5-inch pancake. Make sure your skillet is very hot before pouring in the batter.

Quick Mix Pancakes

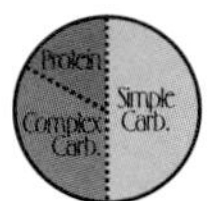

milk or yogurt (protein)
pancake (complex carb.)
fruit topping (simple carb.)

1 3/4 cups Homemade Pancake Mix
1 cup water (or club soda to make pancakes even lighter)
2 egg whites (or 1/4 cup egg substitute), beaten
1 Tbsp. honey

Serve with 1 cup skim milk or yogurt, and 1/4 cup Pourable Fruit (pg. 65) per serving.

Combine pancake mix, water, egg whites and honey; stir gently until completely moistened. Drop by quarter-cupfuls onto a hot nonstick skillet sprayed with cooking spray. Cook until bottoms are lightly browned. Flip and cook until bottoms are set.

Freeze any leftovers in individual freezer bags. When ready to use, toast to thaw and heat.

Makes 6 servings, 2 pancakes per serving.

Per Serving: 284 Calories	
Protein 11.5 gr.	Carb. 49 gr.
Fat 7 gr.	Cal. from fat 22%
Chol. 15 mg.	Sodium 586 mg.

Homemade Pancake Mix

4 cups whole wheat pastry flour
1 tsp. salt
1 cup nonfat dry milk powder
2 1/2 Tbsp. baking powder
1/4 cup canola oil

Mix flour, salt, dry milk and baking powder. Slowly pour in oil, mixing until completely moistened. May be stored in the refrigerator for up to 6 weeks. Use to make Quick Mix Pancakes.

Whole Wheat Waffles

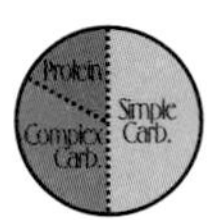

egg white, buttermilk (protein)
flour (complex carb.)
fruit topping (simple carb.)

2 cups whole wheat pastry flour
1 tsp. baking powder
1/2 tsp. baking soda
1/4 tsp. ground cinnamon
2 1/2 cups low-fat buttermilk
1 tsp. honey
1 tsp. vanilla
3 egg whites

Serve with 1/4 cup Strawberry Sauce (pg. 49) or Pourable Fruit (pg. 65) per serving.

Combine first four ingredients in a bowl; stir well. Mix the buttermilk, honey and vanilla in a separate bowl; add to the dry ingredients, stirring until the dry ingredients are moistened.

Beat egg whites with mixer at high speed until soft peaks form. Gently fold them into mixture.

Coat a waffle iron with cooking spray; heat. Spoon 1/3 cup of batter per waffle onto hot waffle iron, spreading batter to edges. Cook 5 minutes or until the steaming stops. Repeat with remaining batter. Place finished waffles on a large baking sheet (lined with a dish towel) in a single layer and hold in 200-degree oven till ready to serve.

Makes 6 servings, 2 waffles each.

Per Serving: 138 Calories	
Protein 8 gr.	Carb. 26 gr.
Fat less than 1 gr.	Cal. from fat 0%
Chol. 1 mg.	Sodium 155 mg.

Pancakes (continued)

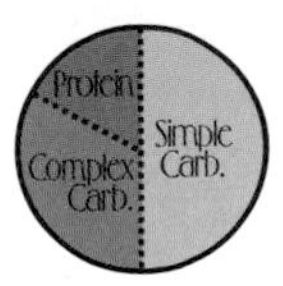

Canadian bacon (protein)
pancakes (complex carb.)
fruit topping (simple carb.)

Danny's Perfect Pancakes

2 cups whole wheat pastry flour
2 tsp. baking soda
1/2 tsp. salt
3/4 cup orange juice
3/4 cup buttermilk
2 egg whites, lightly beaten
1 tsp. vanilla

Serve with 2 Tbsp. Pourable Fruit or Fruited Yogurt Topping (or use purchased all-fruit syrup) and 1 oz. Canadian bacon per serving.

Measure flour, baking soda and salt into medium-sized bowl. Make a well in the center of mixture. Combine juice, buttermilk, egg whites and vanilla; add to well in center of dry ingredients and stir until just moistened.

For each pancake, pour 1/4 cup batter onto hot griddle or nonstick skillet sprayed with cooking spray. Turn pancakes when tops are covered with bubbles and edges look cooked.

While pancakes are cooking, lay Canadian bacon on a plate lined with paper towels and microwave on high for 2 1/4 minutes or until edges curl. Place on plate with 2 pancakes; drizzle pancakes with 2 Tbsp. Pourable Fruit or Fruited Yogurt Topping.

Makes 6 servings, 2 pancakes each.

Per Serving: 262 Calories	
Protein 16 gr.	Carb. 46 gr.
Fat 2.5 gr.	Cal. from fat 8%
Chol. 27 mg.	Sodium 55 mg.

Pourable Fruit

4 cups cut up fresh, ripe fruit (straw berries, bananas, berries, peaches)
1 cup unsweetened apple juice
1/4 cup water
2 Tbsp. cornstarch
1 Tbsp. lemon juice

Blend fresh fruit and apple juice in blender until smooth. Pour into small saucepan and simmer for 5 minutes. Mix cornstarch with water and lemon juice; add to fruit mixture. Simmer until thick. Refrigerate. This fruit will keep in the refrigerator for up to 5 days.

Makes 4 cups, 1/4 cup per serving.

Per Serving: 19 Calories	
Protein 0 gr.	Carb. 4.5 gr.
Fat 0 gr.	Cal. from fat 0%
Chol. 0 mg.	Sodium 1 mg.

Fruited Yogurt Topping

1 cup nonfat plain yogurt
1/4 cup fruit (or 2 Tbsp. all-fruit spread)
ground cinnamon to taste

Combine all ingredients, mixing well.
Makes 6 servings, 1/4 cup per serving.

Per Serving: 26 Calories	
Protein 2 gr.	Carb. 4.5 gr.
Fat less than 1 gr.	Cal. from fat 0%
Chol. 0 mg.	Sodium 29 mg.

Are there pancake toppings beyond maple syrup? Absolutely ! Try these:

- *All fruit spread (sweetened with fruit juices rather than sugar)*
- *Fresh fruit syrup or Pourable Fruit*
- *Bananas blended with cinnamon and orange juice, then warmed*
- *Light or fat-free cream cheese, thinned with all-fruit spread and vanilla*
- *Light cream cheese and fresh fruit*
- *Nonfat cottage cheese and fresh fruit*
- *All-fruit yogurt*
- *Natural peanut butter, thinned with apple juice and warmed*

Lunches & Soups

TWENTY-TWO MEALS

Lunch picks up where breakfast leaves off; it fuels the rest of your day's activities. Like breakfast, lunch should contain a healthy balance of whole grain, complex carbohydrates and low-fat protein to keep your metabolic fires burning brightly and your performance and well-being at their peak. In addition, quick energy-giving, nutrient-filled simple carbohydrates should be part of your lunch in the form of brightly colored fruits and vegetables.

The search for the healthy lunch can be a challenge for many of us because we are at the mercy of the nearest drive-through, cafeteria or restaurant. You don't have much time to grab lunch, let alone think about healthy choices. The temptation is strong to reach for the first appealing thing you see or the "special of the day" — which often turns out not so special at all!

Let the guide to eating at fast food restaurants (pg. 175) direct you to better tasting and healthier fast food that will supply you with "the right stuff" for the long afternoon ahead.

Another option is to pack a lunch. You can do it quickly and be energized with the knowledge that your choice is already made — and it's a smart one.

Pictured: Red Lentil Chili (pg. 91)

Be creative with your brown bag lunches. There is life beyond turkey sandwiches — or even peanut butter and jelly!

Breaking the Rut

Whatever you do, try to stay out of the lunchtime rut — it's an easy ditch to fall into — and live in.

We're in a rut when we settle into a limited variety of meals with which we feel safe and don't have to think about much. We don't want to make decisions; it's just easier to have the same things again and again.

The problem with ruts is that we are set up to overindulge as soon as anything more exciting comes along. Once off track, it becomes very difficult to get back on track — since "on track" means returning to the same old, boring rut.

In addition to the mental reasons ruts are deadly, there are also some nutritional ones. Eating a variety of foods in their whole form provides you with a gamut of vitamins and minerals, including as yet hidden benefits.

Try some of the lunch ideas and recipes that follow to get yourself free from your eating rut and to enjoy a whole new world of food. Think beyond the lunch sandwich altogether — even think beyond bread as the packaging material. Use these guides to help you create your own lunch favorite, possibly in a thermos!

If you make sandwiches in advance, wrap them airtight and refrigerate (they keep for a day that way). You can also freeze meat sandwiches in sandwich bags, then store them in a large freezer-weight bag for up to one month in the freezer. Pull one out of the freezer in the morning, and it will be thawed by lunch. Keep your sandwiches from the soggy blues by packing additions like tomato or pickles in separate plastic bags to tuck in the sandwich just before eating.

Tips for Packing Safety

For safety concerns, how you pack lunch is as important as what you pack. Even the healthiest menu won't prevent the brown-bag bug — food poisoning. Food poisoning symptoms (vomiting, fever, headache, diarrhea and/or stomach cramps) can strike any time from twenty minutes to twenty-four hours after consumption of tainted food.

Lunches carried from home often sit in a desk or locker until noon. That long wait at room temperature makes them a perfect breeding ground for salmonella and other bacterias. The risk of food poisoning soars with the number of these organisms, which give no warning because their toxins are odorless, tasteless and invisible to the naked eye.

Pack Wise to Stay Safe

- Use hot soapy water on hands, countertops, utensils and cutting boards before and after food preparation.
- Keep cold foods cold (below 60 degrees) and hot foods hot (above 125 degrees). Use thermal containers. Give them a headstart by chilling cold containers with ice water or a short freezer visit, and preheating hot containers with boiling water. Make sure the hot food is almost boiling hot when going into the thermos.

THE LUNCHBOX PACKAGE

WRAPPING	CONTENTS	TRIMMINGS
• Whole wheat, rye or pumpernickel bread	• Lean, sliced meats (turkey, chicken breast, roast beef, Canadian bacon, low-fat ham)	• Romaine or leaf lettuce
• Whole grain kaiser or hamburger buns	• Nonfat or low-fat cheese	• Sliced vegetables (peppers, tomato, cucumbers)
• Whole wheat English muffins	• Bean spreads	• Spice sprouts
• Low-fat flour tortilla (preferably whole wheat)	• Tuna or salmon	• Shredded carrots
• Whole wheat bagels	• Boiled egg whites or tofu	• Mustard or light mayonnaise
• Whole wheat pita bread	• Peanut butter and fruit	• Salsa
• Crepes	• Cottage cheese with trail mix	• Sensational spreads (pg. 45)
• Lettuce leaves		
• Focaccia bread		

LUNCH IN A THERMOS

A COLD ONE

Fill a wide-mouthed thermos with ice water for a few minutes; pour out the water and fill with your very cold lunch creation. This will keep it chilled until lunch.

- Roasted Red Pepper and Tortellini Salad (pg. 73)
- Chicken and Pasta Salad (pg. 71)
- Tuscan Bean Salad (pg. 73)
- Confetti Chicken Salad (pg. 81)
- Gazpacho (pg. 87)
- Cottage cheese and fruit
- Fresh fruit shake

A HOT ONE

Fill a wide-mouthed thermos with very hot water for a few minutes; pour out the water and fill with almost boiling food that will be ready for your steaming hot lunch.

- Chili in a Hurry (pg. 90)
- Red Lentil Chili (pg. 91)
- Pasta e Fagioli (pg. 89)
- Smoked Turkey and White Bean Soup (pg. 88)
- Leftover lasagna, spaghetti or any pasta dish
- Macaroni and cheese
- Beef Stew (pg. 119)
- Leftover Risotto (pg. 99)
- Black beans and rice

- Freeze your juice box, water or beverage in a plastic container; it will serve as a cold pack to help keep your foods cool.

If your work site has no refrigerator to store your lunch, you might want to invest in a mini-cooler or an insulated bag with a freezer-pack or frozen beverage. With such care, many sandwiches will stay safe and fresh until lunchtime. If you are taking frozen leftovers, don't remove them from the freezer until you get up in the morning — they will thaw, yet stay cold until lunch.

Use the recipes on the following pages to prepare delicious mid-day meals — whether you are lunching at home or on the run! Then find a quiet spot and enjoy a time of refreshing — body and spirit. With a little creativity and planning, this time can become a welcomed respite to your busy day.

SENSATIONAL SIDES

To round out your lunchbox thermos, you may want to add one of these sensational sides to provide the needed simple carbohydrate or protein.

- Whole or cut fruit
- Black Bean and Corn Salsa (pg. 87)
- Raw veggies and dip
- Mango Salsa (pg. 122)
- Gazpacho (pg. 87)
- Mixed Green Salad with dressing on the side (pg. 99)
- Sliced cucumber salad

Greek Pasta Salad

The exciting flavors of Greek salad: feta, pepperoncinis and a fabulous Greek dressing all bring a taste sensation to this luncheon salad that could easily become a quick and elegant meal. The pasta salad can be made and kept refrigerated for up to five days; the smoked chicken — or shrimp, scallops or turkey, if you prefer — can be added at serving time.

Greek Pasta Salad

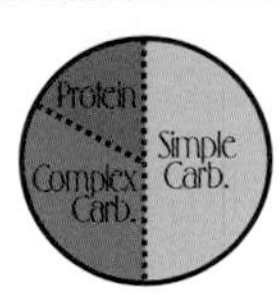

turkey, feta cheese (protein)
pasta (complex carb.)
vegetables (simple carb.)

Greek Pasta

4 cups bowtie pasta, cooked and cooled
1 red bell pepper, finely diced
1 green bell pepper, finely diced
1 yellow pepper, finely diced
1/2 red onion, finely minced
2 Tbsp. chopped fresh herbs (cilantro, basil, rosemary, thyme)
1 cup Greek Vinaigrette
1 tsp. creole seasoning

Combine all ingredients. Allow to marinate at least one hour.

Makes 4 servings.

Per Serving: 204 Calories	
Protein 7 gr.	Carb. 35 gr.
Fat 4 gr.	Cal. from fat 18%
Chol. 0 mg.	Sodium 420 mg.

Greek Vinaigrette

1/4 cup olive oil
1 1/4 cups rice wine vinegar
3/4 cup chicken stock (fat-free/low salt)
1/4 cup Dijon mustard
1/2 cup pepperoncini juice
1 Tbsp. minced garlic
1 Tbsp. minced shallots
1 tsp. creole seasoning
2 Tbsp. chopped fresh herbs (cilantro, basil, rosemary, thyme)
1 Tbsp. chopped fresh oregano (or 1 tsp. dried)

In a large bowl, whisk together ingredients. Refrigerate.

Makes 24 servings, 2 Tbsp. each.

Per Serving: 21 Calories	
Protein 0 gr.	Carb. 1 gr.
Fat 2 gr.	Cal. from fat 66%
Chol. 0 mg.	Sodium 139 mg.

Chicken and Pasta Salad

12 oz. smoked (or roasted) chicken breast
1 recipe of Greek Pasta
2 cups fresh spinach, washed, stemmed and snipped
2 cups romaine or red leaf lettuce
1 cup radicchio leaves,* torn
4 plum tomatoes, quartered
1/2 cup feta cheese, crumbled
1/4 cup Greek Vinaigrette
2 Tbsp. chopped fresh herbs (cilantro, basil, rosemary, thyme)
* ***may use extra lettuce instead***

Cut chicken breast into chunks; mix with Greek Pasta. Place spinach, romaine and radicchio on each of four plates; top with pasta salad. Add tomatoes and crumbled feta cheese. Ladle 1 Tbsp. of Greek Vinaigrette onto each plate, then sprinkle with herbs.

Serves 4.

Per Serving: 357 Calories	
Protein 28 gr.	Carb. 41 gr.
Fat 9 gr.	Cal. from fat 22%
Chol. 0 mg.	Sodium 720 mg.

The best vinaigrettes are made from the most flavorful vinegars, such as balsamic and rice wine vinegar, and are infused with herbs, such as basil, dill, rosemary or tarragon. Those made with fruit, blueberries, cranberries or raspberries are wonderful as well.

Make a lower-fat vinaigrette by replacing half of the oil with defatted chicken stock, vegetable or tomato juice, or fruit juices such as mango or pineapple. You may thicken the dressing by blending it with 1/2 tsp. cornstarch or 1/4 cup cooked rice or 1 to 2 chunks cooked potato.

Chicken Quesadillas

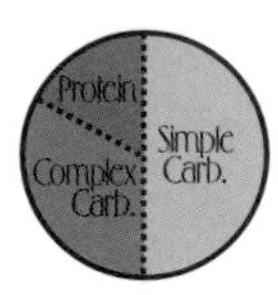

chicken, cheese (protein)
tortilla (complex carb.)
vegetables (simple carb.)

Salsa is a highly seasoned sauce, used either for dipping, topping or as a garnish. Originally made with a base of chopped tomatoes, today's salsas can be made with almost anything, even fruit.

Use warm salsa as a perfect topping for grilled meats or fish, or add 2 to 3 tablespoons salsa to cooked vegetables or salad to give pizzazz — and flavor. Spoon salsa atop baked potatoes or toss some in with hash browns. Use it as sauce for meatloaf to update an old-fashioned favorite. Salsa never lets you down!

Chicken Quesadillas

1 medium onion, sliced
1/2 large green bell pepper, diced
1/2 large red bell pepper, diced
2 Tbsp. chicken stock (fat-free/low salt)
1 tsp. minced garlic
8 large mushrooms, cleaned and sliced
1/8 tsp. cumin
1/8 tsp. crushed red pepper
pinch cayenne pepper
2 Tbsp. rice wine vinegar
1 tsp. chopped fresh cilantro
1 lb. boneless, skinless chicken breast
1 tsp. Mrs. Dash seasoning
1 tsp. creole seasoning
6 burrito-sized, fat-free flour tortillas
3/4 cup grated part-skim cheddar cheese
1 cup mixed lettuces
2 cups Black Bean and Corn Salsa (pg. 87)
3 Tbsp. nonfat sour cream
1/2 cup Spicy Tomato Salsa

Spray a nonstick skillet with cooking spray and heat. Add onion, peppers and chicken stock and quickly sauté. Add garlic, mushrooms, cumin, chili powder and cayenne pepper. Cook for 2 minutes, stirring frequently. Add vinegar and cilantro, and cook until most of the liquid evaporates, about 2 minutes.

Sprinkle chicken breasts with seasonings and grill. Cut crosswise into 1/2-inch strips.

Lay each tortilla on surface of another hot nonstick skillet or griddle. Put 2 Tbsp. vegetable mixture, 2 oz. chicken (1/2 cup) and 2 Tbsp. cheese on one half of each tortilla. Fold over, and grill until browned and crispy and cheese is melted.

Cut each quesadilla into 3 triangles and lay on plate next to lettuce. Top lettuce with 1/3 cup Black Bean and Corn Salsa. Serve with 1/4 cup salsa topped with 1/2 Tbsp. nonfat sour cream.

Makes 6 servings, 3 triangles per serving.

Per Serving: 431 Calories	
Protein 42 gr.	Carb. 50 gr.
Fat 7 gr.	Cal. from fat 15%
Chol. 84 mg.	Sodium 599 mg.

Spicy Tomato Salsa

1 1/2 lbs. plum tomatoes, seeded and diced
1/2 cup finely diced red onion
1 jalapeño, stemmed, seeded and finely diced
1 Tbsp. chopped fresh cilantro
1 tsp. cumin
1 tsp. creole seasoning
1/4 tsp. cracked black pepper
2 cloves garlic, minced
juice of 1 lime

Combine all ingredients in a medium-sized bowl. Refrigerate to allow flavors to blend.

Use 2 Tbsp. per serving.

Per Serving: 15 Calories	
Protein 0 gr.	Carb. 3 gr.
Fat 0 gr.	Cal. from fat 0%
Chol. 0 mg.	Sodium 160 mg.

Terrific Lunchtime Salads

Tuscan Bean Salad

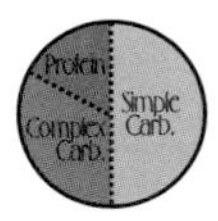

beans, chickpeas (protein)
peppers, peas (complex carb.)
mixed greens (simple carb.)

1 cup cooked black beans, drained
1 cup cooked dark red kidney beans, drained
1 cup cooked chickpeas, drained
2 cloves garlic, minced
2 tsp. minced shallots
8 pieces jarred roasted red peppers, slivered
3 plum tomatoes, quartered
1/3 cup sliced banana peppers
1/2 cup white wine*
1 1/2 cups rice wine vinegar
2 cups chicken stock (fat-free/low salt)
2 tsp. arrowroot (or 1 Tbsp. cornstarch)
2 tsp. Mrs. Dash seasoning
1 tsp. creole seasoning
5 Tbsp. chopped fresh herbs (cilantro, basil, rosemary, thyme), divided
1 bag (12 oz.) baby mixed greens or 3 cups torn lettuce
2 cups spinach or red leaf lettuce
1/2 cup Greek Vinaigrette (pg. 38)
1 cup frozen green peas, thawed
* ***or substitute dealcoholized wine or more chicken stock***

Combine beans, chickpeas, garlic, shallots, red pepper, tomatoes and banana peppers.

In separate bowl, combine white wine, vinegar, chicken stock, arrowroot, seasonings and 3 Tbsp. chopped herbs. Pour over bean mixture, toss gently, then marinate at least 4 hours.

To serve, toss with mixed greens, spinach and Greek Vinaigrette. Add green peas. Sprinkle with remaining chopped herbs.

Serves 4.

Per Serving: 291 Calories	
Protein 16 gr.	Carb. 51 gr.
Fat 4 gr.	Cal. from fat 12%
Chol. 0 mg.	Sodium 502 mg.

Roasted Red Pepper and Tortellini Salad

cheese (protein)
pasta (complex carb.)
melon (simple carb.)

10 oz. light cheese tortellini (purchase in grocery refrigerated sections)
1 jar (7 1/2 oz.) roasted red peppers, drained and sliced
1/4 cup chopped fresh basil or parsley
3 Tbsp. capers, rinsed
2 scallions, trimmed, finely chopped
2 cloves garlic, minced
1/2 cup feta cheese, crumbled
1/4 cup Balsamic Marinade (pg. 42)
1/4 tsp. creole seasoning

Serve with 1/4 cantaloupe, sliced, per serving.

In a large saucepan of boiling water, cook tortellini al dente, 4 to 6 minutes. Drain in a colander and rinse well with cold water.

Transfer to a large bowl; add remaining ingredients.

Serves 4.

Per Serving: 313 Calories	
Protein 19 gr.	Carb. 39 gr.
Fat 9 gr.	Cal. from fat 25%
Chol. 41 mg.	Sodium 763 mg.

Lunches & Soups

TWENTY-TWO MEALS

Your mother sure was right when she told you to "eat your veggies!" Here's why: recent studies show vegetables to be full of nutrients that are champion fighters against disease — including both cancer and heart disease. And the best way to get these super-nutrients is from real foods — not supplements.

Go for bright, vivid colors when shopping for fruits and vegetables — it's a sure sign that they are loaded with protection.

Summer Fiesta Lunch

This sandwich will rewrite your definition of the lunchtime sandwich — and give you an entirely new perspective on tortillas! They aren't just for burritos any longer — they serve as a terrific wrapper for any sandwich filling. Serve with another taste sensation, Pineapple Tomato Salsa, and you'll be ready for a fiesta — not a siesta — after this lunch.

Summer Fiesta Lunch

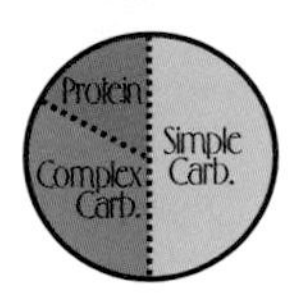

turkey, beans (protein)
tortilla (complex carb.)
pineapple, tomato (simple carb.)

Turkey Tortilla Roll

2 Tbsp. Black Bean Dip*
2 Tbsp. fat-free sour cream
1 burrito size fat-free flour tortilla
1 cup shredded mixed lettuces
2 oz. turkey breast, sliced
4 strips red bell peppers
4 strips green bell peppers
2 tomato slices
1/3 cup Pineapple Tomato Salsa
* ***may use purchased dip or make Black Bean Dip***

Spread Black Bean Dip and fat-free sour cream onto tortilla to cover. Top with lettuce, turkey, peppers and tomatoes.

Roll tortilla tightly burrito style, secure with toothpicks and cut in half.

Serves 1.

Per Serving: 262 Calories	
Protein 24 gr.	Carb. 37 gr.
Fat 2 gr.	Cal. from fat 7%
Chol. 40 mg.	Sodium 433 mg.

Pineapple Tomato Salsa

1 pineapple, diced
1 red bell pepper, cut into strips
2 plum tomatoes, diced
juice of 1 lime
1 Tbsp. chopped fresh cilantro
1/4 tsp. dried coriander seed
1 tsp. creole seasoning
1 radicchio or red cabbage leaf

Mix all ingredients together except radicchio. Refrigerate at least 1 hour to blend flavors. Spoon Pineapple Tomato Salsa onto radicchio leaf placed on plate.

This salsa will keep in the refrigerator for 4 to 5 days.

Makes 4 servings, 1/3 cup each.

Per Serving: 32 Calories	
Protein 0 gr.	Carb. 8 gr.
Fat 0 gr.	Cal. from fat 0%
Chol. 0 mg.	Sodium 268 mg.

Black Bean Dip

2 cans (15 oz. each) black beans, drained and rinsed
4 Tbsp. finely chopped canned or fresh jalapeño peppers
2 Tbsp. red wine vinegar
2 tsp. chili powder (or to taste)
1/2 tsp. creole seasoning
1/4 tsp. cumin
1 Tbsp. minced onion
1 tsp. minced garlic
1 Tbsp. chopped fresh parsley

Place the beans, pepper, vinegar, chili powder and cumin in a blender. Blend the ingredients until they are smooth. Transfer the mixture to a bowl.

Stir in the onion, garlic and parsley, and serve. Makes 12 servings, 1/3 cup per serving.

Per Serving: 117 Calories	
Protein 8 gr.	Carb. 21 gr.
Fat 0 gr.	Cal. from fat 0%
Chol. 0 mg.	Sodium 68 mg.

Fat-free sour cream is a wonderful substitute for regular sour cream. It's made from skim milk, instead of cream, so you avoid the fat naturally without adding extra chemicals or sugars. (Fat-free mayonnaise, on the other hand, is manufactured by adding the chemicals and sugars, so I recommend light mayonnaise instead.)

Super Sandwiches

Leave iceberg lettuce at the store. Instead, come home with the greenest lettuces you can find. Besides romaine, green and red leaf, spinach and watercress, try arugula, Belgian endive, curly endive, frizee, escarole, dandelion greens, mache, mustard greens and radicchio.

Look for greens that are crisp and free of blemishes. Wash and dry, then store by wrapping in dry paper towels in a tightly sealed plastic bag. One pound of greens yields about 6 cups of torn lettuce.

Mango-Chicken Salad Sandwiches

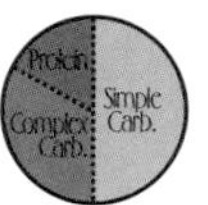

chicken (protein)
English muffin (complex carb.)
mango (simple carb.)

1 1/2 Tbsp. light mayonnaise
1 Tbsp. minced celery
1 Tbsp. chopped fresh cilantro or parsley
2 tsp. fresh lemon juice
1 Tbsp. chopped red bell pepper
1/2 tsp. creole seasoning
2/3 cup peeled and diced mango
1 can (6 oz.) of water-packed chicken, drained*
2 green or red leaf lettuce leaves
2 whole wheat English muffins, split and toasted
1 Tbsp. slivered almonds, toasted
*** *you may substitute fresh crabmeat or water-packed solid white tuna***

Combine the first 6 ingredients in a bowl; stir well. Add mango and chicken; toss gently to coat.

Arrange 1 lettuce leaf on each muffin half, top with 3/4 cup chicken mixture and sprinkle with almonds. Place on plate, laying top half of muffin against sandwich.

Serves 2.

Per Serving: 408 Calories	
Protein 30 gr.	Carb. 51 gr.
Fat 9 gr.	Cal. from fat 20%
Chol. 70 mg.	Sodium 744 mg.

Grilled Vegetable Baguettes

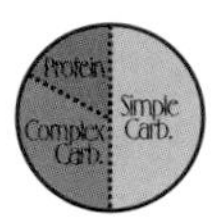

beans (protein)
French bread (complex carb.)
vegetables (simple carb.)

1 cup Balsamic Marinade (pg. 42)
1 eggplant, cut lengthwise into 1/4-inch slices
1 zucchini, cut lengthwise into 1/4-inch slices
1 yellow squash, cut lengthwise into 1/4-inch slices
1 red bell pepper, sliced thin
1 (1 lb.) baguette (a long, thin loaf of French bread)
2 cups Bean and Garlic Pesto (pg. 45)
1 red onion, sliced thin
1 tomato, sliced thin
1 cup loosely packed spinach, washed and stemmed

Serve with mixed greens or Chilled Cucumber Salad (pg. 106).

Marinate sliced eggplant, zucchini, squash and peppers in Balsamic Marinade for at least 1 hour.

Grill or broil eggplant, zucchini, squash and red pepper until crisp tender.

Cut baguette in half lengthwise. Spread cut side of each half with pesto. On bottom half of baguette, layer eggplant, zucchini, squash, red peppers, onion, tomato and spinach. Top with remaining half of baguette and cut into 6 pieces.

Serves 6.

Per Serving: 316 Calories	
Protein 13 gr.	Carb. 55 gr.
Fat 5.5 gr.	Cal. from fat 15%
Chol. 0 mg.	Sodium 470 mg.

Dilled Tortilla Roll

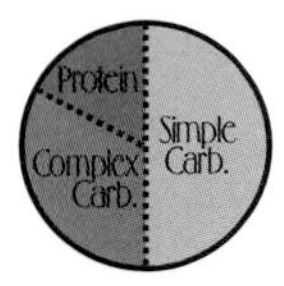

cheese (protein)
tortilla (complex carb.)
cantaloupe (simple carb.)

Dilled Tortilla Roll

1/4 cup fat-free cream cheese
1 tsp. chopped fresh dill
1 tsp. chopped fresh herbs (cilantro, basil, rosemary, thyme)
1/4 tsp. Mrs. Dash Garlic and Herb Seasoning
1/8 tsp. cracked black pepper
2 tsp. lemon juice
1 burrito-sized, fat-free flour tortilla
2 radicchio leaves
1/3 cup shredded lettuce
2 Tbsp. diced, seeded cucumber
1/2 small tomato, diced

Serve with 1/4 cup Cucumber Dill Dressing (pg. 39) for dipping and 1/4 cantaloupe

Mix light cream cheese with dill, herbs, seasoning, pepper and lemon juice.

Spread cheese mixture on flour tortilla; top with radicchio leaves, sprinkle with lettuce, cucumber and tomato. Roll tortilla burrito style and fasten with 2 toothpicks. Cut in half.

Serves 1.

Per Serving: 222 Calories	
Protein 12.5 gr.	Carb. 34 gr.
Fat 4 gr.	Cal. from fat 16%
Chol. 30 mg.	Sodium 357 mg.

Cucumber Dill Dressing

6 oz. light cream cheese
1/3 cup farmer's cheese
1 cup skim milk
1 large cucumber, peeled and seeded
1 1/2 Tbsp. Dijon mustard
2 cloves garlic, minced
1/4 tsp. cracked black pepper
1 tsp. creole seasoning
1 Tbsp. olive oil
juice of 1 lemon
1/2 tsp. Tabasco
2 Tbsp. chopped fresh dill

Blend cheeses together with skim milk. Add other ingredients, except dill, and blend until smooth. Stir in dill.

Makes 24 servings, 1/4 cup each.

Per Serving: 38 Calories	
Protein 1.5 gr.	Carb. 1 gr.
Fat 3 gr.	Cal. from fat 71%
Chol. 3 mg.	Sodium 34 mg.

Flour tortillas are for more than just Mexican food — they are the perfect sandwich wrapper for a variety of fillings. They make terrific pizza crusts and can bake into crispy additions to desserts (pg. 160).

Find tortillas in the refrigerated section of supermarkets, and look for the low-fat and fat-free versions (made without lard). You can also get the whole wheat variety — they are full-flavored and nutritious.

To warm tortillas, wrap them loosely in paper towels or wax paper and pop into the microwave on high for 15 seconds per two tortillas.

Vegetable Tortilla Pizza

Pizza is a can't-do-without tradition for many of us — this tortilla pizza will be a new favorite! Simple to make and fun to eat, it can be topped with any special pizza topping. Here it's crowned with crispy vegetables, just a sprinkling of low-fat cheese and a confetti throw of sliced peppers to bring everyone into the party.

Pizza Pizzazz

Vegetable Tortilla Pizza

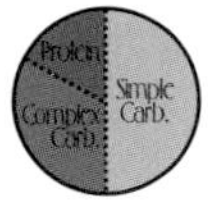

cheese (protein)
tortilla (complex carb.)
vegetables (simple carb.)

2 fajita-sized, fat-free flour tortillas
1/3 cup fat-free mozzarella/Parmesan cheese blend, divided (right column)
1/4 cup Tomato Basil Sauce (pg. 48)
1 Tbsp. chopped fresh herbs (cilantro, basil, rosemary, thyme), divided
6 strips red bell pepper
6 strips green bell pepper
6 strips yellow bell pepper
3 broccoli florets
1/4 small red onion, diced

Preheat oven to 450 degrees.

Lay one tortilla on round wire mesh pan. Sprinkle it with 2 Tbsp. cheese blend; top with remaining tortilla.

Brush the top of tortilla with Tomato Basil Sauce and sprinkle with 1/2 Tbsp. herbs. Lay peppers, broccoli and onions on top of sauce. Sprinkle with the remaining cheese blend.

Bake until lightly browned and crisp, about 5 minutes. Sprinkle with remaining herbs.

Serves 1.

Per Serving: 309 Calories	
Protein 18 gr.	Carb. 48 gr.
Fat 5 gr.	Cal. from fat 14%
Chol. 24 mg.	Sodium 460 mg.

English Muffin Pizzas

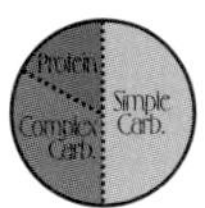

cheese (protein)
English muffin (complex carb.)
eggplant, tomato (simple carb.)

2 egg whites
1/2 cup seasoned dry bread crumbs (purchased)
1 large eggplant, sliced thin
2 tsp. olive oil
4 English muffins, split
1 1/2 cups Tomato Basil Sauce (pg. 48)
1 tomato, sliced thin
2 cups part-skim mozzarella/Parmesan cheese blend (right column)
1/2 tsp. dried basil
1/2 tsp. creole seasoning

Preheat oven to 350 degrees.

Lightly beat egg whites in a pie plate. Place bread crumbs on a piece of wax paper. Dip eggplant into egg whites, then into bread crumbs.

Spray a nonstick skillet with cooking spray. Add olive oil and warm it over medium-high heat. Add eggplant slices and cook until golden, 2 to 3 minutes on each side.

Place muffin halves on a baking sheet. Spread each with 3 Tbsp. of Tomato Basil Sauce. Place 1/4 of the eggplant and tomato slices on each muffin half. Sprinkle each with cheese, basil and seasoning. Bake until cheese melts, 15 to 20 minutes.

Serves 4.

Per Serving: 377 Calories	
Protein 21 gr.	Carb. 54 gr.
Fat 8.5 gr.	Cal. from fat 20%
Chol. 24 mg.	Sodium 622 mg.

Because fat-free cheeses do not melt as quickly or as easily as traditional high-fat cheeses, make your own cheese blends and keep handy. These are two of my favorite blends: a part-skim mozzarella/Parmesan blend, consisting of 3 parts grated part-skim mozzarella and 1 part grated Parmesan; and a blend of part-skim mozzarella with part-skim sharp cheddar cheese, consisting of 3 parts part skim mozzarella and 1 part cheddar.

You can pay the price to buy cheese pre-grated, or grate it ahead of time and refrigerate in a plastic bag until ready to use. Four ounces of block cheese will yield one cup grated.

Pizza or Nachos, Anyone?

Spinach and Mushroom Pita Pizza

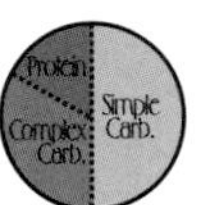

cheese (protein)
pita (complex carb.)
vegetables (simple carb.)

1 oz. (or 1/2 cup dried) assorted mushrooms
4 dried shiitake mushrooms
2 cloves garlic, chopped
1 cup fresh spinach, washed and stemmed
1/2 tsp. creole seasoning
1 tsp. Mrs. Dash seasoning
2 whole wheat pita breads
1/4 cup Tomato Basil Sauce (pg. 48)
2 plum tomatoes, peeled, seeded and quartered
1/2 cup feta cheese, crumbled

Preheat oven to 475 degrees.

Soak the dried mushrooms in cold water until hydrated; squeeze dry. Spray a nonstick skillet with cooking spray and sauté mushrooms, shiitakes and garlic until tender. Add spinach and seasonings. Cover and allow to steam for approximately 1 minute until spinach wilts.

Spray both pitas lightly with cooking spray. Brush with Tomato Basil Sauce. Cover with spinach-mushroom mixture, leaving a 3/4-inch border. Top with tomato quarters and cheese.

Bake until warmed and crispy, 5 minutes.

Serves 2.

Per Serving: 234 Calories	
Protein 11 gr.	Carb. 33 gr.
Fat 7 gr.	Cal. from fat 25%
Chol. 25 mg.	Sodium 755 mg.

Baked Pita Chips

Pita has unlimited possibilities — it can be used as a sandwich pouch, a quick pizza crust or baked to make terrific dipping chips.

Make pita chips by separating pita rounds horizontally. Spray the rounds with cooking spray and lightly season to taste with salt and pepper. Stack the rounds, then cut the stack into 12 wedges. Arrange in a single layer on a nonstick baking sheet and bake at 350 degrees for 8 minutes or until golden brown. Cool on paper towels and store in an airtight container.

Guiltless Nachos

cheese, beans (protein)
chips (complex carb.)
salsa, vegetables (simple carb.)

3 oz. baked tortilla chips (about 1/4 bag)
1/2 cup Black Bean Dip (pg. 75), warmed
1/4 cup nonfat sour cream
1/2 small tomato, chopped
3/4 cup grated part-skim mozzarella
1/4 cup grated part-skim sharp cheddar
1/4 cup spicy salsa (purchased)
1 Tbsp. green onion, sliced thin
2 Tbsp. finely chopped red, green and yellow bell pepper

Lay half of chips onto large oval platter. Spoon half of bean dip and 2 Tbsp. of fat-free sour cream onto chips. Top with remaining chips, then remaining bean dip. Sprinkle with chopped tomato.

Mix together mozzarella and cheddar cheeses; sprinkle onto chips. Place under broiler just until cheese is melted. Spoon on salsa and dot with remaining sour cream.

Sprinkle with green onions and confetti mix of finely chopped peppers.

Serves 2. Can also serve as a whole platter for an appetizer munchie.

Per Serving: 259 Calories	
Protein 21 gr.	Carb. 36 gr.
Fat 4 gr.	Cal. from fat 14%
Chol. 11 mg.	Sodium 724 mg.

Confetti Chicken Salad

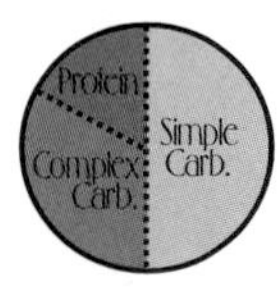

chicken (protein)
corn (complex carb.)
tomatoes, peppers (simple carb.)

Confetti Chicken Salad

12 oz. boneless, skinless chicken breasts
2 cups chicken broth (fat-free/low salt)
1 recipe Cumin-Dijon Dressing
3 ears of corn, cooked and cooled
24 cherry tomatoes, halved
6 radishes, sliced thin
1/2 red bell pepper, sliced
4 cups romaine leaves, torn into bite-sized pieces

Serve with 4 oranges, peeled and sliced.

In a skillet over medium heat, bring chicken and broth to a boil. Reduce heat to medium low. Cover and poach chicken until it is no longer pink, 6 to 8 minutes. Transfer chicken to cutting board and cut into bite-sized pieces. Add Cumin-Dijon Dressing to chicken and toss to coat.

Cut kernels from corn cobs. Add corn, tomatoes, radishes and peppers to chicken. Toss until well combined. Arrange lettuce on a platter and top with the salad. Surround each salad with 1 orange, sliced.

Serves 4.

Per Serving: 312 Calories	
Protein 22 gr.	Carb. 38 gr.
Fat 8 gr.	Cal. from fat 23%
Chol. 48 mg.	Sodium 220 mg.

Cumin-Dijon Dressing

3 Tbsp. lemon juice
1 Tbsp. olive oil
2 Tbsp. chicken stock (fat-free/low salt)
1 Tbsp. red wine vinegar
1 tsp. cumin
1 tsp. Dijon mustard
2 cloves garlic, minced
1/2 tsp. creole seasoning

Whisk lemon juice, oil, chicken stock, vinegar, cumin, mustard, garlic and seasoning in a bowl. Set aside to use with Confetti Chicken Salad.

This dressing may also be used with other salads and is a delicious addition to chicken or turkey sandwiches.

Makes 4 servings, 2 Tbsp. each.

Per Serving: 31 Calories	
Protein 0 gr.	Carb. 0 gr.
Fat 3.4 gr.	Cal. from fat 98%
Chol. 0 mg.	Sodium 150 mg.

To remove corn from its cob, begin by cutting a small piece off the tip to make it flat. Holding the stem edge, stand the cob upright with the flat end on a plate. Use a firm-bladed, very sharp knife to cut downward, removing the corn 3 or 4 rows at a time. To get the "milk" of the corn, use the back of the blade to scrape what's left of the juice from the cobs.

Soup and Sandwich Combo

This isn't just a sandwich — it's a nineties version of the Dagwood! It takes two hands to handle this flavorful, low-fat sandwich, and your appetite will be satisfied with the side of zesty Gazpacho. Any bread you choose would be great in this sandwich, but the marbled rye is particularly interesting and fun.

Soup and Sandwich Combo

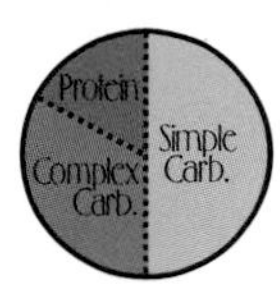

turkey, cheese (protein)
bread (complex carb.)
gazpacho (simple carb.)

Market Club Sandwich

3 thin slices marble rye bread
1/2 Tbsp. light mayonnaise
2 tsp. Dijon mustard
2 green lettuce leaves
2 oz. smoked turkey breast, sliced thin
1 oz. Jarlsberg Lite Swiss cheese
2 slices tomato
1 radicchio leaf

Spread bread with mayo and mustard. Top one slice of bread with one lettuce leaf and 1 oz. turkey, then add second slice of bread. Top with another lettuce leaf, swiss cheese, tomato slice, radicchio leaf and turkey. Top with remaining piece of bread.

Serves 1.

Per Serving: 355 Calories	
Protein 29 gr.	Carb. 38 gr.
Fat 9 gr.	Cal. from fat 24%
Chol. 59 mg.	Sodium 706 mg.

Gazpacho

1 medium red bell pepper, seeded and finely diced
1 medium green bell pepper, seeded and finely diced
1/2 cucumber (European is best) peeled, seeded and finely diced
1/2 small red onion, finely diced
2 tomatoes, finely diced
1 1/2 cups (12 oz.) V-8 juice
1 1/2 cups (12 oz.) tomato juice
1 Tbsp. white wine vinegar
1 clove garlic, minced
1 tsp. Tabasco
1/4 cup chopped fresh basil
1/4 tsp. cumin
1 tsp. creole seasoning

Combine ingredients. Chill. Serve cold. Makes 12 small servings, 1/2 cup each.

Per Serving: 22 Calories	
Protein 1 gr.	Carb. 5 gr.
Fat 0 gr.	Cal. from fat 0%
Chol. 0 mg.	Sodium 312 mg.

Soups make an elegant and exciting first course for any meal you want to make special. Choose one that will complement the flavors of the other dishes in the meal. For example, this zesty, chilled gazpacho is the perfect prelude to this summertime sandwich.

You can shave off a lot of preparation time by using your food processor; it chops and slices vegetables in a fraction of the time it would take to do by hand. Always start with the least moist and messy vegetable. Mushrooms, for example, should be cut and set aside before you chop something moist like peppers or tomatoes. Don't worry about wiping out the bowl between veggies — it's all going into the same pot anyway!

Grilled Turkey Burger

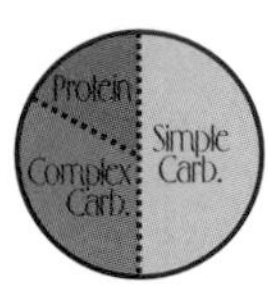

turkey (protein)
bun (complex carb.)
tomato, pineapple (simple carb.)

Ground turkey breast is an excellent substitute for ground beef. You can be assured you are getting only the white meat (no added fat and skin) by taking a package of turkey breast cutlets to the meat counter and asking them to grind them for you. Shop for a few moments, then return to pick up your custom low-fat specialty.

Grilled Turkey Burger

1 Turkey Burger Patty
1 multi-grain hamburger bun
1/2 Tbsp. Garlic Aioli
1 large lettuce leaf
2 slices tomato
2 red onion rings

Serve with 1/3 cup Pineapple Tomato Salsa (pg. 44) in a red cabbage leaf.

Grill Turkey Burger Patty. Place patty on whole wheat bun spread with aioli, lettuce, tomato slices and onion.

Serves 1.

Per Serving: 403 Calories	
Protein 41 gr.	Carb. 44 gr.
Fat 7 gr.	Cal. from fat 16%
Chol. 96 mg.	Sodium 724 mg.

Turkey Burger Patty

3 lbs. ground turkey breast
8 oz. Simply Potatoes hash browns, cooked
1/3 cup chopped fresh parsley
1 Tbsp. Mrs. Dash seasoning
1/2 tsp. black pepper
1/2 cup diced white onions
1 Tbsp. chicken stock (fat-free/low salt)
1 egg white, lightly beaten

Mix all ingredients together in food processor or blender on rough chop until ingredients are blended. Shape into 10 patties.

Makes 10 patties, 5 1/2 oz. each.

Per Serving: 236 Calories	
Protein 36 gr.	Carb. 6 gr.
Fat 5 gr.	Cal. from fat 19%
Chol. 96 mg.	Sodium 294 mg.

Garlic Aioli

1 cup light mayonnaise
1/2 cup nonfat plain yogurt
1/2 tsp. creole seasoning
1 Tbsp. finely chopped shallots
2 tsp. chopped fresh herbs (cilantro, basil, rosemary, thyme)
4 cloves garlic, minced
juice of 1/2 lemon

Mix together all ingredients. Refrigerate.
Makes 25 servings, 1 Tbsp. each.

Per Serving: 28 Calories	
Protein 0 gr.	Carb. 1 gr.
Fat 2.5 gr.	Cal. from fat 80%
Chol. 3 mg.	Sodium 25 mg.

Grilled Fish Sandwich

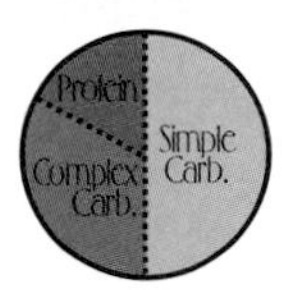

fish (protein)
bun, potato (complex carb.)
vegetables (simple carb.)

Grilled Fish Sandwich

16 oz. grouper or snapper
1/4 cup Balsamic Marinade (pg. 42)
4 multi-grain kaiser or hamburger buns
2 Tbsp. Garlic Aioli (pg. 84)
4 large lettuce leaves
1 red onion, sliced into rings
1 tomato, sliced
sprinkle of chopped fresh herbs (cilantro, basil, rosemary, thyme)

Cut fish into 4 pieces. Marinate in the Balsamic Marinade for up to 1 hour. Grill over hot coals or gas grill until done.

Spread buns with aioli and top with fish, lettuce, onion and tomato slices. Sprinkle with chopped herbs.

Serves 4.

Per Serving: 251 Calories	
Protein 26 gr.	Carb. 24 gr.
Fat 4 gr.	Cal. from fat 14%
Chol. 44 mg.	Sodium 305 mg.

Herbed Potato Salad

1 1/2 lbs. red-skinned potatoes, scrubbed and quartered
1/2 tsp. salt
1 Tbsp. white wine vinegar
1/2 tsp. creole seasoning
2 Tbsp. light mayonnaise
1 Tbsp. Dijon mustard
1/4 cup nonfat sour cream
1/3 cup chopped celery
1 red bell pepper, julienned
1/4 cup chopped green onions
1 Tbsp. chopped fresh parsley
1 Tbsp. chopped fresh dill

In a medium-sized saucepan, cover potatoes with cold water and add salt. Bring to a boil and cook over medium heat until tender, 7 to 9 minutes. Drain in colander and gently transfer to a large bowl. Toss with vinegar and seasoning. Set the potatoes aside to cool.

In a small bowl, whisk together the mayonnaise, mustard and sour cream. Add the dressing and the rest of the ingredients to the potatoes.

Serves 6.

Per Serving: 125 Calories	
Protein 3 gr.	Carb. 25 gr.
Fat 1.5 gr.	Cal. from fat 12%
Chol. 2 mg.	Sodium 142 mg.

Gazpacho

This summer refresher is a delight any time of the year. The unique blend of textures and flavors — cool yet spicy, smooth yet crispy — combined with the vivid colors provides a feast for the senses. The Black Bean and Corn Salsa is an appealing accompaniment — and a fun addition when served as pictured — in a fresh corn husk.

Gazpacho With Salsa

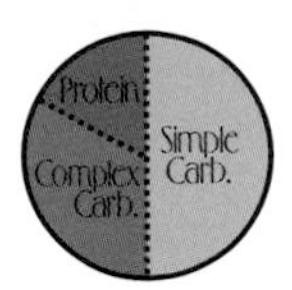

beans (protein)
corn (complex carb.)
tomatoes, vegetables (simple carb.)

Gazpacho*

3 medium red bell peppers, seeded and finely diced
3 medium green bell peppers, seeded and finely diced
1 European cucumber, peeled, seeded and finely diced
1 small red onion, finely diced
6 tomatoes, finely diced
1 can (40 oz.) V-8 juice
1 can (40 oz.) tomato juice
3 Tbsp. white wine vinegar
2 garlic cloves, finely chopped
1 Tbsp. Tabasco
1/4 cup chopped fresh basil
1/2 tsp. cumin

Combine all ingredients. Chill. Serve cold. Makes 12 servings, 1 1/2 cups each.

Per Serving: 66 Calories	
Protein 3 gr.	Carb. 15 gr.
Fat 0 gr.	Cal. from fat 0%
Chol. 0 mg.	Sodium 936 mg.

* **See page 83 for smaller portion recipe.**

Black Bean and Corn Salsa

2 cups black beans, drained and rinsed
1 cup frozen corn kernels, thawed
2 plum tomatoes, diced
1/2 red onion, minced
1 serrano pepper, minced
1 Tbsp. finely chopped cilantro
1 Tbsp. olive oil
4 cloves garlic, minced
juice of 2 limes
1 Tbsp. balsamic vinegar
1 tsp. cumin
2 tsp. hot pepper sauce
1 tsp. creole seasoning

In a large bowl, combine all ingredients and mix well. Allow to marinate at least one hour.

Makes 5 servings, 2/3 cup each.

Per Serving: 158 Calories	
Protein 8 gr.	Carb. 26 gr.
Fat 3 gr.	Cal. from fat 17%
Chol. 0 mg.	Sodium 236 mg.

Have you heard that "soup is good food"? It's true, particularly for the person working toward better portion control. Research has shown that starting your meal with soup, which has a lower caloric density than most solid foods and takes a relatively long time to eat, will often result in your eating less. It gives your brain time to register fullness before it's too late. And don't forget soup is a great one-dish meal — it's one of my favorites.

Soups for Meals

If you don't have time to cook dry beans, you can use canned beans instead. Just empty them into a colander, then rinse and drain them well to lower the salt content.

Pasta and Chickpea Soup

beans, Parmesan cheese (protein)
pasta, beans (complex carb.)
fruit salad (simple carb.)

1 tsp. olive oil
2 cloves garlic, minced
1 can (14 oz.) whole tomatoes, drained
1 Tbsp. chopped fresh rosemary
6 cups chicken stock (fat-free/low salt)
2 cans (19 oz. each) or 4 cups cooked chickpeas, drained and rinsed
6 oz. dry penne pasta
1/2 tsp. creole seasoning
1 tsp. Mrs. Dash seasoning
1/2 cup grated Parmesan cheese

Serve with 1/2 cup mixed cut fruit per serving.

Spray a large stockpot with cooking spray. Add olive oil and heat. Add garlic and cook, stirring, about 1 minute. Add tomatoes and rosemary; simmer for 5 minutes, crushing the tomatoes with stirring spoon. Pour in chicken stock and bring to a simmer over medium heat.

In a small bowl, mash 1 cup of the chickpeas with a fork. Stir the mashed chickpeas into the pot, along with the penne and seasonings. Simmer uncovered until the pasta is tender, 8 to 10 minutes. Stir in the remaining whole chickpeas and heat through. Sprinkle with grated Parmesan.

Makes 8 servings, 1 1/2 cups each.

Per Serving: 195 Calories	
Protein 9 gr.	Carb. 32 gr.
Fat 3 gr.	Cal. from fat 14%
Chol. 16 mg.	Sodium 666 mg.

Smoked Turkey and White Bean Soup

turkey, beans (protein)
beans (complex carb.)
salad, orange (simple carb.)

1 tsp. olive oil
2 cloves garlic, minced
1 can (14 oz.) whole tomatoes, drained
2 Tbsp. chopped fresh basil (or 2 tsp. dried)
6 cups chicken stock (fat-free/low salt)
2 cans (19 oz. each) or 4 cups cooked cannelini or white beans, drained and rinsed
1 lb. smoked turkey, rough chopped
1/2 tsp. creole seasoning
1 tsp. Mrs. Dash seasoning

Serve with Mixed Green Salad With Oranges (pg. 99).

Spray a large stockpot with cooking spray. Add olive oil and bring to low heat. Add garlic and cook, stirring, about 1 minute. Add tomatoes and basil; simmer for 5 minutes, crushing the tomatoes with stirring spoon. Pour in chicken stock and simmer over medium heat.

Stir in cannelini beans and smoked turkey along with the seasonings. Heat through.

Makes 10 servings, 1 1/2 cups each.

Per Serving: 182 Calories	
Protein 19 gr.	Carb. 17 gr.
Fat 4 gr.	Cal. from fat 21%
Chol. 33 mg.	Sodium 560 mg.

Soups for Meals (continued)

Pasta e Fagioli

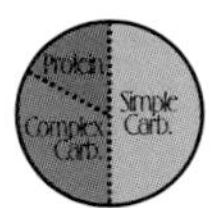

beans (protein)
pasta, bread (complex carb.)
vegetables (simple carb.)

1/2 lb. each uncooked white, black, kidney and pinto beans
2 quarts chicken stock (fat-free/low salt)
1 large yellow onion, chopped
2 cloves garlic, minced
1 cup cabbage, shredded
1 1/2 lbs. plum tomatoes, peeled, seeded and chopped
1 can (4 oz.) tomato paste
1/2 cup balsamic vinegar
2 bay leaves
2 Tbsp. chopped fresh oregano
2 Tbsp. chopped fresh thyme
1 Tbsp. chopped fresh rosemary
1 tsp. cracked black pepper
1 Tbsp. creole seasoning
1 Tbsp. Mrs. Dash seasoning
6 cups cooked whole wheat fettucine

Wash beans and soak in water overnight. Drain.

Spray large saucepan with cooking spray. Quickly saut onion, garlic and cabbage with 2 Tbsp. of chicken stock. Add soaked, drained beans. Add remaining chicken stock and bring to boil. Reduce to simmer and stir occasionally. Add tomatoes, tomato paste, vinegar, herbs and seasonings. Simmer for 1 1/2 hours until beans are soft. Puree 1 cup of the beans and return to pot. Remove bay leaves.

When serving, mound 1/2 cup cooked fettucine into each bowl. Spoon 1 1/2 cups of soup onto pasta.

Makes 12 servings.

Per Serving: 245 Calories	
Protein 15 gr.	Carb. 46 gr.
Fat less than l gr.	Cal. from fat 2%
Chol. 0 mg.	Sodium 353 mg.

Did you plan to use beans but forget the overnight soak? Then try the quick-soak method for the beans. Just cover the beans with water in a large stock pot, bring to a boil and cover. Let boil for 5 minutes, then turn off the heat and let the beans sit on the stove for 1 hour. Rinse well, then add more liquid for the final stage of cooking.

COOKING BEANS

1 Cup Dried Beans	Stock or Water	Cooking Time
Black beans	4 cups	1½ hrs.
Cannelini or white beans	3 cups	1½ hrs.
Garbanzo beans	4 cups	3 hrs.
Great northern beans	3½ cups	3½ hrs.
Kidney beans	3 cups	3 hrs.
Lentils	3 cups	3 hrs.
Lima beans	2 cups	2 hrs.
Navy beans	3 cups	3 hrs.
Pinto beans	3 cups	3 hrs.
Red beans	3 cups	2½ hrs.
Split peas	3 cups	1 hr.

Wash beans and soak in water overnight. Drain and place in large, heavy pot. Cover with stock (or water) and seasonings. Bring slowly to a boil, then reduce heat and simmer, partially covered, until tender. Bean is done when it can be squashed in the roof of the mouth with tongue.

Lunches & Soups

TWENTY-TWO MEALS

Hearty Chili Meals

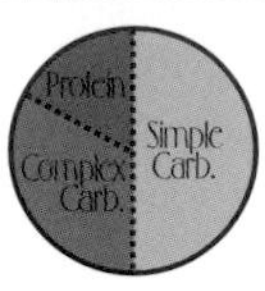

turkey, beans (protein)
rice, beans (complex carb.)
hearts of palm (simple carb.)

To cook ground turkey quickly, crumble ground turkey breast into a hard plastic colander. Cover with paper towel, place colander on a plate to catch juices and microwave on high power for 3 minutes. Stir and break up meat, and microwave for another 2 minutes or until browned.

Chili in a Hurry

1 tsp. olive oil
1 small red onion, chopped
1 red bell pepper, seeded and chopped
1 green bell pepper, seeded and chopped
2 cloves garlic, minced
1 jalapeño pepper, seeded and finely chopped
1 tsp. cumin
1 1/2 Tbsp. chili powder
1 tsp. creole seasoning
1 lb. ground turkey breast
2 cans (28 oz. each) whole tomatoes
1 cup chicken stock (fat-free/low salt)
1 can (15 oz.) black beans, drained

Serve with cooked brown rice, nonfat sour cream and cilantro.

Spray a large, heavy saucepan with cooking spray and heat over medium heat. Add the olive oil, onions and bell peppers; sauté until softened, about 4 to 5 minutes. Add garlic, jalapeño pepper, cumin, chili powder and seasoning; sauté about 2 minutes more.

Add cooked turkey to sauté vegetables and mix together. Add tomatoes and break up with spoon while sauté.

Add chicken stock; reduce heat to low and bring to a simmer, stirring. Cook for another 15 minutes; add drained black beans. Heat through.

When serving, scoop 1/3 cup cooked brown rice into a bowl and ladle 1 1/2 cups of chili on top. Top with 1 Tbsp. nonfat sour cream and garnish with cilantro.

Makes 8 servings.

Per Serving: 255 Calories	
Protein 21 gr.	Carb. 38 gr.
Fat 2 gr.	Cal. from fat 7%
Chol. 35 mg.	Sodium 485 mg.

Hearts of Palm Vinaigrette

1/4 cup orange juice
1 Tbsp. Dijon mustard
2 Tbsp. white wine vinegar
1 tsp. olive oil
2 cloves garlic, minced
1/2 tsp. dried whole basil
1/2 tsp. creole seasoning
4 lettuce leaves
1 can (14.4 oz.) hearts of palm, rinsed and cut into 1/2-inch slices
1/2 small red onion, sliced and separated into rings
2 Tbsp. chopped fresh parsley

Whisk orange juice, mustard, vinegar, olive oil, garlic, basil and seasoning together in a small bowl. Set vinaigrette aside.

Place 1 lettuce leaf on each of 4 salad plates. Arrange hearts of palm and sliced onion on lettuce leaves. Sprinkle evenly with chopped parsley. Drizzle 2 Tbsp. vinaigrette over each salad.

Serves 4.

Per Serving: 33 Calories	
Protein 1 gr.	Carb. 5 gr.
Fat 1 gr.	Cal. from fat 27%
Chol. 1.5 mg.	Sodium 226 mg.

Hearty Chili Meals (continued)

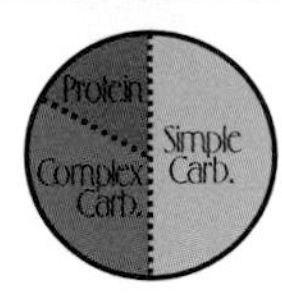

lentils, cheese (protein)
lentils, cornbread (complex carb.)
vegetables (simple carb.)

Red Lentil Chili

$^1/_2$ lb. carrots
1 small zucchini
1 small yellow squash
$^1/_2$ large eggplant
$^1/_2$ large red onion
$^3/_4$ Tbsp. olive oil
12 oz. bag red or brown lentils, rinsed
2 cups chicken stock (fat-free/low salt)
1 tsp. Mrs. Dash seasoning
1 tsp. creole seasoning
2 bay leaves
$^1/_2$ Tbsp. oregano
$^1/_2$ tsp. cumin
1 tsp. chili powder
$^3/_4$ tsp. cayenne
$^3/_4$ tsp. nutmeg
2 cloves garlic, minced
1 jalapeño pepper, chopped
2 cans (32 oz. each) plum tomatoes

Serve with 1 oz. baked tortilla chips and 1 Tbsp. nonfat sour cream per serving or Southwest Cornbread.

In food processor, finely chop carrots, zucchini, squash, eggplant and onion. Spray nonstick skillet with cooking spray. Add olive oil. Heat over medium high heat. Add chopped vegetables. Sauté for 5 minutes. Add lentils, chicken stock, seasonings, herbs, spices, garlic, jalapeño peppers and tomatoes. Simmer for 2 hours.

Makes 10 servings, $1^1/_2$ cups each.

Per Serving: 134 Calories	
Protein 8 gr.	Carb. 26 gr.
Fat 1 gr.	Cal. from fat 8%
Chol. 0 mg.	Sodium 406 mg.

Southwest Cornbread

2 Tbsp. canola oil
$^1/_2$ cup finely chopped onion
1 egg, lightly beaten
1 Tbsp. honey
1 cup skim milk
1 cup whole wheat pastry flour
1 cup yellow cornmeal
1 Tbsp. baking powder
$^1/_2$ tsp. salt
1 cup fresh or frozen corn
$^1/_2$ cup shredded part-skim cheddar cheese

Preheat oven to 375 degrees.

Heat oil in a small skillet. Add onion and sauté for 5 to 8 minutes or until onion is soft.

Beat together egg, honey and milk; set aside.

In a separate bowl, combine flour, cornmeal, baking powder and salt. Add to liquid mixture. Add corn, shredded cheese and onions along with all excess oil. Mix well. Spread into an 8-inch square pan coated with cooking spray.

Bake for 25 to 35 minutes or until brown and firm on top. Cut into 16 pieces.

Makes 16 servings.

Per Serving: 94 Calories	
Protein 5 gr.	Carb. 15 gr.
Fat 1.5 gr.	Cal. from fat 15%
Chol. 2 mg.	Sodium 231 mg.

Lentils are the "quick and easy" legume because they don't need to soak before cooking. After rinsing in a colander, put them in a large stockpot and cover with liquid (chicken stock is best). Cover and simmer till tender, usually about 45 minutes — or a little longer if you've added acidic ingredients like tomatoes and wine, unless you add them when the lentils are almost done. Drain the liquid as soon as lentils are done or they will continue to cook.

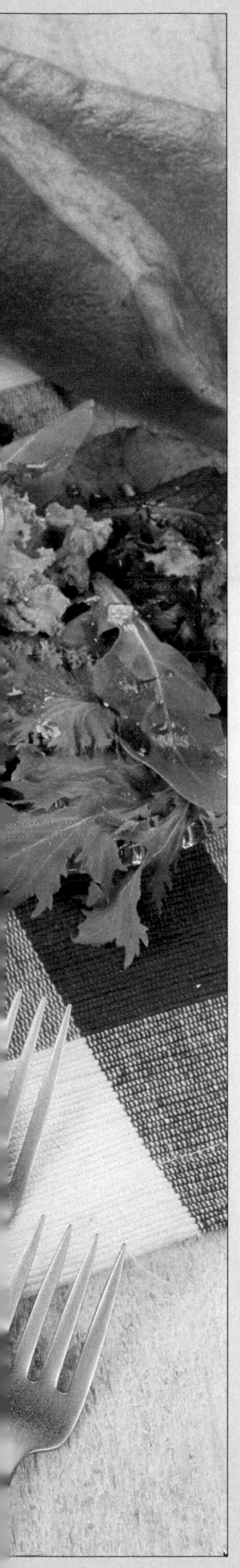

Dinners

FORTY-FOUR MEALS

The good life of cooking and dining is guided by the premise that good health and good food are synonymous. It's an approach to healthy food preparation and presentation that serves up meals that delight and satisfy.

This type of cooking makes eating what we like the same as eating what is good for us. The food is fresh and flavorful, relying on herbs, garlic, fresh vegetables, fruits and small amounts of olive oil. No rich sauces, heavy starches or fat to dull the senses. Meals consist of carefully selected dishes served in appropriate portions.

Each dish is created from natural, wholesome foods that are high in natural fiber and nutrients. The meals are designed to be low in fat and calories, low in cholesterol and sodium, but high on flavor and beauty. And one more thing — they are designed for those of us who don't have the time (or often the energy) to plan and cook a meal after a busy day.

These recipes are personal ones I want to share with you to help you overcome the obstacles to healthy cooking. They are the quickest and easiest ways to turn simple recipes into elegant, complete meals.

All of the meals are planned for important nutrients and balance, for color, for flavor and for texture.

Just as in clothing, some colors in food don't work well together. But a variety of colors can give each plate a pleasing appearance. It's as though each plate becomes an artist's canvas.

A meal that has simple or bland flavors can bore your palate. *The Good Life* meals balance sweet, savory, salty and acidic flavors. Too many complex or strong flavors in a meal can overwhelm the taste buds and the taster.

Texture is how a food feels in your mouth — crispy, crunchy, chewy or soft. Consistency is the food's density and firmness, as well as how it holds together on the plate. It's best to have a variety — too many crisp, crunchy and chewy items can exhaust the eater's jaw, while too many soft or saucy items can form one big glob on the plate. Different shapes and heights also make for better meals.

Variety in temperature of foods brings appeal as well. It adds a contrast that heightens enjoyment. For example, warm, grilled meat on a chilled salad is a celebration!

Pictured: Vegetable Lasagna (pg. 96)

Cooking-Quick Survival Tips

- Keep your pantry, fridge and freezer well-stocked with the basic ingredients for quick and easy food preparation.
- Keep an ongoing grocery list and jot down items as soon as you begin to run low. If you wait until you are completely out of an item, it could cost you an unplanned trip to the store.
- After you have shopped, plan to use the most perishable foods first: fresh seafood, leafy vegetables and some fruits. Saving the hardiest foods for last will help reduce waste and eliminate unnecessary trips to the store.

- Since half the battle is just deciding what to prepare, pick out the meal you are going to try one or two days in advance — and make sure you have the needed ingredients on hand. If you have a family, enlist them in this time of preparing — even allow them the responsibility for a meal or two each week.
- A recipe generally takes longer the first time you prepare it, so when you plan to make a new dish give yourself the extra edge of time.
- These dishes are designed for your time and effort to be spent on one part of the meal. If the entrée requires a bit more time to prepare, it is put together with a simpler side dish.
- Keep a ready-to-cook kitchen: do most of your food preparation on a countertop close to your sink. Declutter your countertops by storing your seldom used appliances in less accessible cabinets. Use the drawer and cabinet closest to your cooking area to store knives, vegetable scrub brushes and peelers, stirring spoons, measuring spoons and cups, mixing bowls, colanders, cutting boards, scales and graters. Keep your food processor and hand-held blender close so they are always handy for quick chopping, mincing or blending.

Trimming Time by Freezing Food

A major part of living the good life is not to spend any unnecessary time in the kitchen! My theory about cooking is, and has always been, "If it takes longer to cook it than to eat it, FORGET IT!" How about you?

One way to streamline your food preparation is to look for the recipes that can be doubled or tripled, then frozen for later use. Nothing can calm frenzied nerves after a busy day — overflowing into a busy night — like a meal that can be pulled out and heated up in a jiffy!

If you're marinating and grilling two chicken breasts, why not do a dozen? Then you can freeze them individually in small plastic zip-top bags. Later they can be popped into the microwave for a quick chicken sandwich or salad. The same goes for any number of dishes — from lasagna to meatloaf.

I also use this theory when I'm picking up takeout. Rather then getting two Chinese meals to bring home, I bring home four and freeze the two extras in small bags for quick meals. Combined with my own flavorful brown rice, it makes a terrific treat days later.

And don't forget about freezing some of the use-in-everything ingredients like stocks, sauces and chopped veggies. They can be frozen in small quantities perfectly sized for your recipes.

Use these tips for fantastic freezing:

- Keep your eyes and mind open for doubling up on recipes, saving you time and effort later. Highlight those recipes to remind you even before you go to the store.
- Choose foods to freeze wisely: Some foods just don't freeze well. The higher the fat content, the shorter its storage potential. And foods that are high in water content will turn to mush, like tomatoes, lettuces and other salad vegetables. Milk and yogurt sauces will curdle.
- Cool food quickly before you freeze it. Don't let your flavor-packed, texture-filled food sit around and lose its quality. Put it in the freezing container, seal it, then cool it in very cold water before freezing.
- Pack it small and flat. I use quart-size, heavy-duty, sealable plastic freezer bags, which can be cleaned and used again and again. Then I pack in individual portion sizes so that I can prepare for one, two or four. A whole pan of lasagna is only helpful if I'm preparing for a crowd.

  Fill bags with food, press out the air, seal and then freeze so they are flat. I then place them in boxes according to proteins, complex carbohydrates and simple carbohydrate vegetables. Just a simple shoebox will do.
- Date each bag. And name it too! I jot down names and dates with a permanent ink pen. Use your frozen foods within six months.

- Defrost carefully. Don't ever leave food out at room temperature for over three hours to thaw. Thaw overnight in the refrigerator or microwave them on defrost (30 percent power) for six to eight minutes per pound of food.
- Combine a frozen meal with a fresh food. This will give you a great balance of aroma, nutrients, color and texture.

After a month of cooking for your immediate meal plus making extra to store in the freezer, it won't be necessary to cook but two or three times a week — because there is always something special waiting for you in that special place!

Tips for Enhancing Family Mealtimes

Sitting down to a table set with a simple placemat and napkin will prepare the stage for a beautiful meal. Too often meals are eaten standing up over the sink (if eaten at all). Not only do our bodies ask, "What did you just do to me?" but our satisfaction meter asks, "Did you just inhale a meal or actually eat one?" Use these tips to enjoy dining, not just eating.

- Schedule a time for regular at-home meals.
- Sit down to the table; put on quiet, relaxing music and dine!
- Concentrate on happy and uplifting conversation or thoughts.
- Don't let the dinner table become a battleground. It should be a place of renewal, both physically and emotionally.
- Turn off the TV!

The dinner table is a great place to engage your family in conversation, which occurs far too rarely with today's busy schedules. Some super conversation starters are:

- Tell me about your day.
- What funny thing happened to you today?
- What do you think you do best?
- What's something nice that happened to you today?
- If you could trade places with anyone, who would you trade with?
- If you had three wishes, what would you wish for?
- What is your favorite sport?
- If you could go anywhere in the world, where would it be?

Take an interest in the answers you hear. Give your undivided attention; listen quietly. Don't criticize, or even comment, until the answer is complete. Acknowledge the other person's feelings with words like *Oh* or *Yes* or *I see*. Really listening will keep your family close on a daily basis.

Often a sympathetic silence is all that is needed; you don't even have to say anything.

What if you're dining alone? Treat yourself just as you would others — as a special guest. And, no eating over the sink allowed!

Dinner can be a magnificent transition from the stresses of the day into the relaxation of your evening. Let the food preparation be the warm-up — lots of tension can be released through chopping vegetables!

Enlist the whole family's help (and friends when they're over) in meal preparation. These occasions allow you to join together in an activity that refreshes and refuels — in all of your arenas.

Get ready — set — cook!

Vegetable Lasagna

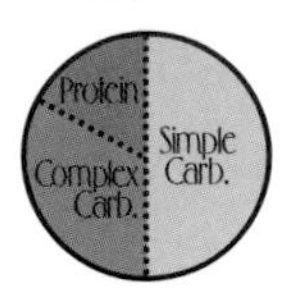

cheeses (protein)
pasta (complex carb.)
vegetables (simple carb.)

Whole grain pasta is more nutritious and satisfying than pasta made from refined flours; you will be full with a much smaller portion and will enjoy the hearty, nutty flavor.

Look for whole wheat or Jerusalem artichoke pastas in your supermarket's natural food section; health food stores will also have a wide variety. Cook in a large pot, in lots of water, for about 1 minute longer than white pastas.

Try them — you'll like them!

Vegetable Lasagna

1/2 small eggplant, sliced very thin
1 large zucchini, sliced lengthwise
1 yellow bell pepper, quartered and flattened
1 red bell pepper, quartered and flattened
1/2 cup Balsamic Marinade (pg. 42)
16 oz. skim milk ricotta cheese
1 cup feta cheese
1 Tbsp. chopped fresh oregano (or 1 tsp. dried)
1 tsp. Mrs. Dash seasoning
1/2 tsp. creole seasoning
2 egg whites
8 oz. dry rotini pasta (spiral), cooked
4 cups Tomato Basil Sauce, heated (pg. 48)
2 Tbsp. chopped fresh parsley

Marinate vegetables in Balsamic Marinade for at least 1 hour or up to overnight. Grill over hot coals or gas grill, or sear on both sides in hot nonstick skillet.

Mix together ricotta, feta, oregano, seasonings and egg whites until relatively smooth.

To assemble, layer individual stacks of vegetables and cheese mix on a clean counter in this order (from the bottom up):

eggplant slice
2 Tbsp. cheese mixture
zucchini slice
2 Tbsp. cheese mixture
yellow pepper quarter
2 Tbsp. cheese mixture
red bell pepper quarter

Toss pasta with 2 cups Tomato Basil Sauce. Place 1/2 cup of this mixture on each plate. Carefully add one of the lasagna stacks to the plate. (Use a spatula to move it.) Top both the pasta and the lasagna with 1/2 cup of reserved Tomato Basil Sauce, and sprinkle with chopped parsley.

Serves 4.

Per Serving: 435 Calories	
Protein 34 gr.	Carb. 55 gr.
Fat 8 gr.	Cal. from fat 16%
Chol. 33 mg.	Sodium 746 mg.

Garlic Dijon Greens

8 cups mixed lettuces
2 tomatoes, quartered
1 cucumber, peeled and sliced
1/2 cup Roasted Garlic Dijon Vinaigrette (pg. 41)

Toss vegetables with dressing.

Serves 4.

Per Serving: 42 Calories	
Protein 1 gr.	Carb. 5 gr.
Fat 2 gr.	Cal. from fat 43%
Chol. 0 mg.	Sodium 110 mg.

Eggplant Rollatini

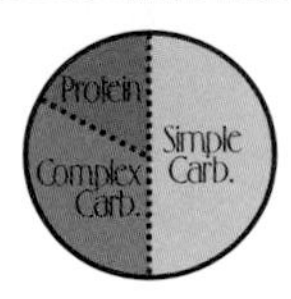

cheeses (protein)
bread crumbs (complex carb.)
vegetables, fruit (simple carb.)

Eggplant Rollatini

1 lb. fresh spinach, washed and stemmed
3/4 lb. eggplant, peeled and cut lengthwise into thin slices
1/2 onion, finely chopped
2 cloves garlic, minced
1/4 tsp. creole seasoning
1 tsp. Mrs. Dash garlic herb seasoning
2 Tbsp. chopped fresh Italian parsley
1 Tbsp. chopped fresh basil
16 oz. skim milk ricotta cheese
1/2 cup feta cheese, crumbled
1 Tbsp. grated Parmesan cheese
1/3 cup dry bread crumbs (purchased)
1 egg (or 1/4 cup egg substitute)
1 egg white, slightly beaten
4 cups Tomato Basil Sauce (pg. 48)

Preheat oven to 400 degrees.

Steam spinach until wilted. Drain well and roughly chop. Reserve. Spray each side of eggplant slices with cooking spray. Bake 10 minutes, flip over and finish baking until tender. Reserve. Reduce oven temperature to 350 degrees.

Spray nonstick skillet with cooking spray. Sauté onions and garlic, adding spinach at end. Let cool. Add seasonings, herbs, cheeses and bread crumbs. Mix in egg and egg white. Chill.

To make rollatini, place 2 heaping tablespoons of spinach-cheese mixture on each eggplant slice. Roll up and place open end down in casserole dish. Cover with 1 cup Tomato Basil Sauce. Bake for 30 minutes.

Place 3 rollatini on each plate. Top with 3/4 cup heated Tomato Basil Sauce.

Serves 4.

Per Serving: 309 Calories	
Protein 30 gr.	Carb. 23 gr.
Fat 5 gr.	Cal. from fat 15%
Chol. 21 mg.	Sodium 785 mg.

Apple Walnut Salad

2 Granny Smith apples, cored and sliced thin
2 Tbsp. chopped walnuts
2 Tbsp. chicken stock (fat-free/low salt)
1 Tbsp. white wine vinegar
2 tsp. walnut oil (or olive oil)
1 Tbsp. finely chopped shallots
1 tsp. Dijon mustard
1/4 tsp. salt
1/4 tsp. cracked black pepper
8 cups washed, dried and torn mixed greens (red leaf, romaine, frizee, radicchio, arugula or bibb)

In a small, dry skillet over low heat, stir walnuts until lightly toasted, about 3 minutes. Transfer to a plate to cool.

In a large salad bowl, whisk together chicken stock, vinegar, oil, shallots, mustard, salt and pepper. Add greens and apples and toss thoroughly. Sprinkle with the toasted walnuts.

Per Serving: 91 Calories	
Protein 2.5 gr.	Carb. 14 gr.
Fat 4 gr.	Cal. from fat 35%
Chol. 0 mg.	Sodium 159 mg.

Choose eggplants that are unspotted, firm, smooth and heavy for their size. A rounder, smoother base will mean fewer bitter seeds.

Keep eggplant refrigerated in a zip-top bag and use in five days or less. Generally, a 1-lb. eggplant will yield 3 to 4 cups chopped.

Remove the bitterness from eggplant by generously salting slices on a baking sheet, covering with paper towels and weighting down with another heavy pan. Rinse and blot dry after 30 minutes.

Bowtie Pasta With Wild Mushroom Sauce

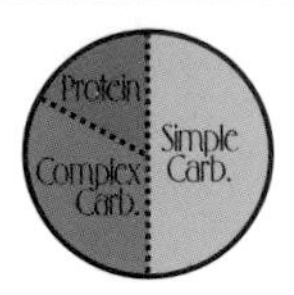

cheese (protein)
pasta (complex carb.)
vegetables (simple carb.)

Wild mushrooms add a rich, exotic flavor to dishes. Look for:

- *Chanterelle (bright yellow-orange and trumpet-shaped)*
- *Enoki (long, spaghetti-like, firm stems with snow-white caps)*
- *Morel (cone-shaped, honeycombed and golden brown)*
- *Oyster (fan-shaped cap; small ones are best)*
- *Porcinis and portobellas (enormous large caps with a rich, beefy taste. Looks wood-like; light brown in color)*
- *Shiitake (dark brown floppy cap 8-10 inches in diameter)*

Rehydrate dried mushrooms by covering and soaking in warm water for about 30 minutes, then rinse and blot with paper towels.

Bowtie Pasta With Wild Mushroom Sauce

2 oz. dried porcini mushrooms
2 tsp. olive oil
2 cloves garlic, minced
1 red onion, sliced thin
1 red bell pepper, cut into strips
2 Tbsp. chopped fresh basil
1 tsp. dried oregano
1/2 tsp. creole seasoning
3/4 cup fresh mushrooms, trimmed and sliced
1 can (14 oz.) plum tomatoes
1 1/2 Tbsp. chopped fresh parsley
12 oz. dry bowtie pasta, cooked
1/2 cup grated Parmesan cheese
2 Tbsp. chopped fresh herbs (cilantro, basil, rosemary, thyme)

In a small bowl, soak dried mushrooms in 1 cup hot water for 15 to 20 minutes. Drain, reserving the soaking liquid. Strain the liquid through a coffee filter; set aside. Rinse and chop the mushrooms.

Spray nonstick skillet with cooking spray. Add olive oil; heat. Add garlic and onions; sauté until translucent, about 3 minutes. Add peppers, herbs and seasoning; sauté another 30 seconds. Add fresh and soaked mushrooms; sauté until mushrooms soften, 3 to 4 minutes.

Pour the reserved soaking liquid into the skillet along with canned tomatoes and about half of the can's juice. Sauté, breaking up the tomatoes with a wooden spoon. Reduce heat to low and simmer about 5 minutes, until juices have been slightly reduced. Stir in parsley and cooked pasta, quickly tossing to coat pasta with sauce. Sprinkle with Parmesan cheese and chopped herbs.

Serves 4.

Per Serving: 354 Calories	
Protein 17 gr.	Carb. 54 gr.
Fat 8 gr.	Cal. from fat 21%
Chol. 67 mg.	Sodium 541 mg.

Squash Creole

1 tsp. olive oil
2 cloves garlic, minced
1 lb. yellow crookneck squash, cut into chunks
1 lb. zucchini squash, cut into chunks
1 red bell pepper, sliced thin lengthwise
1 tsp. Mrs. Dash seasoning
1/2 tsp. creole seasoning
1 Tbsp. chopped fresh herbs (cilantro, basil, rosemary, thyme)
1/4 cup chicken stock (fat-free/low salt)

Spray a nonstick skillet with cooking spray; add the olive oil and heat. Add garlic and lightly sauté about 30 seconds. Add the squash, peppers, seasoning and herbs. Cook until squash is tender, stirring often, adding chicken stock to prevent sticking.

Serves 4.

Per Serving: 50 Calories	
Protein 3 gr.	Carb. 8 gr.
Fat 1.5 gr.	Cal. from fat 24%
Chol. 0 mg.	Sodium 140 mg.

Risotto With Spring Vegetables

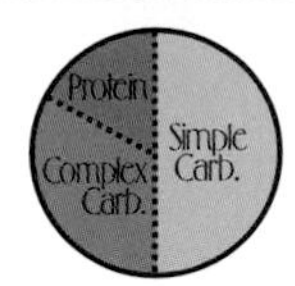

cheeses (protein)
rice (complex carb.)
vegetables, fruit (simple carb.)

Risotto With Spring Vegetables

$5^1/2$ to $6^1/2$ cups chicken stock (fat-free/low salt)
16 baby carrots, shaved and cut in half
8 medium stalks asparagus, trimmed and cut into 2-inch pieces
1 cup sugar snap peas (thawed if frozen)
1 red bell pepper, cut into strips
2 tsp. olive oil
2 cloves garlic, minced
1 red onion, diced
1 cup arborio rice, uncooked
1/2 cup white wine*
1/2 tsp. creole seasoning
1 1/2 Tbsp. chopped fresh basil
1/2 cup grated Parmesan cheese
2 Tbsp. chopped fresh herbs (cilantro, basil, rosemary, thyme)
*** *or substitute dealcoholized wine or more chicken stock***

In a medium-sized stockpot, bring chicken stock to boil over medium heat. Add carrots and cook 3 to 5 minutes until almost tender. Add asparagus and snap peas, and cook 1 minute longer. Remove vegetables with slotted spoon and place in bowl to cool. Reduce heat and keep stock simmering.

Spray a nonstick skillet with cooking spray. Add olive oil; heat. Add garlic and onions, and sauté until translucent, about 3 minutes. Add rice and stir to coat grains. Add wine and cook until most of liquid has been absorbed, about 2 to 3 minutes. Add 1/2 cup simmering chicken stock and cook another 2 to 3 minutes.

Continue adding stock, 1/2 cup at a time, until rice begins to soften, about 15 minutes.

Stir in the seasoning and basil, adding more stock to keep mixture creamy. Stir in reserved vegetables and cheese. Sprinkle with herbs.

Serves 4.

Per Serving: 316 Calories	
Protein 13 gr.	Carb. 52 gr.
Fat 7 gr.	Cal. from fat 19%
Chol. 10 mg.	Sodium 393 mg.

Mixed Green Salad With Oranges

1 small red onion, sliced thin
2 navel oranges, peeled and sliced
4 cups washed, dried and torn mixed greens (red leaf, romaine, frizee, radicchio, arugula or bibb)
1/2 cup Balsamic Marinade (pg. 42)
1 cup whole grain croutons (purchased)
1/4 cup crumbled feta cheese

In a salad bowl, toss together all ingredients with dressing. Divide into fourths and serve on salad plates, allowing orange slices to remain on the top.

Serves 4.

Per Serving: 93 Calories	
Protein 3.5 gr.	Carb. 14 gr.
Fat 2 gr.	Cal. from fat 20%
Chol. 6 mg.	Sodium 229 mg.

Risotto is a creamy, classic Northern Italian dish made with short-grain, highly starched rice, such as arborio.

Start risotto by sautéeing rice in a small amount of olive oil for a few minutes until it is opaque.

Add hot liquid to rice 1/2 cup at a time, stirring constantly until the rice absorbs the liquid before adding more liquid.

Keep the broth over low heat, ready to be added. Stir in extra ingredients a few minutes before serving.

Risotto is wonderful with lamb shanks and wild mushrooms.

French Country Meal

Home-style cooking is updated in this hearty menu with fresh and rustic flavor. The Cornish hens have been flavorfully marinated with herbs, then roasted to a golden brown. Served with marinated tomatoes on a bed of new potatoes, carrots and sugar snap peas, this is a simple and elegant meal that brings comfort and joy in any season.

French Country Meal

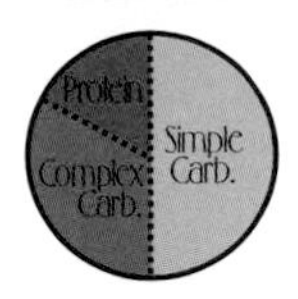

game hens (protein)
potatoes (complex carb.)
carrots, snap peas, tomatoes (simple carb.)

Cornish Game Hens

2 Cornish hens, halved lengthwise
2/3 cup white wine Worcestershire sauce
2 cloves garlic, minced
2 Tbsp. chopped fresh rosemary
1 tsp. Mrs. Dash seasoning
1/2 tsp. creole seasoning

Preheat oven to 375 degrees.

Remove skin from Cornish hens where possible. Place in small roasting pan and top with remaining ingredients. Let marinate for at least 1 hour.

Place hens in oven for 45 minutes or until juices run clear when pierced with fork. Brush occasionally with marinade in pan. See picture for beautiful plate presentation.

Serves 4.

Per Serving: 150 Calories	
Protein 25 gr.	Carb. 0 gr.
Fat 4 gr.	Cal. from fat 28%
Chol. 74 mg.	Sodium 202 mg.

Marinated Tomatoes

4 tomatoes
1/2 cup Balsamic Marinade
2 Tbsp. chopped fresh basil
1 tsp. cracked black pepper
1/2 tsp. creole seasoning

Slice each tomato into 5 to 7 slices and marinate in Balsamic Marinade for up to 1 hour. Sprinkle with basil, pepper and seasoning.

Serves 4.

Per Serving: 34 Calories	
Protein 1 gr.	Carb. 5 gr.
Fat 1 gr.	Cal. from fat 26%
Chol. 0 mg.	Sodium 168 mg.

Sautéed Carrots and New Potatoes

1 lb. (8 to 10) small red-skinned potatoes, quartered
1 tsp. olive oil
2 cloves garlic, minced
1 cup baby carrots, shaved
1/2 tsp. Mrs. Dash seasoning
1/2 tsp. creole seasoning
1 Tbsp. chopped fresh herbs (cilantro, basil, rosemary, thyme)
1/4 cup chicken stock (fat-free/low salt)
1/2 lb. frozen sugar snap peas, thawed

Place red-skinned potatoes in microwaveable dish with 1/4 cup water. Microwave on high power for 4 minutes; drain.

Spray a nonstick skillet with cooking spray, then add olive oil. Heat. Add garlic to pan; lightly sauté. Add potatoes, carrots, herbs and seasonings. Sauté for 5 minutes, adding chicken stock as needed; add sugar snap peas and sautée until crisp tender.

Serves 4.

Per Serving: 117 Calories	
Protein 4 gr.	Carb. 23 gr.
Fat 1.5 gr.	Cal. from fat 11%
Chol. 0 mg.	Sodium 167 mg.

Fresh herbs give pizzazz to a dish that dried herbs just can't match. They are easy to grow and easy to buy. Look for those with a clean, fresh fragrance and bright color. You can keep them for up to 5 days in the refrigerator by wrapping them loosely in a damp paper towel and sealing them airtight in a plastic bag.

Just before using herbs, wash them, then blot with a paper towel. Kitchen shears are great for snipping fresh herbs into small pieces.

Grilled Chicken Over Mixed Greens

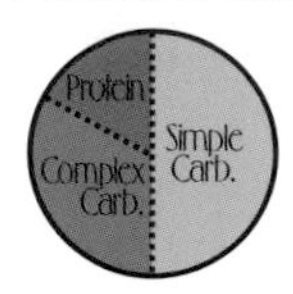

chicken, beans (protein)
corn, beans (complex carb.)
greens (simple carb.)

Marinating low-fat meats and vegetables before grilling will help to keep them moist and full of flavor. When marinated meats hit the high heat of the grill, the outside is seared, sealing the flavor and moisture inside.

Vinegars, wines, fruit juices and yogurts are great main ingredients for low-fat marinades. Combine with garlic or shallots and your favorite herbs and spices for extra pizzazz.

Grilled Chicken Over Mixed Greens

1/2 cup Balsamic Marinade (pg. 42)
4 boneless, skinless chicken breast halves (1 lb.)
12 cups mixture of torn romaine, bibb and red leaf lettuces
1 cup Citrus Vinaigrette (pg. 39)
2 Tbsp. chopped fresh herbs (cilantro, basil, rosemary, thyme)
3 tomatoes, cut into quarters

Marinate the chicken breasts in Balsamic Marinade for at least 1 hour. Grill, or sear in hot skillet, basting with marinade to keep moist.

Toss lettuce mixture with Citrus Vinaigrette. Place grilled chicken on top and sprinkle all with chopped herbs.

Garnish with tomato quarters.

Serves 4.

Per Serving: 259 Calories	
Protein 31 gr.	Carb. 18 gr.
Fat 7 gr.	Cal. from fat 24%
Chol. 72 mg.	Sodium 248 mg.

Black Bean and Corn Salsa

1 can (16 oz.) or 2 cups black beans, drained and rinsed
8 oz. frozen corn kernels, thawed
2 plum tomatoes, diced
1/2 red onion, minced
1 serrano or jalapeño pepper, seeded and minced
1 Tbsp. finely chopped cilantro
1 Tbsp. olive oil
4 cloves garlic, minced
juice of 1 lime
1 Tbsp. balsamic vinegar
1 tsp. cumin
2 tsp. hot pepper sauce
1 tsp. creole seasoning

In a large bowl, combine all ingredients and mix well. Allow to marinate at least one hour.

Makes 10 servings, 1/3 cup each.

Per Serving: 79 Calories	
Protein 4 gr.	Carb. 13 gr.
Fat 1.5 gr.	Cal. from fat 17%
Chol. 0 mg.	Sodium 118 mg.

Breast of Chicken Nicoise

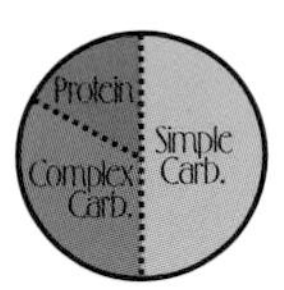

chicken (protein)
couscous (complex carb.)
vegetables (simple carb.)

Breast of Chicken Nicoise

4 boneless, skinless chicken breast halves (1 lb.)
1 tsp. Mrs. Dash garlic herb seasoning, divided
1 tsp. creole seasoning, divided
1/2 cup fennel, cut into strips
1/2 cup leeks, cut into strips
1 tsp. olive oil
2 cloves garlic, minced
1/2 cup cucumber, cut in strips
1 1/2 cups chicken stock (fat-free/low salt)
1/2 cup white wine*
1 large tomato, seeded and cut into strips
1/4 cup chopped fresh basil leaves
8 Nicoise olives, quartered
2 Tbsp. chopped fresh parsley
* ***or substitute dealcoholized wine or more chicken stock***

Clean chicken breasts of all fat and tendons. Season with 1/2 tsp. Mrs. Dash and 1/8 tsp. creole seasoning. Grill, or sear in hot skillet, on each side until done.

Meanwhile, steam fennel and leeks. Spray sauté pan with cooking spray; add olive oil and heat. Add garlic and quickly sauté. Add steamed vegetables and cucumber, and quickly sauté. Add chicken stock and wine, then add tomato, remaining seasonings, basil and olives. Simmer until reduced by half.

Place grilled chicken breasts on plate. Sprinkle with chopped parsley. Cover with vegetables and sauce.

Serves 4.

Per Serving: 209 Calories	
Protein 28 gr.	Carb. 11 gr.
Fat 6 gr.	Cal. from fat 25%
Chol. 72 mg.	Sodium 384 mg.

Herbed Couscous

1 1/4 cups chicken stock (fat-free/low salt)
1 tsp. olive oil
1/2 tsp. Tabasco
1/4 tsp. salt
1 tsp. Mrs. Dash seasoning
1 cup quick-cooking couscous
1 Tbsp. chopped fresh parsley
1/8 tsp. cracked black pepper

In small saucepan, combine chicken stock, olive oil, Tabasco, salt and seasoning, and bring to a boil. Stir in couscous and remove from heat. Cover with a tight-fitting lid and let stand for 5 minutes. Uncover and fluff with fork to separate. Stir in parsley and pepper.

Serves 4.

Per Serving: 183 Calories	
Protein 5 gr.	Carb. 35 gr.
Fat 1 gr.	Cal. from fat 7%
Chol. 0 mg.	Sodium 141 mg.

Chicken Marco

Inspired by a creation of Marco Barbitta, chef and owner of the Trading Post Cafe in Taos, New Mexico, this dish is a delightful blend of flavors, colors and textures. The vegetables are quickly sautéed in a tasty herbal broth and served atop vibrant saffron rice. The marinated grilled breast of chicken is the crowning touch!

Chicken Marco

chicken (protein)
rice (complex carb.)
vegetables (simple carb.)

Chicken Marco

2/3 cup Balsamic Marinade (pg. 42)
4 boneless, skinless chicken breast halves (1 lb.)
2 cloves garlic, minced
2 tsp. shallots, minced
1 cup broccoli florets, blanched
1 each red, green and yellow pepper, cut into strips
1 1/2 cups red beans, cooked and drained
1 1/2 cups chickpeas, cooked and drained
2 plum tomatoes, cut into quarters
1 cup chicken stock (fat-free/low salt)
1 cup white wine*
1 tsp. creole seasoning
1 tsp. Mrs. Dash seasoning
2 Tbsp. chopped fresh herbs (cilantro, basil, rosemary, thyme)
2 cups fresh spinach leaves, washed and stemmed
12 radicchio leaves
* ***or substitute dealcoholized wine or more chicken stock***

Marinate chicken breasts in Balsamic Marinade for at least 1 hour. Grill chicken breasts until done.

Spray a nonstick skillet with cooking spray. Heat. Add garlic and shallots to pan; lightly sauté. Add blanched broccoli, peppers, beans, chickpeas, tomatoes, chicken stock, wine, seasonings and herbs. Lightly sauté, allowing liquid to reduce. Add spinach and radicchio at end of cooking to allow to wilt with heat.

To serve, spoon 1/2 cup saffron rice onto each plate. Top with a fourth of sautéed vegetable mixture. Add a grilled chicken breast, and spoon skillet broth over chicken and rice.

Serves 4.

Per Serving: 371 Calories	
Protein 41 gr.	Carb. 42 gr.
Fat 6 gr.	Cal. from fat 14%
Chol. 72 mg.	Sodium 559 mg.

Saffron Rice

1 tsp. olive oil
2 cloves garlic, minced
1 3/4 cups chicken stock (fat-free/low salt)
4 to 5 saffron threads (or 1/4 tsp. powder)
1/8 tsp. cumin
1/2 tsp. creole seasoning
1 Tbsp. chopped fresh parsley (or 1 tsp. dried)
2 cups instant brown rice

Spray a medium saucepan with cooking spray; add olive oil and heat. Add minced garlic and lightly sauté about 1 to 2 minutes, then add chicken stock, saffron, cumin, seasoning and parsley. Let come to a boil, then stir in brown rice. Boil for 1 minute, turn down heat to low and cover. Simmer for 5 minutes; uncover saucepan and fluff rice with fork. Cover again, and let sit for another 5 minutes.

Serves 4.

Per Serving: 126 Calories	
Protein 2.5 gr.	Carb. 24 gr.
Fat 2 gr.	Cal. from fat 15%
Chol. 0 mg.	Sodium 136 mg.

Saffron is the world's most expensive spice. You can buy it in threads or powder, or in a less expensive "imitation" form such as turmeric. The powder loses its flavor easily and should be bought in very small quantities (that's all anyone can afford, anyway!).

When using the threads, crush just before using. Heat will release saffron's flavor essence, so mixing it with 1 Tbsp. of very hot water and letting it stand for 10 minutes will increase its impact.

Chicken Curry Over Rice

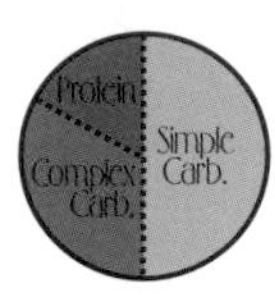

chicken (protein)
rice (complex carb.)
cucumber (simple carb.)

Canned, unsweetened coconut milk — not to be confused with the sweetened coconut "cream" used in sweet drinks — can be found in your supermarket's Asian food section or in a specialty market. It is made from simmering coconut "meat" in water, and adds a subtle flavor and silky texture to many soups and sauces.

Chicken Curry Over Rice

1/4 cup unsweetened coconut milk
2 tsp. cornstarch
1 lb. boneless, skinless chicken breasts
1/2 tsp. creole seasoning
1 tsp. canola oil
1 small onion, chopped
1 red bell pepper, cored, seeded and julienned
2 cloves garlic, minced
1 jalapeño pepper, seeded and finely chopped
4 tsp. curry powder
1 tsp. cumin
1 tsp. ground coriander
1 cup evaporated skim milk
juice of 1 lime
1/4 cup chopped fresh cilantro
2 cups brown rice, cooked

In a small bowl, whisk together coconut milk and cornstarch until smooth; set aside.

Spray a large, heavy saucepan with cooking spray and heat over medium heat. Cut chicken into 2-inch chunks and season with creole seasoning. Add to saucepan, quickly sautéeing until browned. Remove chicken from pan and set aside.

To same saucepan, add canola oil, onions and red bell peppers, reserving a few pieces of pepper for garnish; sauté until softened, about 5 minutes. Add garlic, jalapeño pepper, curry powder, cumin and coriander; sauté about 2 minutes more.

Reduce heat to low and stir in coconut milk mixture and evaporated skim milk. Bring to a simmer, stirring. Cook for another 5 minutes, then add chicken. Heat through, stirring in lime juice and cilantro. Serve over brown rice. Garnish with reserved red pepper.

Serves 4.

Per Serving: 359 Calories	
Protein 35 gr.	Carb. 34 gr.
Fat 8 gr.	Cal. from fat 23%
Chol. 74 mg.	Sodium 278 mg.

Chilled Cucumber Salad

2 cucumbers (European, if available)
2 Tbsp. rice wine vinegar
1/2 tsp. sugar
1/2 tsp. creole seasoning
1 tsp. Mrs. Dash seasoning
1 Tbsp. fresh chopped dill (or 1 tsp. dried)

Peel cucumbers and cut in half lengthwise. With a teaspoon, scrape out and discard seeds. Cut the cucumbers crosswise into 1/4-inch slices.

Place in a medium-size bowl along with the vinegar, sugar, seasonings and dill. Toss to combine and refrigerate until serving time.

Serves 4.

Per Serving: 21 Calories	
Protein 1 gr.	Carb. 5 gr.
Fat 0 gr.	Cal. from fat 0%
Chol. 0 mg.	Sodium 137 mg.

Chicken Paella

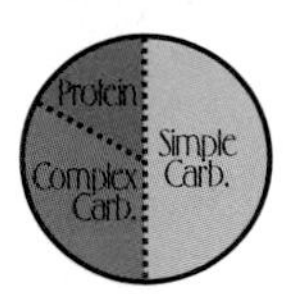

chicken (protein)
rice, peas (complex carb.)
spinach salad (simple carb.)

Chicken Paella

1 lb. boneless, skinless chicken breast, trimmed of fat and cut into chunks
1/4 cup white wine Worcestershire sauce
2 tsp. olive oil
2 cloves garlic, minced
1 small onion, diced
1 cup arborio (or medium grain) rice
2 cups chicken stock (fat-free/low salt)
1/4 tsp. crushed saffron threads (or 1/8 tsp. powdered)
1/2 tsp. creole seasoning
1 tsp. Mrs. Dash seasoning
1 cup frozen peas, thawed
1/3 cup jarred, roasted red peppers, drained and cut into strips

Marinate chicken breasts in Worcestershire sauce for up to 1 hour.

Spray a large nonstick skillet with cooking spray. Add olive oil and heat over medium-high heat. Add garlic and onions and sauté 30 seconds, then add marinated chicken chunks. Sauté until slightly browned on the outside and opaque inside, 3 to 4 minutes. Remove chicken from skillet and set aside.

To skillet, add rice and stir to coat well. Stir in chicken stock, saffron and seasonings. Cover and cook over low heat for 20 minutes. Gently stir in cooked chicken, green peas and roasted red peppers. Cover again and cook, stirring occasionally, until rice is tender, about 5 minutes more. Serve immediately.

Serves 4.

Per Serving: 414 Calories	
Protein 32 gr.	Carb. 55 gr.
Fat 6 gr.	Cal. from fat 13%
Chol. 72 mg.	Sodium 616 mg.

Spinach Salad With Horseradish Dressing

12 oz. fresh spinach, washed and stemmed
1/2 cup grated carrots
1/2 cup grated zucchini
1/2 red onion, sliced thin
1 cup Horseradish Dressing (pg. 40)

Dry spinach in a salad spinner or on a towel.

Toss all remaining ingredients together with dressing and spinach.

Serves 4.

Per Serving: 84 Calories	
Protein 5 gr.	Carb. 16 gr.
Fat 0 gr.	Cal. from fat 0 %
Chol. 0 mg.	Sodium 176 mg.

Choose spinach leaves that are small, firm and dark green; if purchasing spinach by the bag, look for one marked "baby" or "salad" spinach.

To prepare, first discard any leaves that are wilted or discolored. Soak the spinach twice, holding the leaves by the stem and gently swishing the leaves underwater. Stem the spinach by folding each leaf lengthwise, then holding it in one hand, rib side out, and with the other hand pulling the stem off the leaf. Dry the spinach in a salad spinner or by wrapping the leaves in paper towels.

Taste of India Dinner

It sounds nouvelle, but chicken and lentils are actually a centuries-old pairing. Simmered with vegetables, the lentils make a rich bed for the chicken breast and red peppers, which are gently placed on top. If they're available, the red or French lentils give the dish a more delicate flavor.

Taste of India Dinner

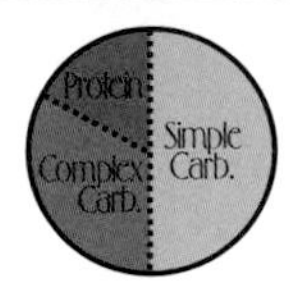

chicken, lentils (protein)
lentils (complex carb.)
vegetables (simple carb.)

Chicken and Sweet Pepper Brochettes

4 wooden skewers
1 lb. boneless, skinless chicken breast, cut into large chunks
2 red bell peppers, cut into 12 chunks
2 yellow bell peppers, cut into 12 chunks
1 onion, cut into 12 pieces
1/2 cup Balsamic Marinade (pg. 42)
1/2 tsp. Mrs. Dash seasoning
1 tsp. creole seasoning
1/2 cup Yogurt Sauce (right column)
2 tsp. chopped fresh cilantro

Serve with a green salad.

Skewer chunks of chicken and vegetables onto wooden skewers that have been soaked in water. Marinate in Balsamic Marinade for at least 1 hour or up to overnight. Sprinkle with seasonings and grill over hot coals.

Make a bed of Seasoned Lentil Sauté in the center of each of four plates. Place grilled skewers on top. Add a tablespoon of Yogurt Sauce and sprinkle with chopped cilantro.

Serves 4.

Per Serving: 203 Calories	
Protein 31 gr.	Carb. 11 gr.
Fat 3.5 gr.	Cal. from fat 16%
Chol. 73 mg.	Sodium 377 mg.

Seasoned Lentil Sauté

1 Tbsp. shallots, chopped
2 cloves garlic, minced
2 cups red or brown lentils, cooked in chicken stock (fat-free/low salt)
1/2 cup red bell pepper, finely minced
1/2 cup yellow bell pepper, finely minced
1 tsp. Mrs. Dash seasoning
1/2 tsp. creole seasoning
1 cup white wine*
2 cups chicken stock (fat-free/low salt)
*** *or substitute dealcoholized wine or more chicken stock***

Spray nonstick pan with cooking spray; heat. Add shallots and garlic; heat through. Add lentils, peppers, seasonings, wine and chicken stock. Gently cook until heated through and chicken stock is reduced slightly.

Serves 4.

Per Serving: 118 Calories	
Protein 8 gr.	Carb. 22 gr.
Fat 0 gr.	Cal. from fat 0%
Chol. 0 mg.	Sodium 165 mg.

Savory Yogurt Sauce

This sauce is a flavorful topping to grilled meats. Put into a squirt bottle and get creative.

1 cup nonfat plain yogurt
2 Tbsp. skim milk
*2 Tbsp. white wine**
juice of 1 lime
2 Tbsp. Dijon mustard
1 Tbsp. honey
1 1/2 tsp. curry
1 tsp. turmeric
1/2 Tbsp. Mrs. Dash seasoning
1 Tbsp. chopped cilantro
1 tsp. chopped fresh mint

Combine all ingredients in a blender. Chill.

* or substitute dealcoholized wine or more chicken stock

Chicken Laurent

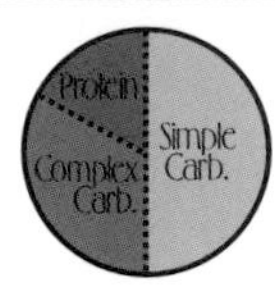

chicken (protein)
rice (complex carb.)
asparagus, red onion (simple carb.)

Shallots taste like a combination of onion and garlic, but are milder than both. They are formed more like garlic than onion, with a head comprised of multiple cloves, each covered with a thin, papery skin. Choose shallots that are plump and firm with dry skins. Avoid those that are wrinkled or sprouting. Store in a cool, dry well-ventilated place for up to one month.

When a recipe calls for one shallot, it usually means one clove, not the whole head.

Chicken Laurent

4 boneless, skinless chicken breast halves (1 lb.)
1/4 cup white wine Worcestershire sauce
2 tsp. olive oil
2 cloves garlic, minced
2 tsp. shallots, minced
1 tsp. Mrs. Dash seasoning
1/2 tsp. creole seasoning
1 lb. asparagus, trimmed
1 red onion, sliced thin
1/3 cup white wine*
2/3 cup chicken stock (fat-free/low salt)
2 tsp. cornstarch
*** *or substitute dealcoholized wine or more chicken stock***

Preheat oven to 375 degrees.

Marinate chicken breasts in Worcestershire sauce for at least 15 minutes.

Place asparagus spears with 1/4 cup water in a glass baking dish; cover with vented plastic wrap. Microwave on high to blanch for 3 to 4 minutes.

Spray nonstick ovenproof skillet with cooking spray. Add olive oil and heat. Add garlic and shallots to pan; lightly sauté. Add marinated chicken breasts and brown on both sides, sprinkling with seasonings. Lay asparagus and red onion slices on top of chicken.

Stir together wine and chicken stock in a small stock pot; add cornstarch mixed with 1 Tbsp. cold water. Stir over moderate heat until thickened. Pour over chicken and vegetables.

Bake in oven for 30 minutes.

Serves 4.

Per Serving: 214 Calories	
Protein 30 gr.	Carb. 11 gr.
Fat 6 gr.	Cal. from fat 24%
Chol. 72 mg.	Sodium 338 mg.

Quick Brown Rice Pilaf

1 tsp. olive oil
1/2 red onion, diced
2 cloves garlic, minced
1 3/4 cups chicken stock (fat-free/low salt)
1/2 tsp. creole seasoning
1 Tbsp. chopped fresh herbs (cilantro, basil, rosemary, thyme)
2 cups instant brown rice

Spray a medium saucepan with cooking spray; add olive oil and heat. Add diced onion and garlic, and lightly sauté about 1 to 2 minutes; then add chicken stock, seasoning and herbs.

Let mixture come to a boil, then stir in brown rice. Let boil for 1 minute, turn down heat to low and cover. Let simmer for 5 minutes, uncover skillet and fluff rice with fork. Cover again. Let sit for another 5 minutes.

Serves 6.

Per Serving: 126 Calories	
Protein 2.5 gr.	Carb. 24 gr.
Fat 2 gr.	Cal. from fat 15%
Chol. 0 mg.	Sodium 136 mg.

Turkey Carbonara

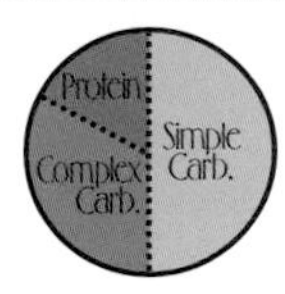

turkey, cheeses (protein)
pasta (complex carb.)
vegetables, fruit (simple carb.)

Turkey Carbonara

8 oz. dried linguine, preferably whole wheat
2 strips turkey bacon, chopped
1 shallot, minced
2 cloves garlic, minced
8 oz. smoked turkey, cut into chunks
1/2 cup frozen green peas, thawed
2 Tbsp. chopped fresh herbs (cilantro, basil, rosemary, thyme)
2 cups Carbonara Sauce
1 tsp. Mrs. Dash seasoning
1/2 tsp. creole seasoning
2 Tbsp. chopped fresh basil
1 plum tomato, diced

Serve with a green salad and 1/2 cup chopped mixed fruit.

In a large stockpot, cook pasta in boiling salted water until done, preferably al dente (slightly firm). Set aside.

Spray large sauté pan with cooking spray; heat. Add turkey bacon pieces, then shallots and garlic. Begin to cook over low heat. Add smoked turkey.

Add pasta, peas and fresh herbs, and sauté quickly. Then add Carbonara Sauce. Bring to a simmer and add seasonings. Serve immediately, sprinkled with basil and tomato.

Serves 4.

Per Serving: 383 Calories	
Protein 33 gr.	Carb. 40 gr.
Fat 9 gr.	Cal. from fat 22%
Chol. 86 mg.	Sodium 537 mg.

Carbonara Sauce

1 Tbsp. olive oil
2 Tbsp. all-purpose or whole wheat flour
2 cups skim milk
1/4 cup white wine*
1/4 cup skim milk ricotta cheese
1 tsp. Mrs. Dash garlic herb seasoning
1/2 tsp. creole seasoning
1/4 cup grated Parmesan cheese
* ***or substitute dealcoholized wine or chicken stock (fat-free/low salt)***

Spray a nonstick skillet with cooking spray. Add olive oil and heat. Add flour, stirring with oil until blended.

Add skim milk; bring to a boil and simmer slowly until thickened, stirring often. Add white wine, ricotta and seasonings. Stir over low heat until smooth. Stir in Parmesan cheese.

Makes 6 servings, 3/4 cup each.

Per Serving: 79 Calories	
Protein 8 gr.	Carb. 5.5 gr.
Fat 2.5 gr.	Cal. from fat 29%
Chol. 4 mg.	Sodium 215 mg.

Cheese can turn stringy, rubbery or grainy when exposed to high heat. Avoid this by first shredding or cutting cheese into small pieces and stirring into the sauce toward the end of cooking. Cook over low heat until cheese melts. Low-fat cheeses will melt more slowly than traditional ones; be gentle!

Turkey With a Thai Twist

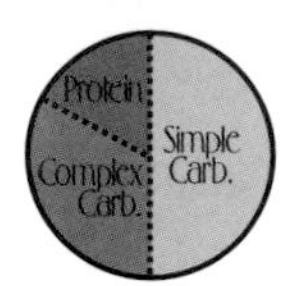

turkey (protein)
waffles (complex carb.)
broccoli, tomatoes(simple carb.)

Corn Waffles With Turkey Breast Cutlets

4 turkey breast cutlets (1 lb.)
1/2 cup Balsamic Marinade (pg. 42)
12 oz. purchased whole wheat pancake or waffle mix (or Homemade Pancake Mix, pg. 64)
2 cups frozen corn kernels, thawed
2 Tbsp. chopped chives
2 cups broccoli florets, cooked
1 cup Thai dressing
1 red pepper, minced
12 tomato slices (about 2 large tomatoes)

Clean turkey cutlets of skin and fat. Marinate in Balsamic Marinade overnight. Grill turkey. Set aside.

Spray waffle iron with cooking spray. Prepare waffle mix according to package directions; add corn and chives. Cook in waffle iron 3 to 5 minutes, until golden brown and cooked through.

Place one waffle and one turkey cutlet on each of four plates. Drizzle Thai Dressing over the turkey. Place broccoli on plate. Sprinkle all with minced pepper. Serve with sliced tomatoes.

Serves 4.

Per Serving: 356 Calories	
Protein 34 gr.	Carb. 42 gr.
Fat 7 gr.	Cal. from fat 18%
Chol. 59 mg.	Sodium 370 mg.

Thai Dressing

3/4 cup lime juice
3/4 cup chicken stock (fat-free/low salt)
1/2 cup honey
1/4 cup fish sauce*
1 Tbsp. oyster sauce*
1 tsp. chili sauce
2 Tbsp. grated fresh ginger
3 Tbsp. chopped fresh cilantro
* ***These are found in the Oriental section of your grocery store.***

Combine all ingredients in a blender.

Use additional dressing to create an exotic Oriental salad for another night. Dressing will keep refrigerated up to 2 weeks.

Makes 10 servings, 1/4 cup each.

Per Serving: 65 Calories	
Protein 0 gr.	Carb. 16 gr.
Fat 0 gr.	Cal. from fat 0%
Chol. 0 mg.	Sodium 216 mg.

Chicken Au Poivre

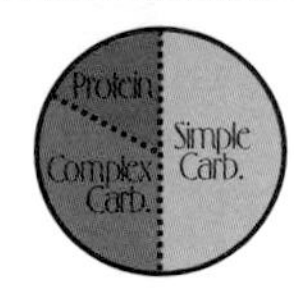

chicken (protein)
orzo (complex carb.)
vegetables (simple carb.)

Chicken Au Poivre

4 boneless, skinless chicken breast halves (1 lb.)
1 tsp. cracked black pepper
1/2 tsp. Mrs. Dash seasoning
1 tsp. olive oil
2 cloves garlic, minced
1 small red onion, finely chopped
1/4 cup fennel, sliced into 1/2 -inch slices
1/4 cup sun-dried tomatoes, slivered
2 tsp. capers, rinsed
2 cups cooked orzo
2 shiitake mushrooms, sliced
1 cup white wine*
2 cups chicken stock (fat-free/low salt)
2 Tbsp. lemon juice
4 leaves basil
1 tsp. creole seasoning
* ***or substitute dealcoholized wine or more chicken stock***

Rub chicken with pepper and Mrs. Dash. Grill over hot coals, or sear in hot skillet until done. Set aside.

Spray nonstick skillet with cooking spray. Add olive oil and heat on medium high. Sauté garlic, onion and fennel until all begin to soften, about 3 to 4 minutes. Add sun-dried tomatoes, capers and orzo; stir. Add mushrooms, white wine, chicken stock, lemon juice, basil and creole seasoning. Cook gently for another 3 to 4 minutes or until liquids begin to reduce. Pour entire mixture, including juice, onto plate.

Top with the grilled chicken and 1 Tbsp. of Basil Sauce per serving.

Serves 4.

Per Serving: 340 Calories	
Protein 32 gr.	Carb. 36 gr.
Fat 7.5 gr.	Cal. from fat 20%
Chol. 72 mg.	Sodium 820 mg.

Basil Sauce

1/2 cup white wine*
2 Tbsp. chopped fresh basil
2 Tbsp. lemon juice
1/2 tsp. cracked black pepper
* ***or substitute dealcoholized wine or chicken stock (fat-free/low salt)***

Mix together all ingredients.
Makes 10 servings, 1 Tbsp. each.

Per Serving: 9 Calories	
Protein 0 gr.	Carb. 2 gr.
Fat 0 gr.	Cal. from fat 0%
Chol. 0 mg.	Sodium 7 mg.

Fresh fennel has a broad, bulb-shaped base with celery-like stems and bright green leaves. The aromatic and flavorful bulbs and stems can be used raw in salads or cooked in a variety of ways: braised, sautéed, boiled, or marinated and grilled. The greenery can be used as a garnish or snipped and used as a last-minute flavor enhancer.

Favorite Summer BBQ

The days are long and lazy; it's time to enjoy the simple pleasure of cooking outdoors and eating relaxed meals on the deck. A down-home, all-American meal is in order: BBQ chicken, grilled corn on the cob and cole slaw make the perfect combination.

Favorite Summer BBQ

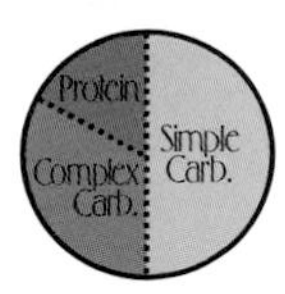

chicken (protein)
corn (complex carb.)
cabbage, apple, mango (simple carb.)

BBQ Breast of Chicken

1/2 cup Jamaican Marinade (pg. 43)
4 boneless, skinless chicken breast halves (1 lb.)
1 cup Citrus BBQ sauce (pg. 42)
1 1/3 cups Apple Chutney

Marinate chicken breasts in Jamaican Marinade for at least 1 hour. Grill, basting with Citrus BBQ sauce. Serve over Apple Chutney.

Serves 4.

Per Serving: 252 Calories	
Protein 28 gr.	Carb. 26 gr.
Fat 4 gr.	Cal. from fat 14%
Chol. 72 mg.	Sodium 410 mg.

Tricolor Coleslaw

2 cups red cabbage, shredded
2 cups green cabbage, shredded
1 cup carrots, grated
1/2 cup Citrus Vinaigrette (pg. 39)
2 Tbsp. chopped fresh herbs (cilantro, basil, rosemary, thyme)
1/2 tsp. creole seasoning
1 tsp. Mrs. Dash seasoning

In a large bowl, combine all ingredients, tossing well. Refrigerate until chilled.

Serves 4.

Per Serving: 49 Calories	
Protein 1 gr.	Carb. 8 gr.
Fat 1.5 gr.	Cal. from fat 29%
Chol. 1 mg.	Sodium 273 mg.

Grilled Corn on the Cob

4 ears of corn (with husks intact)

Carefully peel back husks but do not detach. Remove silk; replace the husks back over the corn (leave a small bit exposed) and secure the top by pulling two pieces of husk to the front and tying into a bow-tie knot.

Microwave on high for 4 minutes.

Place exposed side of the corn on the grill, periodically turning for even cooking, until the ears are tender when pierced, about 8 minutes.

Serves 4.

Per Serving: 83 Calories	
Protein 2 gr.	Carb. 19 gr.
Fat 0 gr.	Cal. from fat 0%
Chol. 0 mg.	Sodium 13 mg.

Apple Chutney

1 Granny Smith apple, thinly julienned
1 cup Mango Chutney (pg. 47)

Mix together and refrigerate to blend flavors. Makes 4 servings, 1/3 cup each.

Per Serving: 47 Calories	
Protein 0 gr.	Carb. 12 gr.
Fat 0 gr.	Cal. from fat 0%
Chol. 0 mg.	Sodium 272 mg.

Corn is best and sweetest when cooked in the husks. Gently pull back the husks, remove the silk, then replace the husks, tying them together at the top with a string or a strip of the husk itself. Cook as you would husked corn, even when boiling. Don't overcook the corn, or it will get tougher, as it will if cooked in salted water.

When grilling corn, soak the corn in cold water for 15 minutes so that the husks don't burn while grilling. As an alternative, microwave for 4 to 5 minutes before grilling to greatly reduce cooking time.

Grilled Lamb Chop and Couscous

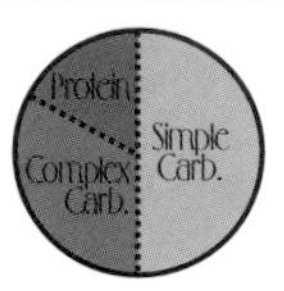

lamb (protein)
couscous (complex carb.)
vegetables (simple carb.)

Removing most of the excess fat from lamb cuts is not only good for your health, but it also reduces any strong lamb flavor some diners don't enjoy.

If lamb is a bit strong for you, even without the fat, try marinating for 2 hours before cooking. This will also tenderize the meat.

Grilled Lamb Chops and Couscous

4 lamb chops (5 oz. each)
3/4 cup Balsamic Marinade (pg. 42)
1/2 cup quick couscous (purchased)
2 cups chicken stock (fat-free/low salt)
2 Tbsp. chopped fresh herbs (cilantro, basil, rosemary, thyme)
1 tsp. Mrs. Dash seasoning
1 tsp. creole seasoning
1/2 eggplant, sliced
1 small zucchini, sliced
1 small yellow squash, sliced
1 red bell pepper, quartered
1 tsp. olive oil
1/2 medium onion, minced
2 cloves garlic, minced
2 Tbsp. sliced mushroom
2 cups broccoli florets, blanched
2 cups beef stock (fat-free/low salt)
1 tsp. cracked black pepper
1 Tbsp. chopped fresh basil
1 Tbsp. chopped fresh oregano

Trim all fat from lamb chops. Marinate at least 3 hours in 1/2 cup Balsamic Marinade.

Cook couscous according to package directions with chicken stock, herbs and seasonings.

Marinate eggplant, zucchini, squash and bell pepper in 1/4 cup marinade. Grill (or roast in 400-degree oven until slightly charred), then dice.

Spray skillet with cooking spray. Add oil and heat. Sauté onions and garlic. Add mushrooms, broccoli and grilled vegetables; quickly sauté. Add beef stock, black pepper, herbs and cooked couscous; quickly sauté, leaving dish moist.

Grill marinated lamb chop (or sear in a hot skillet). Serve over vegetable couscous mixture.

Serves 4.

Per Serving: 248 Calories	
Protein 21 gr.	Carb. 22 gr.
Fat 8 gr.	Cal. from fat 29%
Chol. 52 mg.	Sodium 198 mg.

Sliced Fennel and Asparagus Salad

1 whole fennel bulb
10 to 12 asparagus spears
2 tsp. olive oil
juice of 1 lemon
1/2 tsp. creole seasoning
1 tsp. Mrs. Dash seasoning
1 small tomato, diced

Trim base from fennel bulb. Remove and discard the fennel stalks and any discolored parts from the bulb. Stand the bulb upright and cut vertically into very thin slices.

Slice asparagus into 2-inch pieces. Place in microwavable bowl with 1/4 cup water; micro-wave on high for 2 to 3 minutes or until crisp tender. Immerse in icewater bath to chill quickly.

In a small bowl, whisk together the oil, lemon juice and seasonings. Add the sliced fennel, asparagus and diced tomato.

Serves 4.

Per Serving: 86 Calories	
Protein 3.5 gr.	Carb. 14 gr.
Fat 2.5 gr.	Cal. from fat 26%
Chol. 0 mg.	Sodium 152 mg.

Veal Picatta

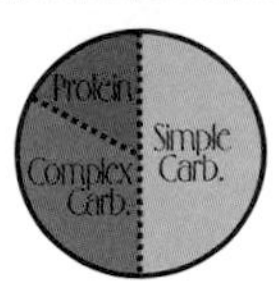

veal (protein)
orzo (complex carb.)
squash (simple carb.)

Veal Picatta

1/4 cup white wine Worcestershire sauce
4 slices veal, about 1 inch thick (1 lb.)*
1 tsp. Mrs. Dash seasoning, divided
1 tsp. creole seasoning, divided
1/3 cup all purpose flour
2 tsp. olive oil
2 cloves garlic, minced
2 Tbsp. chopped fresh herbs (cilantro, basil, rosemary, thyme)
1/2 cup chicken stock (fat-free/low salt)
1 lemon, peeled and cut into segments
1/2 tsp. sugar
1 Tbsp. capers, rinsed
* ***may substitute pork cutlets, trimmed of fat***

Serve with Squash Creole (pg. 98).

Pound veal slices to tenderize. Marinate in white wine Worcestershire sauce up to 1 hour.

Combine flour, 1/2 tsp. Mrs. Dash and 1/2 tsp. creole seasoning in a shallow dish. Lightly dredge marinated veal slices in the flour mixture, shaking off the excess.

Spray a nonstick skillet with cooking spray, then add olive oil; heat. Add the veal to the pan and cook until the outside is golden brown, about 2 to 3 minutes each side. Transfer to a platter and keep warm. Add garlic to the same skillet; lightly sauté. Add remaining seasonings and herbs; then stir in more chicken stock and bring to a boil. Stir while cooking for 1 minute.

Add lemon segments, sugar and capers; cook for 30 seconds more.

Serves 4.

Per Serving: 212 Calories	
Protein 24 gr.	Carb. 11 gr.
Fat 7 gr.	Cal. from fat 32%
Chol. 93 mg.	Sodium 401 mg.

Herbed Orzo

8 oz. package of orzo
1 tsp. olive oil
2 cloves garlic, minced
1/2 cup chicken stock (fat-free/low salt)
1/2 tsp. creole seasoning
1 tsp. Mrs. Dash seasoning
1 tsp. chopped fresh basil

In a large stockpot, cook orzo in salted water according to package directions until done.

Spray a nonstick skillet with cooking spray, then add olive oil. Heat. Add garlic and sauté for 30 seconds. Then add remaining ingredients and cooked orzo, lightly sautéeing to coat. Serve immediately.

Serves 6.

Per Serving: 101 Calories	
Protein 2 gr.	Carb. 21 gr.
Fat 1 gr.	Cal. from fat 9%
Chol. 0 mg.	Sodium 141 mg.

Grilled Sirloin and New Potato Salad

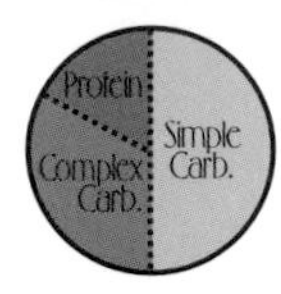

steak (protein)
potatoes, toast (complex carb.)
peppers, greens (simple carb.)

When buying meat, all cuts should be lean and trimmed of visible fat. The leanest cuts of beef and veal are the round, loin, sirloin and extra-lean ground beef. The leanest pork is from the tenderloin, leg and shoulder. The leanest lamb is from the leg, loin and rib. Poultry should be skinless.

Grilled Sirloin and New Potato Salad

1/3 cup Balsamic Marinade (pg. 42)
3/4 lb. lean sirloin*, trimmed of all fat
2 red bell peppers, cut in half lengthwise
1 large red onion, cut into thick slices
8 red-skinned potatoes, halved
1/2 tsp. creole seasoning
1/2 tsp. Mrs. Dash seasoning
12 cups washed, dried and torn mixed greens (red leaf, romaine, frizee, radicchio, arugula or bibb)
1/2 cup Honey-Orange Vinaigrette (pg. 38)
2 Tbsp. chopped fresh herbs (cilantro, basil, rosemary, thyme)
* ***may use skinless, boneless chicken breasts***

Marinate meat, peppers and onions in Balsamic Marinade for up to 3 hours.

Microwave potatoes and 1/4 cup water in a glass dish, covered with plastic wrap (vented) on high for 4 minutes.

Carefully place meat, cooked potatoes and other vegetables on grill and sprinkle with seasonings. Cook for 4 minutes. Turn over meat and vegetables, and cook until the meat is done and vegetables are slightly charred, about another 3 to 4 minutes. Slice the grilled peppers and sirloin into strips and toss with other grilled vegetables, lettuces and Honey-Orange Vinaigrette.

Serves 4.

Per Serving: 329 Calories	
Protein 25 gr.	Carb. 41 gr.
Fat 8 gr.	Cal. from fat 22%
Chol. 57 mg.	Sodium 249 mg.

Garlic Toasts

4 slices (1/2-inch thick) French, Italian or sourdough bread
garlic-flavored cooking spray
1 large garlic clove, cut in half
1/4 cup Balsamic Marinade (pg. 42)

Prepare a grill. Spray the bread slices with garlic-flavored cooking spray and place on grill. Grill bread, turning once, until well toasted on both sides, about 2 to 3 minutes per side. Rub one side of each slice with the cut side of the garlic clove and brush with Balsamic Marinade.

Serves 4.

Per Serving: 93 Calories	
Protein 3 gr.	Carb. 18 gr.
Fat 1 gr.	Cal. from fat 10%
Chol. 0 mg.	Sodium 214 mg.

Beef Stew

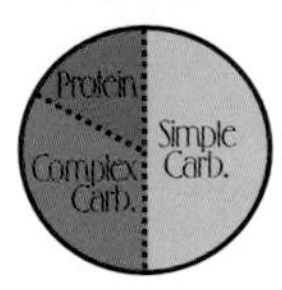

beef (protein)
bread (complex carb.)
vegetables (simple carb.)

Beef Stew

1 lb. top sirloin of beef, trimmed of all fat and cut into chunks
1/4 cup Balsamic Marinade (pg. 42)
1/4 lb. baby carrots, shaved
1 zucchini, cut into 1/2-inch slices
1 cup green beans, trimmed
1 tsp. Mrs. Dash seasoning, divided
1 tsp. creole seasoning, divided
1 red onion, chopped
1 cup red wine*
1 1/2 cups beef stock (fat-free/low salt)
1 Tbsp. chopped fresh basil
1 tsp. dried crushed thyme
1/4 tsp. crushed black pepper
2 whole plum tomatoes, quartered
1 Tbsp. chopped fresh chives
**** or substitute dealcoholized wine or beef stock (fat-free/low salt)***

Marinate beef overnight in Balsamic Marinade.

In a large saucepot, place carrots, zucchini and green beans with 1/2 cup water. Steam for 7 to 8 minutes or until crisp tender.

Season beef with 1/2 tsp. Mrs. Dash and 1/2 tsp. creole seasoning. Spray nonstick skillet with cooking spray. Sear beef with onions in the hot skillet. Add red wine and stir; then remove beef. To the same skillet, add steamed vegetables, beef stock, basil, thyme, pepper and remaining seasonings.

Simmer over medium-high heat until liquid is reduced about halfway. Add beef back to pan and sauté quickly to heat through. Add tomatoes. Sprinkle with fresh chives when serving.

Serves 4.

Per Serving: 261 Calories	
Protein 29 gr.	Carb. 16 gr.
Fat 9 gr.	Cal. from fat 32%
Chol. 76 mg.	Sodium 354 mg.

Chopped Tomato Salad With Garlic Toasts

2 medium ripe tomatoes, chopped
1 medium red bell pepper, chopped
1 medium yellow bell pepper, chopped
1 small red onion, chopped
2 tsp. capers
3 Tbsp. chopped fresh basil
1 Tbsp. balsamic vinegar
2 tsp. freshly squeezed lemon juice
2 cloves garlic, minced
1 tsp. dried oregano
1/2 tsp. creole seasoning
freshly ground black pepper to taste
1 recipe of Garlic Toasts (pg. 118)

Mix together all ingredients but garlic toast in a large bowl; cover and refrigerate 1 hour.

Equally divide and place a mound of salad on each serving plate with 1 slice hot garlic toast alongside.

Serves 4.

Per Serving: 121 Calories	
Protein 4 gr.	Carb. 24 gr.
Fat 1 gr.	Cal. from fat 11%
Chol. 0 mg.	Sodium 310 mg.

Vegetables cooked to the point of mushiness require a lot of seasoning to give them any taste at all, which creates the need some people have for bacon grease and lard.

But steaming vegetables to a crisp tender stage allows the full flavor to be present in the vegetable, and the use of herbs and spices complements the fresh taste. Adding a garlic clove or onion slice to the steaming water or stock increases the flavor even more.

A Taste of the Tropics

Fruit, fruit juices, herbs and spices are the flavor ribbons that wind through this meal from the tropics. The meat is marinated for tenderness and zest, then placed on a vibrant salsa of mango and red pepper. A bowlful of Caribbean rice and beans makes the perfect accompaniment.

A Taste of the Tropics

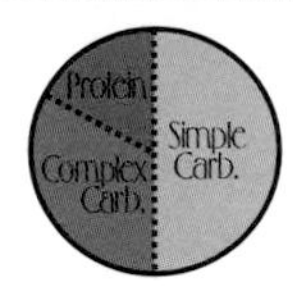

beef, black beans (protein)
rice, black beans (complex carb.)
mango, spinach (simple carb.)

Beef Tip Skewers

1 1/2 lbs. beef sirloin, cut into chunks
3/4 cup Balsamic Marinade (pg. 42)
12 wooden skewers
1 tsp. creole seasoning
1/2 cup Pickapeppa sauce (or hot pepper sauce)
2 cups Mango Salsa (pg. 122)
6 pineapple slices
3 Tbsp. tomato, finely chopped
3 Tbsp. chopped fresh parsley

Trim all visible fat from beef. In a large bowl, marinate sirloin chunks in Balsamic Marinade for at least 3 hours; skewer evenly onto wooden skewers that have been soaked in water. Sprinkle with seasoning and grill, brushing with Pickapeppa sauce to coat.

Grill about 4 minutes on one side; turn and grill another 4 minutes or until desired doneness. Spoon 1/3 cup Mango Salsa on each plate. Top with beef skewers, 2 per serving.

Cut each pineapple slice into 3 triangles; arrange around beef tips. Sprinkle with tomatoes and chopped parsley.

Serves 6.

Per Serving: 245 Calories	
Protein 27 gr.	Carb. 22 gr.
Fat 9 gr.	Cal. from fat 36%
Chol. 76 mg.	Sodium 718 mg.

Rice and Black Beans

1 tsp. olive oil
1/2 red onion, diced
2 cloves garlic, minced
1 cup chicken stock (fat-free/low salt)
1 1/2 cups tomato sauce
1 cup long-grain brown rice, uncooked
1/2 cup black beans, drained and rinsed
1/2 tsp. cumin
1/2 tsp. creole seasoning

Spray saucepan with cooking spray; add olive oil and heat. Add diced onions and sauté. Add chicken stock and tomato sauce. When boiling, add rice. Simmer for 1 minute; then cover and steam until done, about 40 to 45 minutes.

Combine black beans with cumin and seasoning. Microwave 1 1/2 minutes on high. Using a large slotted spoon, smash beans until half are mush. Combine with hot, cooked rice.

Serves 6.

Per Serving: 161 Calories	
Protein 4 gr.	Carb. 33 gr.
Fat 1 gr.	Cal. from fat 6%
Chol. 0 mg.	Sodium 460 mg.

(Meal continued on the next page.)

A Taste of the Tropics (continued)

Tropical Spinach Salad

12 oz. fresh spinach, washed and stemmed
3 navel oranges, peeled and sectioned
1 whole carrot, cut lengthwise into strips
1 cup Honey-Orange Vinaigrette
2 tomatoes, diced fine
2 Tbsp. dry-roasted pistachios, shelled

Toss spinach, orange sections and carrot strips with Honey-Orange Vinaigrette. Sprinkle with diced tomato and pistachios.

Serves 4.

Per Serving: 138 Calories	
Protein 4 gr.	Carb. 26 gr.
Fat 2 gr.	Cal. from fat 13%
Chol. 0 mg.	Sodium 184 mg.

Honey-Orange Vinaigrette

1/2 cup orange juice
1 Tbsp. honey
1/2 cup balsamic vinegar
1/2 tsp. creole seasoning
1 tsp. Pickapeppa sauce (or hot pepper sauce)
juice of 1/2 lemon
1 Tbsp. chopped fresh herbs (cilantro, basil, rosemary, thyme)

Mix together all ingredients. Refrigerate.
Makes 10 servings, 2 Tbsp. each.

Per Serving: 12 Calories	
Protein 0 gr.	Carb. 3 gr.
Fat 0 gr.	Cal. from fat 0%
Chol. 0 mg.	Sodium 53 mg.

Mango Salsa

2 whole ripe mangos, peeled and diced
juice of 2 limes
1/2 cup orange juice
1 large red bell pepper, diced
1/2 tsp. five spice powder
1/2 Tbsp. minced shallots, diced fine
1/4 cup honey
1 tsp. creole seasoning

Mix together all ingredients. Refrigerate at least 1 hour to blend flavors.

Makes 8 servings, 1/3 cup each.

Per Serving: 77 Calories	
Protein 0 gr.	Carb. 20 gr.
Fat 0 gr.	Cal. from fat 0
Chol. 0 mg.	Sodium 135 mg.

Super Supper Burger

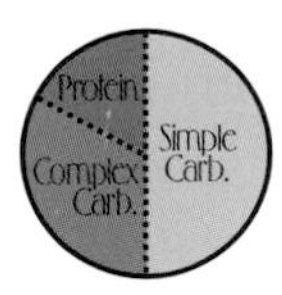

turkey (protein)
bread (complex carb.)
tomato, cucumbers (simple carb.)

Super Supper Burger

$1^1/_2$ lbs. ground turkey breast
1 small green bell pepper, chopped
1 small onion, minced
1 Tbsp. grated horseradish
1 Tbsp. Dijon mustard
1 tsp. creole seasoning
$^1/_4$ cup chili sauce (or salsa)*
1 round unsliced loaf Italian or sourdough bread, 8 inches in diameter, preferably whole wheat
2 large leaves of lettuce
*** *either one can be purchased in any grocery store***

Preheat oven to 350 degrees.

In a large bowl, mix all ingredients except chili sauce and bread. Press meat mixture into an ungreased 9-inch pie plate. Spread chili sauce on top.

Bake uncovered 45 minutes or until meat is no longer pink in the center. Drain immediately upon removing from oven. Let stand 5 minutes. Cut bread crosswise into halves (like a large bun). Carefully place pie-size burger on one bread half. Top with lettuce and other half of bread. Cut into six wedges.

Serves 6.

Per Serving: 259 Calories	
Protein 28 gr.	Carb. 26 gr.
Fat 5 gr.	Cal. from fat 17%
Chol. 52 mg.	Sodium 712 mg.

Spicy Tomato and Cucumber Salad

2 large tomatoes, cut into wedges
1 cup diced cucumber
$^1/_2$ cup finely chopped red onion
1 clove garlic, minced
2 Tbsp. chopped fresh cilantro
2 Tbsp. red wine vinegar
2 tsp. chopped fresh hot green chili pepper (or $^1/_4$ tsp. crushed red pepper)
1 tsp. honey
$^1/_2$ tsp. creole seasoning

In a medium-sized bowl, mix together all ingredients. Cover and refrigerate about 2 hours or until chilled.

Makes 6 servings.

Per Serving: 28 Calories	
Protein 1 gr.	Carb. 6 gr.
Fat 0 gr.	Cal. from fat 0%
Chol. 0 mg.	Sodium 96 mg.

Ripen tomatoes with an apple in a paper bag pierced with a few holes. Once ripened, store tomatoes, stem down, at room temperature away from direct sunlight. Never refrigerate tomatoes! Cold temperatures make the flesh pulpy and destroy the flavor.

If you are using canned tomatoes in a recipe, go for canned Italian plum tomatoes — they have a wonderful flavor that sometimes even beats fresh, out-of-season tomatoes.

Nineties Meatloaf

meat (protein)
oats, potatoes (complex carb.)
tomatoes, broccoli (simple carb.)

Nineties Meatloaf

2 lbs. ground round (or ground turkey breast)
3/4 cup chopped onion
2 cloves garlic, minced
2 cups old-fashioned oats, uncooked
2 Tbsp. tomato puree
2 tsp. Dijon mustard
1 tsp. creole seasoning
1 Tbsp. Worcestershire sauce
2 egg whites (or 1/4 cup egg substitute)
2 Tbsp. skim milk
1/2 cup tomato sauce (or salsa)

Preheat oven to 375 degrees.

Spray two loaf pans with cooking spray. Mix together all ingredients except tomato sauce; shape into 2 loaves place in loaf pans.

Bake about 1 hour or until no longer pink in center. Drain off all juices immediately upon removing from oven. One loaf may be frozen for a later meal.

Spread with even amounts of tomato sauce or salsa. Cut each loaf into 6 slices.

One loaf makes 6 servings, 1 slice per serving.

Per Serving: 175 Calories	
Protein 24 gr.	Carb. 13 gr.
Fat 3 gr.	Cal. from fat 17%
Chol. 47 mg.	Sodium 278 mg.

Oven Potato Casserole

4 cups thinly sliced Idaho potatoes
1 red onion, sliced thin
2 large tomatoes, sliced thin
1 tsp. creole seasoning
1/2 cup part-skim cheddar cheese, shredded

Preheat oven to 350 degrees.

Alternate layers of potatoes, onions and tomatoes in baking dish. Lightly sprinkle each layer with seasoning.

Bake for 30 minutes (or microwave on high for 12 minutes). Top with cheese in the last 5 minutes of cooking and allow to melt, gently browning.

Makes 6 servings.

Per Serving: 99 Calories	
Protein 4 gr.	Carb. 18 gr.
Fat 1.5 gr.	Cal. from fat 15%
Chol. 5 mg.	Sodium 229 mg.

Seasoned Broccoli

1 1/2 lbs. fresh broccoli, trimmed
1/3 cup chicken stock (fat-free/low salt)
1 tsp. Mrs. Dash seasoning
3/4 tsp. creole seasoning

Microwave broccoli in chicken stock and seasonings for 7 to 8 minutes or until crisp tender.

Serves 6.

Per Serving: 48 Calories	
Protein 4 gr.	Carb. 8 gr.
Fat 0 gr.	Cal. from fat 0%
Chol. 0 mg.	Sodium 168 mg.

Savory Round Roast

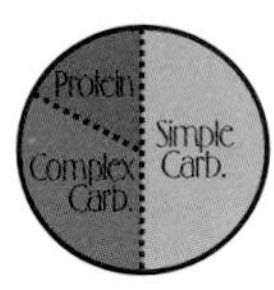

roast (protein)
polenta (complex carb.)
green beans (simple carb.)

Savory Round Roast

1 boneless round roast (about 4 lbs.), trimmed of all fat
1 tsp. ground ginger
1 tsp. creole seasoning
1 tsp. Mrs. Dash garlic herb seasoning
1 Tbsp. chopped fresh basil (or 1 tsp. dried)
2 cloves garlic, minced
2 medium chopped onions
1 cup tomato puree
1 cup dry red wine*
** or substitute dealcoholized wine or defatted beef stock (fat-free/low salt)*

Serve with Green Beans and Mushrooms (pg. 155).

Preheat oven to 325 degrees.

Spray nonstick skillet with cooking spray; heat. Brown roast on both sides in skillet. Transfer to a rack in a roasting pan and season with ginger, seasonings and basil.

Add garlic and onions to tomato puree and spread over the top of roast. Slowly pour wine over the top.

Cover tightly and bake for $2^{1}/_{2}$ to 3 hours or until meat is tender, basting several times.

Makes 16 servings. Remaining servings may be frozen in plastic freezer bags for later meals.

Per Serving: 202 Calories	
Protein 26 gr.	Carb. 3 gr.
Fat 8 gr.	Cal. from fat 40%
Chol. 76 mg.	Sodium 250 mg.

Polenta Wedges

4 cups water
1 cup frozen whole kernel corn, thawed (or 2 ears fresh corn, cooked)
1 tsp. creole seasoning
1 tsp. olive oil
1 Tbsp. fresh whole rosemary (or 1 tsp. dried)
1 cup stone ground cornmeal (or polenta)

Spray a 9 x 13-inch rectangular baking pan with cooking spray.

In a medium saucepan, heat all ingredients except cornmeal to boiling. Gradually add cornmeal, stirring constantly. Cook over medium-low heat 8 to 12 minutes, stirring occasionally, until mixture pulls away from sides of saucepan. Pour into baking dish. Cool 15 minutes. Cover and refrigerate 1 hour or until firm. Can be refrigerated up to 3 days.

When ready to serve, cut polenta into six squares; cut each square diagonally into 2 triangles. Spray a large nonstick skillet with cooking spray and heat over medium heat. Brown triangles in skillet for about 5 minutes on each side or until light brown.

Serves 6.

Per Serving: 55 Calories	
Protein 1 gr.	Carb. 11 gr.
Fat 1 gr.	Cal. from fat 18%
Chol. 0 mg.	Sodium 182 mg.

Polenta is made from coarse ground cornmeal. It may be used as a grain side dish or in desserts. Polenta can be found in health food stores.

Most cornmeal in supermarkets is steel-ground, which means the husk and germ have been almost completely removed.

Stone-ground cornmeal retains some of the corn's hull and germ, making it more nutritious. To make polenta without lumps, whisk the cornmeal into the cold liquid before heating and cooking.

Speedy Pork Roast

This beautiful menu is a perfect match for any special occasion. It is elegant in presentation, yet simple and quick in preparation. The marinated, seared pork tenderloin goes perfectly with fluffy cinnamon-scented sweet potatoes. And asparagus is the vegetable that heralds freshness.

Speedy Pork Roast

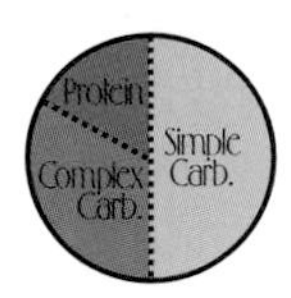

pork (protein)
sweet potatoes (complex carb.)
asparagus (simple carb.)

Seared Pork Tenderloin

1 1/2 lbs. pork tenderloin, trimmed of all visible fat
1/2 cup white wine Worcestershire sauce
1/2 tsp. creole seasoning
2 Tbsp. chopped fresh herbs (cilantro, basil, rosemary, thyme)
1 tsp. Mrs. Dash seasoning
2 garlic cloves, minced
1 large red onion, sliced thin

Preheat oven to 400 degrees.

Marinate pork tenderloin in Worcestershire sauce, seasonings, herbs and garlic for at least 1 hour.

Sear pork on both sides in hot ovenproof skillet, then top with sliced onions. Place whole skillet in oven for 15 minutes or until internal temperature reaches 150 to 170 degrees. May pour on additional marinade while roasting.

Serves 4.

Per Serving: 148 Calories	
Protein 25 gr.	Carb. 1 gr.
Fat 4 gr.	Cal. from fat 26%
Chol. 78 mg.	Sodium 190 mg.

Cinnamon Sweet Potatoes

4 sweet potatoes
cinnamon

Preheat oven to 400 degrees.

Wash and scrub sweet potatoes. Place in oven for 35 minutes. (You may add the skillet of pork tenderloins to the oven after 20 minutes.)

Cut open sweet potatoes and push ends together to "mash" toward center and fluff. Sprinkle with cinnamon.

Serves 4.

Per Serving: 118 Calories	
Protein 2 gr.	Carb. 27 gr.
Fat 0 gr.	Cal. from fat 0%
Chol. 0 mg.	Sodium 12 mg.

Fresh Asparagus

1 lb. fresh asparagus, trimmed
1/4 cup chicken stock (fat-free/low salt)
1 tsp. Mrs. Dash seasoning
1/2 tsp. creole seasoning

Microwave asparagus in chicken stock and seasonings for about 7 to 8 minutes or until crisp tender.

Serves 4.

Per Serving: 48 Calories	
Protein 4 gr.	Carb. 8 gr.
Fat 0 gr.	Cal. from fat 0%
Chol. 0 mg.	Sodium 140 mg.

Cooking pork to 137 degrees will kill trichinosis. To allow for a safety margin, however, most experts recommend an internal temperature of 150 to 165 degrees. This range will produce pork that's juicy and tender. Pork cooked to temperatures above 170 degrees will be dry and overcooked. Use a meat thermometer (purchased at the supermarket or department store's kitchen section) to check for doneness.

Pork Chops Portofino

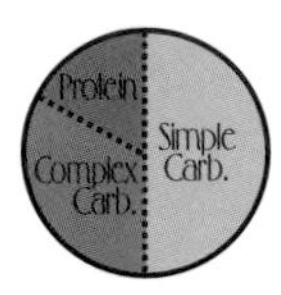

pork chops, cheese (protein)
bread crumbs, orzo (complex carb.)
broccoli, grapes (simple carb.)

Pork Chops Portofino

Use sun-dried tomatoes for added depth of flavor without the fat; their dark red color and crinkled flesh are an especially welcome boost to sauces.

Buy sun-dried tomatoes packaged in plastic; soak back to life in boiling water for 2 minutes, then drain.

4 center cut pork chops (about 1¼ lbs.), trimmed of fat
½ cup feta cheese
¼ cup skim milk ricotta cheese
2 Tbsp. sun-dried tomatoes, slivered
⅛ tsp. cracked black pepper
1 Tbsp. fresh Italian parsley (or parsley)
1 tsp. Mrs. Dash seasoning
2 large egg whites
¼ cup water
⅔ cup dried Italian bread crumbs (purchased)
2 Tbsp. grated Parmesan cheese
½ tsp. creole seasoning

Serve with 2 cups cooked orzo and a side of Frosted Grapes (pg. 132)

Preheat oven to 400 degrees.

Mix together cheeses, tomatoes, pepper, parsley and Mrs. Dash to make stuffing; set aside.

Place the pork chops on a cutting board. With a sharp knife, make a horizontal slit along the long edge of each chop opposite the bone, nearly cutting through to the opposite side. Open the chop so it forms a butterfly. Place one-fourth of the cheese mixture on half of each chop, leaving a ¼-inch space between the filling and the edges of the meat. Close the chop carefully and set aside. Repeat with the remaining pork chops.

Whisk together egg whites and water in a bowl. In a shallow pan, stir together bread crumbs, Parmesan cheese and creole seasoning.

Spray a shallow roasting pan with cooking spray. Carefully dip each chop in the crumb mixture, then in the egg white mixture and back again in the crumb mixture. Gently lift into the baking pan and bake for 40 to 45 minutes, until crisp and lightly browned on the outside and juices run clear.

Serves 4.

Per Serving: 274 Calories	
Protein 32 gr.	Carb. 15 gr.
Fat 8 gr.	Cal. from fat 26%
Chol. 93 mg.	Sodium 535 mg.

Tuscan Broccoli

1 tsp. olive oil
2 cloves garlic, minced
2 Tbsp. capers, rinsed
½ tsp. creole seasoning
1 tsp. Mrs. Dash seasoning
1 Tbsp. chopped fresh rosemary (or 1 tsp. dried)
1 bunch (1¼ lbs.) broccoli, cut into florets and trimmed of tough stalks
½ cup chicken stock (fat-free/low salt)

Spray a large nonstick skillet with cooking spray. Add olive oil and heat over medium heat. Add garlic, capers, seasonings and rosemary, and sauté until the garlic is golden, about 30 seconds. Add the broccoli florets and chicken stock. Reduce heat and cook covered until broccoli is crisp tender and cooking liquid is reduced, about 5 to 7 minutes. Ladle into serving dish, tossing together.

Serves 4.

Per Serving: 57 Calories	
Protein 4 gr.	Carb. 8 gr.
Fat 1 gr.	Cal. from fat 16%
Chol. 0 mg.	Sodium 688 mg.

Marinated Pork Tenderloin

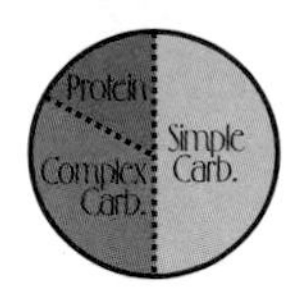

pork (protein)
black beans, rice (complex carb.)
vegetables (simple carb.)

Marinated Pork Tenderloin

1 1/2 lbs. pork tenderloin, trimmed of fat
1/4 cup low-sodium soy sauce
2 Tbsp. ginger
2 cups red wine*
1/4 cup Dijon mustard
2 Tbsp. chopped fresh basil
juice of 1 lemon
1 carrot, quartered
1 cup green beans, trimmed
1 small red onion, chopped
4 shiitake mushrooms (optional)
2 Tbsp. chopped fresh herbs (cilantro, basil, rosemary, thyme)
1 tsp. creole seasoning
2 tsp. Mrs. Dash seasoning
* ***or substitute dealcoholized wine or chicken stock (fat-free/low salt)***

Serve with Rice and Black Beans (pg. 121).

Mix soy, ginger, wine, mustard, basil and lemon juice for marinade. Marinate pork overnight.

Preheat oven to 400 degrees.

In a microwavable dish, place carrots, green beans, onions and mushrooms with 1/2 cup water. Cover with plastic wrap and vent. Microwave on high for 4 to 5 minutes.

Spray a nonstick ovenproof skillet with cooking spray; heat over medium-high heat. Add the marinated tenderloin (reserve remaining marinade) and sear on both sides.

Transfer skillet to oven; cook to medium pink or an internal temperature of 150 to 170 degrees.

Remove pork from pan. In same pan, sauté the vegetables with fresh herbs and seasonings. Add pork. Add 2 Tbsp. of reserved pork marinade; cook for 3 to 4 minutes.

Serves 4.

Per Serving: 201 Calories	
Protein 27 gr.	Carb. 13 gr.
Fat 4 gr.	Cal. from fat 18%
Chol. 79 mg.	Sodium 725 mg.

Fresh Vegetables With Creamy Herb Dip

2 oz. fat-free cream cheese, softened
2 Tbsp. nonfat sour cream
2 Tbsp. chopped fresh chives (or scallions)
1 Tbsp. chopped fresh dill
1/2 tsp. creole seasoning
1 tsp. Mrs. Dash seasoning
1 tsp. prepared horseradish
2 cups trimmed and sliced fresh vegetables (carrots, broccoli, cucumbers, celery, zucchini, yellow squash, red and green bell pepper strips)

Place cream cheese in a small bowl and stir in nonfat sour cream until smooth. Mix in chives, dill, seasonings and horseradish. Spoon into small bowl. Surround bowl with vegetables.

Serves 4.

Per Serving: 26 Calories	
Protein 3.5 gr.	Carb. 3 gr.
Fat 0 gr.	Cal. from fat 0%
Chol. 1 mg.	Sodium 208 mg.

Southern Pork Salad

A dish of pork and black-eyed peas is soul food in the South — the original comfort food. Lean and tender pork is marinated in Balsamic Marinade, then seared. Combined with the black-eyed peas and spinach, it becomes a new version of the time-tested favorite.

Southern Pork Salad

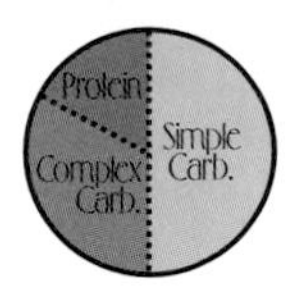

pork (protein)
black-eyed peas, corn (complex carb.)
spinach, peppers (simple carb.)

Seared Pork and Black-Eyed Pea Salad

1 lb. pork tenderloin or medallions, cut into strips
1/2 cup Balsamic Marinade (pg. 42)
2 cloves garlic, minced
1 each red and green bell peppers, quartered
2 cups Black-Eyed Pea and Corn Salad
12 oz. fresh spinach, washed and stemmed
1 Tbsp. chopped fresh herbs (cilantro, basil, rosemary, thyme)
2 plum tomatoes, quartered

Marinate pork strips in 1/4 cup Balsamic Marinade for up to 1 hour.

Spray a nonstick skillet with cooking spray. Add garlic and lightly sauté. Add pork to skillet, sautéeing 2 to 3 minutes until no pink remains. Add the remaining marinade, the peppers and the Black-Eyed Pea and Corn salad to skillet, lightly tossing to heat.

Line plate with spinach; top with pork salad mixture, allowing peppers to lie on top. Garnish with herbs and tomato quarters.

Serves 4.

Per Serving: 304 Calories	
Protein 32 gr.	Carb. 31 gr.
Fat 7 gr.	Cal. from fat 21%
Chol. 78 mg.	Sodium 332 mg.

Black-Eyed Pea and Corn Salad

16 oz. (or 2 cups frozen) black-eyed peas
1/4 cup chicken stock (fat-free/low salt)
1 cup frozen corn kernels, thawed
2 plum tomatoes, diced
3/4 red onion, minced
1 serrano pepper, minced
2 Tbsp. finely chopped cilantro
1 tsp. olive oil
4 cloves garlic, minced
juice of 1 lime
1/4 cup Balsamic Marinade (pg. 42)
1 tsp. cumin
2 tsp. hot pepper sauce
1 tsp. creole seasoning

Follow package instructions to cook black-eyed peas in 1/4 cup chicken stock; cool. Combine all ingredients. Allow to marinate at least one hour.

Makes 8 servings, 1/2 cup per serving.

Per Serving: 85 Calories	
Protein 4 gr.	Carb. 15 gr.
Fat 1 gr.	Cal. from fat 10%
Chol. 0 mg.	Sodium 170 mg.

Just like the commercials say, today's pork is leaner — some cuts are even leaner than beef. And, thanks to modern technology, trichinosis in pork is no longer an issue. Take precautions, however, by thoroughly washing in hot, soapy water anything (hands, knives, cutting boards, etc.) that comes in contact with raw pork. Never taste uncooked pork. Leftover pork dishes should be refrigerated within 2 hours of cooking and used within 2 days.

Grilled Citrus BBQ Pork Chops

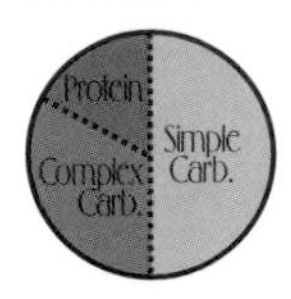

pork chops (protein)
plantains (complex carb.)
spinach, grapes (simple carb.)

Five spice is a blend of equal parts of cinnamon, cloves, fennel seed, star anise and Szechuan peppercorns. It has a pungent, slightly sweet licorice flavor and is used in Oriental cuisine, especially for meat, fish and salsas. Five spice can be found in the supermarket's spice aisle or Asian section, or in a specialty foods store.

Citrus BBQ Pork Chops

1/2 cup Jamaican Marinade (pg. 43)
4 pork chops (7 oz. each) with bone (or 1 1/2 lbs. center-cut pork chops)
1/4 cup Citrus BBQ Sauce (pg. 42)
1 tsp. olive oil
1 small onion, sliced thin
2 cloves garlic, minced
1 ripe plantain, sliced thin
1 cup orange juice
1/2 tsp. five spice powder (or cinnamon)
1 Tbsp. honey

Trim pork chops of all fat. Marinate pork chops in Jamaican Marinade for 3 to 4 hours. Grill, basting with Citrus BBQ Sauce.

While pork chops are grilling, spray a nonstick pan with cooking spray; add olive oil and heat. Add onions, garlic and plantain, and sauté with orange juice, five spice powder and honey until it begins to caramelize (make a syrup). Serve the chops with plantains.

Serves 4.

Per Serving: 276 Calories	
Protein 26 gr.	Carb. 30 gr.
Fat 5.5 gr.	Cal. from fat 19%
Chol. 78 mg.	Sodium 326 mg.

Sautéed Spinach

1 tsp. olive oil
2 cloves garlic, minced
1 lb. fresh spinach, washed and stemmed
1/2 tsp. creole seasoning
juice of 1 lemon
1 Tbsp. low-sodium soy sauce

Spray a nonstick skillet with cooking spray; add oil and heat over medium-high heat. Add garlic and stir until golden, about 30 seconds. Add spinach and toss until just wilted, 2 to 4 minutes. Add seasoning, lemon juice and soy sauce; toss to blend. Serve immediately.

Serves 4.

Per Serving: 41 Calories	
Protein 3.5 gr.	Carb. 4.5 gr.
Fat 1 gr.	Cal. from fat 22%
Chol. 0 mg.	Sodium 351 mg.

Frosted Grapes

1 lb. red and/or green grapes, stemmed

Wash grapes and pat dry. Place on a pan in freezer for 45 minutes. Remove from freezer and let sit for 2 minutes before serving.

Makes 8 servings, about 12 grapes each.

Per Serving: 40 Calories	
Protein 0 gr.	Carb. 10 gr.
Fat 0 gr.	Cal. from fat 0%
Chol. 0 mg.	Sodium 1 mg.

Tropical Seafood and Spinach Salad

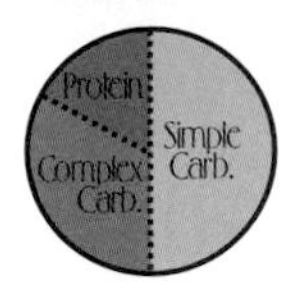

seafood (protein)
bread (complex carb.)
spinach, peppers (simple carb.)

Tropical Seafood and Spinach Salad

8 oz. fresh white fish (snapper, grouper, sea bass or halibut), cut into chunks
1 lb. large shrimp
1/2 cup Jamaican Marinade (pg. 43)
2 red bell peppers, cut into chunks
12 oz. fresh spinach, washed and stemmed
3 oranges, peeled and sectioned
1 whole carrot, cut lengthwise into strips
1 cup Honey-Orange Vinaigrette (pg. 38)
2 tomatoes, diced fine
1/4 cup dry-roasted pistachios, shelled

Marinate seafood in Jamaican Marinade for at least 1 hour. Put on wood skewers (which have been soaked in water) with red pepper chunks. Grill, basting with more marinade.

Toss spinach, oranges and carrots with Honey-Orange Vinaigrette. Spoon onto large plate; top with seafood skewer. Sprinkle with diced tomato and pistachios.

Serves 4.

Per Serving: 272 Calories	
Protein 33 gr.	Carb. 26 gr.
Fat 4 gr.	Cal. from fat 13%
Chol. 186 mg.	Sodium 490 mg.

Focaccia Bread

2 1/2 to 3 cups all-purpose flour
3/4 cup chopped onions
1 Tbsp. olive oil
3 tsp. crushed dried rosemary leaves, divided
1/2 tsp. salt
1/2 tsp. cracked black pepper
1 pkg. of quick-acting dry yeast
2 cups very warm water (120 degrees)
2 to 2 1/2 cups whole wheat flour
Stone ground cornmeal
1 tsp. olive oil

Mix 2 cups flour with onions, 1 Tbsp. oil, 1 tsp. rosemary, salt, pepper and yeast in a large bowl. Add warm water. Use an electric mixer to beat on low for 1 minute, then medium for 1 minute, scraping the bowl frequently. Stir in remaining all-purpose flour, then whole wheat flour, 1 cup at a time.

Turn dough onto lightly floured surface; gently roll in flour to coat. Knead about 10 minutes or until smooth and elastic. Spray large bowl with cooking spray. Place dough in bowl, turning to coat top. Cover and let rise in a warm place about 1 1/2 hours or until double.

Spray jelly roll pan with cooking spray; sprinkle lightly with cornmeal. Punch down dough. Press into pan. Cover and let rise in warm place 30 minutes or until almost double.

Heat oven to 400 degrees. Press dough to edges of pan. Brush lightly with oil; sprinkle with 2 tsp. rosemary. Bake 30 to 35 minutes or until golden brown. Remove from pan. Cool on wire rack.

Makes 16 servings.

Per Serving: 135 Calories	
Protein 4 gr.	Carb. 28 gr.
Fat 1 gr.	Cal. from fat 6%
Chol. 0 mg.	Sodium 70 mg.

Light Seafood Stew

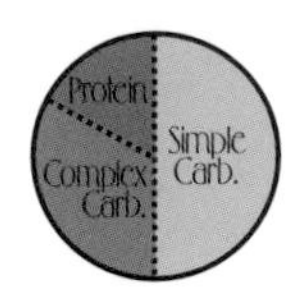

seafood, goat cheese (protein)
bread (complex carb.)
vegetables (simple carb.)

The number-one rule for buying seafood is this: be choosy when you shop! Seafood may not have seen its ocean home for 8 days, yet it still may be legally labeled as "fresh."

Fresh fish should be resting on top of ice in a case kept at lower than 33 degrees. Cuts of fish should hold together well and be unblemished and shiny. Fish should not be spongy to the touch or smelly to the nose!

Light Seafood Stew

4 small potatoes, medium diced
1/2 cup diced onion
1/2 cup diced celery
6 cups chicken stock (fat-free/low salt)
1 cup frozen green peas, thawed
1/2 cup Spanish sherry or white wine*
2 tsp. saffron
1 tsp. creole seasoning
2 tsp. Mrs. Dash seasoning
2 Tbsp. chopped fresh herbs (cilantro, basil, rosemary, thyme)
1 tsp. Tabasco
2 tsp. Worcestershire sauce
20 mussels, washed
20 clams, washed
2 lbs. any fresh fish
1/3 cup chopped chives
* ***or substitute dealcoholized wine or more chicken stock***

Steam potatoes, onion and celery; add to chicken stock. Add peas, sherry, saffron, seasonings, herbs, Tabasco and Worcestershire sauces. Add mussels and clams and cook until opened.

Add fish and poach in stock lightly. Ladle into soup bowls. Sprinkle with chives.

Makes 10 servings, 1 1/2 cups each.

Per Serving: 243 Calories	
Protein 36 gr.	Carb. 13 gr.
Fat 3.5 gr.	Cal. from fat 14%
Chol. 75 mg.	Sodium 384 mg.

Baguette With Warm Goat Cheese

6 oz. goat cheese
2 Tbsp. chopped fresh herbs (cilantro, basil, rosemary, thyme)
1/4 tsp. creole seasoning
juice of 1/2 lemon
2 large tomatoes, sliced
1/4 cup bread crumbs (purchased)
1 baguette (a long narrow loaf of French bread)
1/4 cup Balsamic Marinade (pg. 42)
1 cup Tomato Basil Sauce (pg. 48)

Preheat oven to 375 degrees.

Mix goat cheese with herbs, seasoning and lemon juice. Place tomato slices on pan. Top each with 2 Tbsp. goat cheese mixture; sprinkle with 1 Tbsp. bread crumbs and brown in oven.

Slice baguette diagonally into 12 pieces. Dip each slice into Balsamic Marinade; toast under broiler until golden brown. Lay slices beside tomatoes, with warm Tomato Basil Sauce for dipping.

Makes 6 servings, 2 pieces of bread and 2 slices of tomato each.

Per Serving: 193 Calories	
Protein 7 gr.	Carb. 30 gr.
Fat 5 gr.	Cal. from fat 23%
Chol. 15 mg.	Sodium 426 mg.

Pasta Shrimp Pomodoro

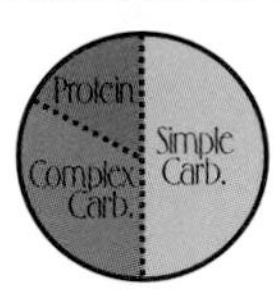

shrimp (protein)
pasta (complex carb.)
vegetables, salad (simple carb.)

Pasta Shrimp Pomodoro

1½ lbs. shrimp, peeled and deveined
¼ cup white wine Worcestershire sauce
8 oz. dry angel hair pasta
2 tsp. olive oil
2 cloves garlic, minced
1 small red onion, chopped
1 each yellow, orange and red bell peppers, cut into strips
1 tsp. Mrs. Dash seasoning
1 tsp. creole seasoning
1 tsp. dried oregano
½ tsp. dried basil
1 can (32 oz.) whole tomatoes
2 Tbsp. grated Parmesan cheese

Marinate shrimp in Worcestershire sauce for at least 15 minutes.

In a large saucepan, cook pasta in salted water until done. Drain.

Spray a nonstick skillet with cooking spray. Lightly sauté half of the garlic and half of the onions. Add shrimp and sear on one side for 1 minute; then turn and sear on other side.

Spray another skillet with cooking spray and add olive oil; heat. Add remaining garlic and onions; sauté. Then add peppers, seasonings and herbs. Allow peppers to soften, then add tomatoes, breaking up tomatoes with spatula while heating. Allow to simmer and reduce for about 4 to 5 more minutes. Add shrimp, stirring all together. Sprinkle with Parmesan cheese. Serve over cooked pasta.

Serves 4.

Per Serving: 394 Calories	
Protein 30 gr.	Carb. 54 gr.
Fat 6 gr.	Cal. from fat 16%
Chol. 225 mg.	Sodium 540 mg.

Salad of Field Greens

4 radicchio leaves
1 cup arugula or watercress, washed
1 head endive, sliced
½ cup Green Goddess Dressing (pg. 39)
2 plum tomatoes, seeded and diced
1 cucumber, peeled, seeded and sliced

Cut radicchio leaves in half. Place on plate.

Toss arugula and endive in dressing. Mound on top of radicchio. Sprinkle with tomato and cucumber.

Serves 4.

Per Serving: 40 Calories	
Protein 3 gr.	Carb. 7 gr.
Fat 0 gr.	Cal. from fat 0%
Chol. 1 mg.	Sodium 70 mg.

Cooking Pasta

To cook pasta, use four quarts of water per pound of pasta.

Have the water boiling rapidly before adding a touch of salt, then pasta. Squeeze lemon into the water to prevent pasta from sticking together.

Perfectly cooked pasta should be al dente *— tender, but still firm to the bite. Pasta to be cooked further in another dish should be cooked for one-third less time initially.*

Drain pasta well; only rinse if it's to be used in salad.

Jamaican Grouper

Caribbean cuisine is based on the treasures of the region's soil — extravagantly colored fruits and richly textured vegetables. This cuisine lends itself to cooking the healthy way — fresh and flavorful! This fish is seared with a full-bodied sauce that has an exotic taste of the islands.

Jamaican Grouper

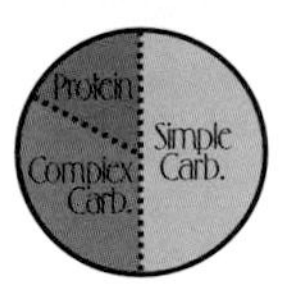

grouper (protein)
rice (complex carb.)
pineapple, raisins, green beans (simple carb.)

Jamaican Grouper

1/2 cup white wine Worcestershire sauce
4 grouper fillets (5 oz. each)
1 tsp. olive oil
1 tsp. creole seasoning
2 cups Jamaican Sauce
1/2 cup chicken stock (fat-free/low salt), if needed
1 Tbsp. chopped fresh herbs (cilantro, basil, rosemary, thyme)

Marinate grouper in Worcestershire sauce.

Spray a nonstick skillet with cooking spray. Add olive oil and heat. Sprinkle grouper with seasoning and lightly sear on both sides.

Add Jamaican Sauce to skillet and allow grouper to finish cooking while sauce is reducing. Add chicken stock, if necessary, to keep grouper from burning.

Serve grouper with pan sauces.

Serves 4.

Per Serving: 199 Calories	
Protein 30 gr.	Carb. 11 gr.
Fat 3 gr.	Cal. from fat 14%
Chol. 53 mg.	Sodium 598 mg.

Jamaican Sauce

1 tsp. olive oil
2 cloves garlic, minced
1 Tbsp. minced shallots
1 tsp. creole seasoning
2 cups beef stock (fat-free/low salt)
1/4 diced fresh pineapple (about 1/2 cup)
2 Tbsp. Jamaican dark rum (optional)
1/2 tsp. five spice powder
1 Tbsp. honey
2 Tbsp. golden raisins
1 Tbsp. Pickapeppa sauce (or hot pepper sauce)
1 Tbsp. chopped fresh herbs (cilantro, basil, rosemary, thyme)

Spray a nonstick skillet with cooking spray. Add olive oil and heat. Sprinkle garlic and shallots with seasoning and quickly sauté 1 to 2 minutes. Add stock and allow to reduce while adding remaining ingredients. Add extra stock as needed.

Makes 2 cups, 1/4 cup per serving.

Per Serving: 31 Calories	
Protein 0 gr.	Carb. 8 gr.
Fat less than 1 gr.	Cal. from fat 0%
Chol. 0 mg.	Sodium 134 mg.

(Meal continued on the next page.)

All fish contain wonderfully healthy oils that lower total cholesterol while increasing your level of the good HDL cholesterol. Those highest in disease-preventing oils, Omega-3's, are cold-water fish and hard shellfish, such as salmon, albacore tuna, swordfish, sardines and mackerel.

These fish oils have also been shown to reduce the tendency of the blood to clot and to decrease triglycerides — and even to help battle arthritis!

So have you had your fish today?

Jamaican Grouper (continued)

Saffron Rice

- 1 tsp. olive oil
- 2 cloves garlic, minced
- 1 3/4 cups chicken stock (fat-free/low salt)
- 4 to 5 saffron threads (or 1/4 tsp. powder)
- 1/8 tsp. cumin
- 1 tsp. creole seasoning
- 1 Tbsp. chopped fresh parsley (or 1 tsp. dried)
- 2 cups instant brown rice

Spray a medium saucepan with cooking spray. Add olive oil and heat. Add garlic and lightly sauté about 1 to 2 minutes, then add chicken stock, saffron, cumin, seasoning and herbs. Bring to a boil, then stir in brown rice. Boil for 1 minute; turn down heat to low and cover. Simmer for 5 minutes; uncover saucepan and fluff rice with fork. Cover again and let sit for another 5 minutes.

Serves 4.

Per Serving: 126 Calories	
Protein 2.5 gr.	Carb. 24 gr.
Fat 2 gr.	Cal. from fat 15%
Chol. 0 mg.	Sodium 136 mg.

Roasted Green Beans and Peppers

- 3/4 lb. green beans, trimmed
- 1 large red bell pepper, cut into long thin strips
- 1 tsp. olive oil
- 1/2 tsp. creole seasoning
- 1 tsp. Mrs. Dash seasoning

Preheat oven to 450 degrees.

Place green beans and peppers on a baking sheet and toss with olive oil and seasonings. Spread the vegetables in an even layer. Roast for about 12 minutes or until the vegetables are browned and tender. Stir midway.

Serves 4.

Per Serving: 57 Calories	
Protein 2 gr.	Carb. 10 gr.
Fat 1 gr.	Cal. from fat 16%
Chol. 0 mg.	Sodium 140 mg.

Herb-Crusted Orange Roughy

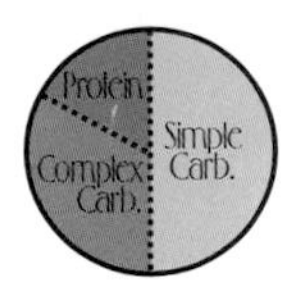

fish (protein)
potatoes, bread crumbs (complex carb.)
broccoli (simple carb.)

Herb-Crusted Orange Roughy

4 orange roughy fillets (5 oz. each)
1/4 cup white wine Worcestershire sauce
1 tsp. creole seasoning
1/2 cup dried bread crumbs (purchased)
2 Tbsp. chopped fresh herbs (cilantro, basil, rosemary, thyme)
1/4 cup Dijon mustard
2 cups broccoli florets, steamed until crisp tender
1/2 cup Tomato Basil Sauce (pg. 48)
1 Tbsp. parsley, chopped

Marinate orange roughy in Worcestershire sauce for at least 15 minutes, or up to 1 hour.

Preheat oven to 375 degrees.

Season fish with seasoning and roll in bread crumbs. Spread mustard on top of fish and roll in bread crumbs once more.

Spray a nonstick skillet with cooking spray; heat. Sear fish in hot skillet on both sides, then transfer to oven and roast until done and browned.

Serve on bed of Tomato Basil Sauce with steamed broccoli. Sprinkle with chopped parsley.

Serves 4.

Per Serving: 291 Calories	
Protein 36 gr.	Carb. 29 gr.
Fat 4 gr.	Cal. from fat 14%
Chol. 53 mg.	Sodium 723 mg.

Herb-Roasted Potatoes

2 lbs. (about 5 large) red-skinned potatoes, scrubbed and quartered
2 cloves garlic, minced
2 tsp. olive oil
1/2 tsp. creole seasoning
1 tsp. Mrs. Dash seasoning
1 Tbsp. chopped fresh rosemary (or 1 tsp. dried)

Preheat oven to 450 degrees.

Spray a shallow roasting pan with cooking spray. Add potatoes, garlic, olive oil, seasonings and rosemary, and spread in an even layer. Bake until the potatoes begin to brown, 20 to 30 minutes, turning them once midway through roasting.

Serves 4.

Per Serving: 139 Calories	
Protein 2 gr.	Carb. 27 gr.
Fat 2 gr.	Cal. from fat 15%
Chol. 0 mg.	Sodium 139 mg.

A baked potato doesn't have to be piled with butter and sour cream to be delicious. Here are some low-fat suggestions for seasoning these packages of power:

- *nonfat yogurt, sour cream or blended-till-smooth nonfat cottage cheese (or ricotta) mixed with chopped chives, fresh dill, parsley, scallions, horseradish or minced green pepper*
- *salsa and herbs*
- *dried herbs mixed with a little lemon juice or balsamic vinegar*
- *fresh grated Parmesan cheese*
- *Dijon mustard or low-fat salad dressing*

Curried Shrimp

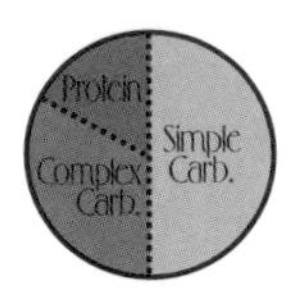

shrimp (protein)
cornsticks (complex carb.)
vegetables (simple carb.)

The curry powder we buy in the grocery store bears little resemblance to the freshly ground original Indian version, but it still packs a lot of flavor. Each brand varies, so find the one you like best.

A pinch of curry adds an exotic touch to soups, vegetables, rices, salad dressings and salads. Start with a light touch! You can always add more to your liking; too much can overpower a dish.

Curried Shrimp

1 lb. large shrimp, peeled and deveined
1/2 cup Balsamic Marinade (pg. 42)
1 tsp. curry powder
1 tsp. olive oil
1 small onion, finely chopped
2 cloves garlic, minced
1 tsp. creole seasoning
1 cup white wine*
2 Tbsp. grenadine
1/4 cup white wine Worcestershire sauce
1 to 1 1/2 cups chicken stock (fat-free/low salt)
3 plum tomatoes, cut into eighths
1 lb. frozen corn kernels, thawed
2 Tbsp. chopped fresh herbs (cilantro, basil, rosemary, thyme)
1 lemon
* ***or substitute dealcoholized wine or more chicken stock***

Serve with a salad tossed with Parmesan Peppercorn Dressing (pg. 40).

Marinate shrimp in Balsamic Marinade for up to 1 hour. Sprinkle with curry powder.

Spray large nonstick skillet with cooking spray. Add olive oil and heat. Add onion and garlic, and sauté. Add drained shrimp. Sprinkle with seasoning. Turn shrimp as it browns.

Add white wine, grenadine and Worcestershire sauce. Add 1 cup chicken stock, tomatoes, corn and fresh herbs. Reduce liquid by one half, adding more chicken stock as needed. Squeeze lemon juice over all.

Serves 4.

Per Serving: 227 Calories	
Protein 22 gr.	Carb. 28 gr.
Fat 3 gr.	Cal. from fat 12%
Chol. 166 mg.	Sodium 733 mg.

Cheesy Cornsticks

1/3 cup skim milk
2 egg whites, lightly beaten
1 Tbsp. olive oil
1/3 cup whole wheat pastry flour
1/2 cup stone ground cornmeal
1/4 cup grated Parmesan cheese
2 tsp. baking powder
1/2 tsp. sugar
1/4 tsp. salt

Preheat oven to 425 degrees.

Spray a muffin pan or cast-iron cornstick mold with cooking spray.

Combine milk, egg whites and oil in a measuring cup; stir briskly with a fork until mixed. In a medium-sized bowl, whisk together flour, cornmeal, cheese, baking powder, sugar and salt. Make a well in the center of the dry mixture and pour in the milk mixture. Stir until just combined.

Spoon a heaping tablespoon of the batter into each of 8 cornstick molds or divide the batter among 4 muffin cups. Bake for 10 to 12 minutes or until set and lightly browned.

Makes 8 cornsticks.

Per Serving: 83 Calories	
Protein 4 gr.	Carb. 10 gr.
Fat 3 gr.	Cal. from fat 32%
Chol. 2 mg.	Sodium 231 mg.

Roasted Cod With Vegetables

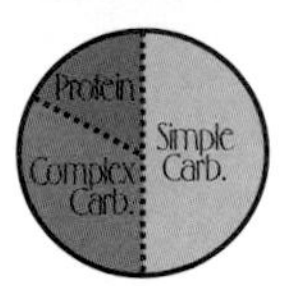

codfish (protein)
rice, green peas (complex carb.)
vegetables, salad (simple carb.)

Roasted Cod With Vegetables

4 codfish fillets (5 oz. each)
1/2 cup Balsamic Marinade (pg. 42)
1 large stalk celery, diced
1 red bell pepper, diced
1 carrot, diced
1/2 cup diced fennel
1/2 cup diced red onion
1 tsp. creole seasoning
3 cups chicken stock (fat-free/low salt)
1/2 cup white wine*
2 whole tomatoes, seeded and chopped
1 can (4 oz.) tomato paste
1 tsp. Mrs. Dash seasoning
2 cups green peas
* ***or substitute dealcoholized wine or more chicken stock***

Preheat oven to 350 degrees.

Marinate codfish in Balsamic Marinade. Spray a large, nonstick ovenproof skillet with cooking spray. Sear codfish over medium-high heat on both sides. Then put skillet in oven for 6 to 8 minutes to finish cooking.

Steam celery, bell pepper, carrot and fennel over boiling water, or microwave, covered and vented, on high power with 1/4 cup water for 3 to 4 minutes.

Spray another pan with cooking spray; heat. Quickly sauté onions; add creole seasoning and steamed vegetables. Sauté lightly; add chicken stock and wine. Cook and reduce by half.

Add tomatoes and tomato paste; cook for 1 minute. Add Mrs. Dash and cook until vegetables are done. Add green peas. Pour broth and vegetables into bowl; top with codfish.

Serves 4.

Per Serving: 291 Calories	
Protein 29 gr.	Carb. 37 gr.
Fat 3 gr.	Cal. from fat 9%
Chol. 35 mg.	Sodium 706 mg.

Crunchy Jicama and Melon Salad

1 medium jicama, julienned
1 medium cantaloupe, cut into 1/2-inch cubes
3 Tbsp. lime juice
3 Tbsp. chopped fresh mint (or 1 Tbsp. dried)
1 tsp. grated lime peel
2 tsp. honey
1/4 tsp. salt

In a medium-sized bowl, mix together all ingredients. Cover and refrigerate 2 hours or until chilled.

Makes 4 servings.

Per Serving: 62 Calories	
Protein 1 gr.	Carb. 15 gr.
Fat 0 gr.	Cal. from fat 0%
Chol. 0 mg.	Sodium 91 mg.

Jicama is a large root vegetable with a thin brown skin and white crunchy flesh. Its nutty, sweet flavor resembles water chestnuts and is great both raw and cooked. It's good raw added to fruit and vegetable salads. It also adds crunch when sliced thin for sandwiches. Cooked, it can be used in stir-frys. Or it can be boiled and mashed like potatoes, added to soups and stews at the end of their cooking, or just sautéed on its own.

Shop for a jicama that's heavy for its size and free of blemishes. One pound yields about 3 cups chopped. Store jicama in a plastic bag in the refrigerator for up to 2 weeks. Pull off skin with a sharp knife just before using.

Tropical Shrimp Salad

The beauty of this meal is that its preparation does not require a great deal of time: The shrimp is cooked quickly, and the salsa is prepared ahead of time. The focaccia bread accompaniment can either be purchased or prepared in advance, making a perfectly balanced meal.

Tropical Shrimp Salad

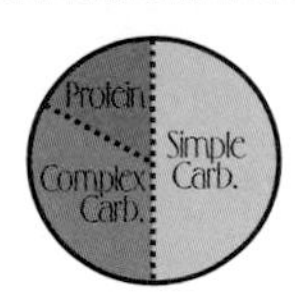

shrimp (protein)
bread (complex carb.)
salsa, vegetables (simple carb.)

Shrimp Salad St. Lucia

1¼ lbs. large shrimp
¼ cup white wine Worcestershire sauce
1 tsp. olive oil
1 tsp. creole seasoning
1 cup Mango Salsa
8 cups washed, dried and torn mixed greens (red leaf, romaine, frizee, radicchio, arugula or bibb)
½ cup Citrus Vinaigrette (pg. 39)
2 tomatoes, cut into wedges
2 lemons, sliced thin
2 Tbsp. chopped fresh herbs (cilantro, basil, rosemary, thyme)

Serve with Focaccia Bread (pg. 133).

Peel all but tails of shrimp; devein. Marinate shrimp in Worcestershire sauce for at least 1 hour.

Spray a nonstick skillet with cooking spray. Add olive oil and heat. Sprinkle shrimp with seasoning and quickly sauté in hot pan until done.

To serve, spoon 3 small pools of salsa on each plate. Toss torn lettuce leaves with Citrus Vinaigrette. Place lettuce in middle of plate. Then arrange shrimp and tomato wedges on top of salad.

Garnish with lemon slices and sprinkle with chopped herbs.

Serves 4.

Per Serving: 341 Calories	
Protein 27 gr.	Carb. 48 gr.
Fat 4.5 gr.	Cal. from fat 12%
Chol. 166 mg.	Sodium 625 mg.

Mango Salsa

2 whole ripe mangoes, peeled and diced
juice of 2 limes
½ cup orange juice
1 large red bell pepper, diced
½ tsp. five spice powder
½ Tbsp. minced shallots
¼ cup honey
1 tsp. creole seasoning

Mix together all ingredients. Refrigerate at least 1 hour to blend flavors.

Makes 8 servings, ¼ cup each.

Per Serving: 77 Calories	
Protein 0 gr.	Carb. 20 gr.
Fat 0 gr.	Cal. from fat 0%
Chol. 0 mg.	Sodium 135 mg.

You may have heard that eating shellfish raises your cholesterol. Forget that thought: it's just a well-traveled rumor!

Shellfish can actually protect arteries and blood vessels by lowering bad-type blood cholesterol and providing the heart with many other protective functions. Shellfish is actually a heart champion. Up-to-date analysis shows low levels of cholesterol in oysters, mussels, clams and scallops. Crab and shrimp have slightly higher levels, though still modest amounts, and all are extremely low in fat.

The heart-healthy key is to cook and serve seafood without any added saturated fat such as butter or typical frying oils.

Pan-Seared Swordfish

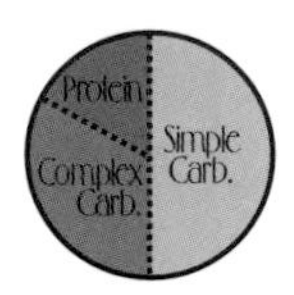

swordfish (protein)
potatoes (complex carb.)
vegetables, salad (simple carb.)

Ginger root has tough, tan-colored skin that must be removed. Look for smooth skin; wrinkled and cracked means old and dry. Store ginger root in the freezer in a zip-top, heavy-duty freezer bag; it's easier to peel and grate while frozen. Slice off as much as you need and return the rest of the root to the freezer.

When you peel ginger, be careful to remove only the skin; most of the flavor is just under the surface.

Daikon radishes, often called Japanese or Oriental radishes, are long and mild. They may be pickled, or shredded and used as a garnish. Or they may be used in salads to add new and creative textures.

Pan-Seared Swordfish With Mixed Vegetables

4 swordfish steaks (5 oz. each)
1 eggplant, sliced in 1/4-inch slices
1/2 cup white wine Worcestershire sauce
8 red-skinned potatoes, quartered
1 cup green beans, cut in 1-inch diagonal pieces, blanched
1 cup wax beans, cut in 1-inch diagonal pieces, thawed
1 tsp. olive oil
1 yellow bell pepper, cut into strips
1 red bell pepper, cut into strips
1 cup frozen sugar snap peas, thawed
1 tsp. creole seasoning
1 cup Herbal Vinaigrette (pg. 38)

Marinate swordfish and eggplant slices in Worcestershire sauce for up to 1 hour.

In a microwavable dish, place potatoes, green beans and wax beans with 1/4 cup water. Cover dish with plastic wrap and vent. Microwave on high for 4 to 5 minutes.

Spray large sauté pan with cooking spray; add oil and heat. Sauté marinated swordfish and eggplant on both sides until done. Remove fish. In same pan, sauté peppers for one minute. Add snap peas, then beans and potatoes, seasoning and Herbal Vinaigrette.

Serve the fish on top of the vegetables.

Serves 4.

Per Serving: 345 Calories	
Protein 28 gr.	Carb. 39 gr.
Fat 8.5 gr.	Cal. from fat 22%
Chol. 43 mg.	Sodium 502 mg.

Asian Daikon Salad

1/4 cup rice wine vinegar
1 Tbsp. sesame oil
1 Tbsp. low-sodium soy sauce
1/4 cup chicken stock (fat-free/low salt)
2 tsp. grated ginger root
1/2 tsp. creole seasoning
3 cups diagonally sliced daikon radishes (about 4 medium)
1 1/2 cups sliced mushrooms (about 4 ounces)
1/3 cup sliced green onions
8 red leaf lettuce leaves
2 Tbsp. sesame seeds, toasted

In a tightly covered container, shake together vinegar, oil, soy sauce, stock, ginger root and seasoning. Pour over daikon slices, mushrooms and onions; toss until evenly coated. Cover and refrigerate until chilled, about 2 hours. Serve on lettuce leaves. Sprinkle with sesame seeds.

Makes 8 servings.

Per Serving: 47 Calories	
Protein 1 gr.	Carb. 4 gr.
Fat 3 gr.	Cal. from fat 57%
Chol. 0 mg.	Sodium 152 mg.

Pan-Roasted Crab Cakes

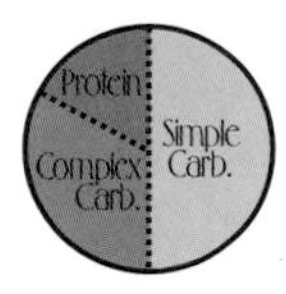

crab (protein)
bread crumbs (complex carb.)
Tropical Salsa, salad (simple carb.)

Pan-Roasted Crab Cakes

1 lb. lump crabmeat*
3 Tbsp. light mayonnaise
2 cloves garlic, minced
1/2 cup egg substitute (or 2 eggs), lightly beaten
1 red bell pepper, diced fine
1 green bell pepper, diced fine
1 carrot, diced fine
1 tsp. creole seasoning
1 cup fine bread crumbs
* ***may substitute canned salmon, drained***

Serve with Tropical Salsa (pg. 44), 1/3 cup per serving.

Mix crab meat with mayonnaise, garlic, egg substitute, vegetables, seasoning and bread crumbs. Shape into 8 cakes.

Spray a nonstick skillet with cooking spray; heat. Brown the cakes until golden brown and cooked through.

Place 2 warm crab cakes atop 1/3 cup of salsa on large plate. Serve Mixed Greens surrounding crab cake.

Serves 4.

Per Serving: 343 Calories	
Protein 22 gr.	Carb. 48 gr.
Fat 7 gr.	Cal. from fat 18%
Chol. 15 mg.	Sodium 657 mg.

Mixed Greens With Citrus Vinaigrette

12 cups washed, dried and torn mixed greens (red leaf, romaine, frizee, radicchio, arugula or bibb)
1/2 cup Citrus Vinaigrette (pg. 39)
4 green onions, leaves curled
2 Tbsp. chopped fresh herbs (cilantro, basil, rosemary, thyme)
2 plum tomatoes, diced

Just before serving, toss lettuce leaves with Citrus Vinaigrette. Top with curly-leaved onion and sprinkle lightly with herbs and diced tomatoes.

Serves 4.

Per Serving: 71 Calories	
Protein 3 gr.	Carb. 10 gr.
Fat 2 gr.	Cal. from fat 25%
Chol. 0 mg.	Sodium 79 mg.

Canned crab is available flaked, or as lump or claw meat. Once opened, refrigerate and use within 2 days.

If canned crabmeat tastes metallic, let it soak in ice water for 5 minutes, then drain and blot before using.

Always use your fingers to pick through crabmeat — fresh or canned — to make sure no tiny pieces of shell were left in it.

Poached Salmon

Salmon atop a colorful and flavorful Black Bean and Corn Salsa is tonight's main course, enhanced by the vivid colors and textures of spinach and asparagus — an unexpected yet delicious way to enjoy the subtle flavors of these vegetables. It's served with a Waldorf Salad in disguise — made over in a delightful way.

Poached Salmon

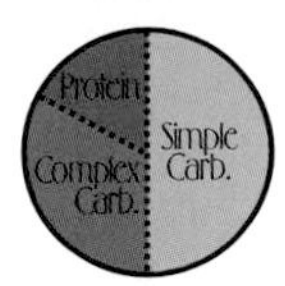

salmon, black beans (protein)
corn, black beans (complex carb.)
vegetables, fruit (simple carb.)

Poached Salmon Over Black Beans and Corn

4 salmon fillets (5 oz. each)
Poaching stock:
1 cup white wine*
2 cups chicken stock (fat-free/low salt)
1 whole shallot, quartered
2 cloves garlic, minced
2 sprigs fresh thyme
2 bay leaves
1/4 tsp. cracked black pepper
1/2 tsp. creole seasoning
1 lb. asparagus, trimmed of tough stalks
2 cups Black Bean and Corn Salsa (pg. 44)
2 cups fresh spinach leaves, washed and stemmed
1 Tbsp. chopped chives
1 lemon, sliced
* ***or substitute dealcoholized wine or more chicken stock***

In a large nonstick skillet, bring poaching stock to boil. Add salmon and asparagus spears; simmer 5 to 7 minutes until done.

Spoon Black Bean and Corn Salsa onto plate. Add fresh spinach leaves and place poached salmon and asparagus spears on top of the leaves.

Sprinkle with chopped chives and garnish with twisted lemon slice.

Serves 4.

Per Serving: 340 Calories	
Protein 38 gr.	Carb. 38 gr.
Fat 4 gr.	Cal. from fat 11%
Chol. 51 mg.	Sodium 405 mg.

Waldorf Salad

2 large apples, cut into chunks
1/2 cup unsweetened pineapple chunks
1/2 stalk celery, chopped
1/2 cup carrots, shredded
1 small orange, peeled and sectioned
1/4 cup golden raisins
1/4 cup orange juice
1 1/4 cups nonfat vanilla yogurt
3 Tbsp. chopped walnuts

Combine all fruits along with vegetables and orange juice. Add yogurt, mixing well. Chill. Top with chopped walnuts for serving.

Makes 6 servings.

Per Serving: 114 Calories	
Protein 2 gr.	Carb. 22 gr.
Fat 2 gr.	Cal. from fat 18%
Chol. 0 mg.	Sodium 53 mg.

Poaching cooks food in simmering liquid. It produces a particularly delicate flavor in foods and keeps them moist.

Don't throw out a poaching liquid. It can be used either to make a sauce for the poached food or as a soup base.

If you're not going to use a poaching liquid within a couple of days, freeze it for up to six months. Be sure to label it though, so you don't have a mystery package!

Spicy Scallops and Cucumber Salad

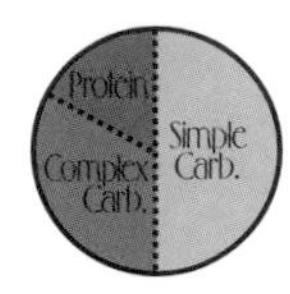

scallops (protein)
roll (complex carb.)
vegetables (simple carb.)

Cooking with garlic:

One fresh medium garlic clove yields 1/2 tsp. minced garlic or 1/8 tsp. garlic powder or dried minced garlic.

Crushing, mincing, pressing or pureeing garlic releases essential oils and produces a more assertive flavor than slicing garlic cloves or leaving them whole. To give just a hint of flavor to a salad, rub a cut garlic clove in the bowl.

Peel a garlic clove by placing the flat side of a large knife on top of a clove and giving it a gentle smack with your fist. The jolt will separate the skin from the clove for easy removal.

Minced garlic, purchased in a jar from the supermarket's produce section, takes advantage of the splendor of garlic without the chop-chop. The flavor is not the same, but the convenience may make up for the difference!

Spicy Scallops and Cucumber Salad

16 sea scallops, washed and drained
1/2 cup white wine Worcestershire sauce
1 tsp. creole seasoning
2 tsp. Mrs. Dash seasoning
1 medium European cucumber, peeled, seeded and sliced diagonally
2 large tomatoes, seeded and cut into strips
1 large red onion, cut into strips
4 cups mixed radicchio, bibb and endive lettuces
1 cup Cucumber Dill Dressing (pg. 39)
2 Tbsp. chopped cilantro
1 lemon, cut into wedges

Serve with whole grain rolls or bread.

Marinate scallops in Worcestershire sauce for up to 1 hour. Toss scallops in seasonings. Spray a nonstick pan with cooking spray. Sear scallops in pan until cooked through.

Toss dressing with cucumbers, tomatoes and red onions. Place salad on bed of lettuces. Drizzle one wedge of lemon juice over salad.

Add hot scallops to top of salad. Garnish with lemon wedge and chopped cilantro. Serve immediately with a whole grain roll.

Serves 4.

Per Serving: 299 Calories	
Protein 27 gr.	Carb. 32 gr.
Fat 6 gr.	Cal. from fat 21%
Chol. 42 mg.	Sodium 502 mg.

Cucumber Dill Dressing

6 oz. fat-free cream cheese, softened
1 1/2 oz. farmer's cheese
1 cup skim milk
1 cup cucumbers, peeled, seeded and chopped
1 1/2 Tbsp. Dijon mustard
2 cloves garlic, minced
1/4 tsp. cracked black pepper
1 tsp. creole seasoning
1 Tbsp. olive oil
juice of 1 lemon
1/2 tsp. Tabasco sauce
2 Tbsp. chopped fresh dill

Blend cheeses together with skim milk. Add remaining ingredients, except dill, and blend until smooth. Stir in dill.

Makes 1 1/2 quarts, 24 servings, 4 Tbsp. each.

Per Serving: 38 Calories	
Protein 1.5 gr.	Carb. 1 gr.
Fat 3 gr.	Cal. from fat 71%
Chol. 3 mg.	Sodium 34 mg.

Herbed Shrimp Pasta Primavera

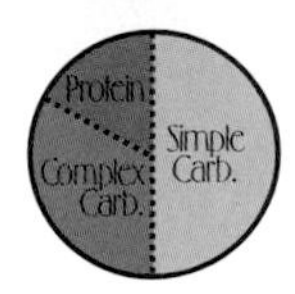

shrimp, beans (protein)
pasta (complex carb.)
vegetables, salad (simple carb.)

Herbed Shrimp Pasta Primavera

1 1/2 lbs. shrimp, peeled and deveined
1/4 cup white wine Worcestershire sauce
8 oz. dry bowtie pasta
2 tsp. olive oil
2 cloves garlic, minced
2 shallots, minced
1 each yellow, green and red bell peppers, cut into strips
1 tomato, cut into strips
1 cup broccoli florets, blanched
1 cup garbanzo beans
2 cups chicken stock (fat-free/low salt)
1 cup white wine*
1 tsp. creole seasoning
1 tsp. Mrs. Dash seasoning
1 cup skim milk
1/3 cup shredded, part-skim mozzarella cheese
4 Tbsp. grated Parmesan cheese, divided
2 Tbsp. chopped fresh herbs (cilantro, basil, rosemary, thyme)
* ***or substitute dealcoholized wine or more chicken stock***

Marinate shrimp in Worcestershire sauce for at least 15 minutes.

In a large saucepan, cook bowtie pasta in salted water. Drain.

Spray a nonstick pan with cooking spray. Add olive oil and heat over medium-high heat. Lightly sauté garlic and shallots; add marinated shrimp and sauté 1 minute. Add vegetables, garbanzo beans, chicken stock, white wine and seasonings and let cook for another 1 to 2 minutes until liquid reduces slightly. Mix together mozzarella and 2 Tbsp. of the Parmesan cheese. Add to pan with skim milk and cooked pasta; toss to heat.

Sprinkle all with the remaining 2 Tbsp. grated Parmesan and the fresh herbs.

Serves 4.

Per Serving: 382 Calories	
Protein 33 gr.	Carb. 52 gr.
Fat 5 gr.	Cal. from fat 12%
Chol. 209 mg.	Sodium 775 mg.

Caesar Salad

12 cups romaine lettuce, torn
1/2 cup Caesar Salad Dressing (pg. 40)

Toss lettuce with dressing. Serve immediately.

Serves 4.

Per Serving: 54 Calories	
Protein 2 gr.	Carb. 6 gr.
Fat 2.5 gr.	Cal. from fat 42%
Chol. 2.5 mg.	Sodium 60 mg.

Garlic cooks in about 30 seconds. If sautéeing with onions, add the garlic at the end to keep it from becoming overbrowned and bitter.

When roasted, garlic turns golden and butter-soft, with a mild, slightly sweet and nutty flavor. Roast a whole head or individual cloves by trimming off stem ends and placing cut side down on pan sprayed with cooking spray. Loosely wrap in aluminum foil, drizzling with a scant teaspoon of olive oil and bake at 400 degrees for 25-30 minutes or until soft.

Roast a half-dozen heads at one time; cool and squeeze out the individual cloves. Place the cloves in a freezer bag, press the bag flat and freeze. To use, pry off cloves with the tip of a knife; thaw for 1-2 minutes, mash and use.

Seafood and Pasta

This dish of shrimp and mussels in a rich tomato broth atop pasta is a lively blend of color, flavor and texture. Accompany with a broccoli salad — chilled, fresh and spicy — to balance the meal.

Seafood and Pasta

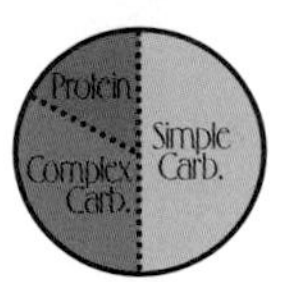

seafood (protein)
pasta (complex carb.)
broccoli (simple carb.)

Mediterranean Seafood Stew

1/2 lb. large shrimp
6 oz. white fish (grouper, snapper or sea bass)
1/2 cup white wine Worcestershire sauce
2 tsp. olive oil
2 cloves garlic, minced
1 small red onion, diced
2 cups chicken stock (fat-free/low salt)
4 cups Tomato Basil Sauce (pg. 48)
1 tsp. creole seasoning
2 Tbsp. chopped fresh herbs (cilantro, basil, rosemary, thyme)
juice of 1 lime
1 dozen clams, washed
1 dozen mussels, washed
10 oz. dry angel hair pasta
4 rosemary sprigs (optional)

Marinate shrimp and fish in Worcestershire sauce for up to 1 hour.

Spray large nonstick skillet with cooking spray. Add olive oil; heat. Add garlic and onions; sauté until translucent. Add shrimp and fish; lightly sauté. Add chicken stock, Tomato Basil Sauce, seasoning and fresh herbs; squeeze in juice of 1 lime. Add mussels and clams, and cook lightly until they open.

Meanwhile, cook angel hair pasta according to package directions. Drain. Serve 1 cup of pasta topped with an even portion of stew. Top with rosemary sprig.

Serves 4.

Per Serving: 418 Calories	
Protein 42 gr.	Carb. 47 gr.
Fat 6 gr.	Cal. from fat 14%
Chol. 176 mg.	Sodium 555 mg.

Fresh Broccoli Salad

2 bunches fresh broccoli, trimmed and cut into small pieces
1 cup chopped fresh parsley
2 to 3 green onions, sliced
1/2 cup nonfat cottage cheese (or ricotta)
1/4 cup light mayonnaise
1/2 cup skim milk
2 cloves garlic, minced
1 tsp. Mrs. Dash seasoning
1/2 tsp. creole seasoning
3/4 tsp. dill weed

Blanch broccoli for 5 minutes in boiling water. Immerse quickly in ice water to chill; drain. Toss with parsley and green onions.

Make dressing by blending cottage cheese, mayonnaise, milk, garlic and seasonings in blender until smooth. Stir in dill. Toss with vegetables and chill well.

Makes 8 servings.

Per Serving: 76 Calories	
Protein 3 gr.	Carb. 16 gr.
Fat 0 gr.	Cal. from fat 0%
Chol. 1 mg.	Sodium 54 mg.

Shell shrimp by holding the tail fin in one hand and peeling away the shell starting with the bottom "feet." The tail may be left on.

Generally, small to medium shrimp don't need deveining except for eye-appeal. However, the vein of larger shrimp will contain noticeable grit and should be removed.

Devein by cutting a shallow slit down the middle of the outside curve with a sharp, pointed knife. Pull out the dark vein, then rinse the slit under cold, running water.

A Traditional Holiday Dinner

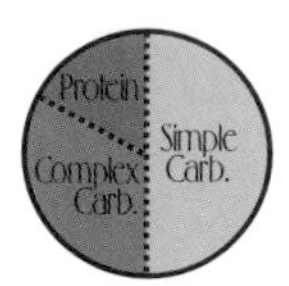

turkey (protein)
dressing, sweet potatoes (complex carb.)
green beans, chutney, fruit salad (simple carb.)

Antipasto Cups With Creamy Herb Dip

2 medium red bell peppers
2 medium yellow bell peppers
2 medium green bell peppers
2 medium carrots, quartered and cut into 3-inch strips (or shaved baby carrots)
1 medium zucchini, quartered and cut into 3-inch strips
12 radish roses (pg. 15, garnishing tips)
12 scallion brushes (pg. 15, garnishing tips)
6 pepperoncini peppers
2 oz. part-skim mozzarella, cubed
1½ cups Creamy Herb Dip (pg. 46)

Cut the top off each pepper, reserving it for other uses; remove seeds. Cut a thin slice from the bottom of each pepper, if necessary, to help the pepper stand upright to become a cup for the remaining ingredients.

Arrange equal amounts of cut carrots, zucchini, radishes, onion fans, peppers and cheese in each pepper cup. Chill thoroughly. Serve with Creamy Herb Dip.

Serves 6.

Per Serving: 90 Calories	
Protein 8 gr.	Carb .10 gr.
Fat 2 gr.	Cal. from fat 20%
Chol. 6 mg.	Sodium 205 mg.

Roast Turkey With Gravy

1 whole turkey, thawed
celery leaves
thin onion slices
garlic cloves

Before roasting, place a thin layer of celery leaves and thin slices of onion between the skin and the breast meat of the turkey. This will add rich flavor to the meat and absorb much of the fat from the skin.

Roast turkey according to package directions, basting with lower-salt chicken stock.

One serving is 3 oz. turkey.

Per Serving: 158 Calories	
Protein 27 gr.	Carb. 0 gr.
Fat 5.5 gr.	Cal. from fat 34%
Chol. 72 mg.	Sodium 180 mg.

A Traditional Holiday Dinner (continued)

Turkey Gravy

turkey giblets
1 qt. water
1 onion, cut in pieces
1 stalk celery, cut in pieces
2 Tbsp. canola oil
2 cloves garlic, minced
1 Tbsp. cornstarch
1 bay leaf
1/2 cup white wine*
1 tsp. Mrs. Dash seasoning
1/2 tsp. salt
1/4 tsp. cracked black pepper
*** *or substitute dealcoholized wine or more chicken stock***

First, make turkey stock. Remove the giblets from the bird and wash well. Boil giblets together with neck in 1 quart of water with onion and celery. Drain off broth and refrigerate to defat.

To make gravy, heat canola oil in a medium saucepan. Add garlic and cook for 30 seconds. Stir in cornstarch until smooth. Add 3 cups turkey stock, bay leaf, wine and seasonings. (Purchased or homemade chicken stock may be substituted for turkey stock.) Cook over low heat, stirring, until gravy thickens, about 5 minutes. Remove bay leaf.

Makes 15 servings, 1/4 cup each.

Per Serving: 20 Calories	
Protein 0 gr.	Carb. 0 gr.
Fat 2 gr.	Cal. from fat 100%
Chol. 0 mg.	Sodium 120 mg.

Cranberry Chutney

2 cups chopped fresh cranberries
1 cup peeled, chopped Granny Smith apples
3 Tbsp. brown sugar
2 Tbsp. chopped prunes
2 Tbsp. chopped onions
1/2 tsp. ground cinnamon
1/4 tsp. five spice powder
1/3 cup apple-cranberry juice
3 Tbsp. red wine vinegar
2 tsp. lemon juice

Combine all ingredients in a medium saucepan. Bring mixture to a boil. Cover, reduce heat and simmer for 30 minutes, stirring frequently. Uncover and cook, stirring, for 5 minutes or until mixture is thickened.

Makes 8 servings, 1/3 cup each.

Per Serving: 84 Calories	
Protein 0 gr.	Carb. 21 gr.
Fat 0 gr.	Cal. from fat 0%
Chol. 0 mg.	Sodium 15 mg.

(Holiday Dinner recipes continue through page 155.)

There's nothing like the holidays to bring out the worst in our old eating habits and attitudes about food. Holidays are like mini-vacations — a time to let go. And for centuries holidays have centered around the sharing of food.

The good news is that a lifestyle of good health doesn't mean eliminating food from your holiday celebrations. Holiday food doesn't have to be sinful to be enjoyable, nor does the meal have to be the center of the celebration. The dinner should be just one part of a glorious time that celebrates life!

Learn how to prepare old, unhealthy classics in new healthy ways. Add some guaranteed-to-please new favorites. Here is a traditional holiday menu that will please even your most skeptical guests.

A Traditional Holiday Dinner (continued)

You'll love this great tasting, yet lower-fat dressing. The traditional recipe had 225 calories and 13 grams of fat (50 percent of its calories). This version has only 135 calories and 1 gram of fat (6 percent of its calories).

Calories and/or fat are reduced by using defatted chicken or turkey stock, cornbread dressing cubes instead of traditional higher fat cornbread, egg substitute in place of whole eggs, and cooking spray instead of oil.

The original sweet potato casserole recipe scored a whopping 737 calories and 36 grams of fat (42 percent of calories from fat). This version has 178 calories and 3.5 grams of fat (18 percent of calories).

Cornbread Dressing

3 cups chicken stock (fat-free/low salt) or homemade turkey stock (pg. 153)
1 cup finely chopped celery
1/2 cup chopped onions
2 Tbsp. snipped fresh parsley (or 2 tsp. dried)
1 tsp. ground sage
1 1/2 tsp. poultry seasoning
1/2 tsp. cracked black pepper
1/2 tsp. salt
2 packages (12 oz. each) unseasoned cornbread stuffing cubes
1/2 cup egg substitute (or 4 egg whites)

Preheat oven to 350 degrees.

Lightly spray a medium nonstick skillet with cooking spray. Add the celery and onions. Cook over medium heat until tender. Stir in herbs, seasoning and spices.

Lightly spray a large casserole dish with cooking spray. Place the cornbread cubes in casserole. Add onion and celery mixture, 2 cups of the broth and egg substitute. Gently toss. Drizzle with remaining broth to moisten bread thoroughly; gently toss again to mix well.

Bake uncovered for 30 to 40 minutes or until heated through.

Makes 10 servings.

Per Serving: 135 Calories	
Protein 4 gr.	Carb. 27 gr.
Fat 1 gr.	Cal. from fat 6%
Chol. 0 mg.	Sodium 320 mg.

Sweet Potato Casserole

3 cups cooked and cubed sweet potatoes
1/4 cup sugar
4 egg whites
1 tsp. vanilla
1 tsp. cinnamon
Topping:
1/2 cup brown sugar
3 Tbsp. flour
1 Tbsp. melted butter
1/4 cup chopped pecans

Preheat oven to 350 degrees.

Spray a 1 1/4-quart casserole dish with cooking spray. Set aside until ready to use.

In a food processor or with electric mixer, mix potatoes, sugar, egg whites, vanilla and cinnamon. Spoon into prepared casserole dish.

Make topping by rubbing together, with your fingers, the brown sugar, flour and butter until crumbly. Stir in pecans. Sprinkle the mixture on top of sweet potatoes.

Bake approximately 30 minutes until golden brown.

Makes 8 servings.

Per Serving: 178 Calories	
Protein 5 gr.	Carb. 31 gr.
Fat 3.5 gr.	Cal. from fat 18%
Chol. 1 mg.	Sodium 188 mg.

A Traditional Holiday Dinner (continued)

Green Beans and Mushrooms

2 lbs. green beans
2 tsp. olive oil
2 cloves garlic, minced
2 Tbsp. minced shallots
1/2 tsp. dried basil
1/2 tsp. dried rosemary
1/2 tsp. Mrs. Dash seasoning
2 Tbsp. chopped fresh parsley
1/2 tsp. creole seasoning
1/2 lb. (8 oz.) fresh mushrooms, trimmed
2 Tbsp. white wine Worcestershire sauce

Trim ends from green beans; break into smaller pieces if desired. Steam in chicken stock until crisp tender.

Spray nonstick skillet with cooking spray; add olive oil and heat over medium-high heat. Add garlic and shallots; cook for about 1 minute. Add herbs and seasonings, and sauté another 30 seconds; then add mushrooms and Worcestershire sauce. Continue to sauté for about 3 to 4 minutes, then add steamed green beans. Toss together and serve.

Makes 8 servings.

Per Serving: 53 Calories	
Protein 2 gr.	Carb. 9 gr.
Fat 2 gr.	Cal. from fat 17%
Chol. 0 mg.	Sodium 229 mg.

Mom's Tropical Fruit Salad

2 packets of unflavored gelatin
4 cups unsweetened white grape juice
1 large can (28 oz.) unsweetened, crushed pineapple
2 packages (8 oz. each) fat-free cream cheese
1 small can of mandarin oranges, rinsed and drained

In a medium saucepan, add gelatin to 1 cup white grape juice and let dissolve. Place pan on burner and gently heat on medium-high, adding remaining juice and drained juice from canned pineapple. Stir constantly, and remove from heat as the mixture begins to thicken. Add two packages of softened cream cheese and beat with electric mixer or in food processor. Add pineapple and mandarin oranges.

Let chill 3 to 4 hours or until firm. Cut into pieces to serve.

Makes 16 servings.

Per Serving: 68 Calories	
Protein 4 gr.	Carb. 13 gr.
Fat 0 gr.	Cal. from fat 0%
Chol. 15 mg.	Sodium 125 mg.

Calories and/or fat are reduced by using egg whites instead of whole eggs; by lowering the amount of sugar and adding cinnamon instead; by lowering the amount of butter and adding flour to thicken; by using fewer nuts; and by using cooking spray rather than butter.

The original fruit salad recipe contained 336 calories and 13 grams of fat (38 percent of calories). The new version, with no added sugar, is trimmed down to only 68 calories and 0 grams of fat (0 percent of calories).

Calories, sugar and/or fat are reduced by using unflavored gelatin and 100-percent pure juice instead of already flavored gelatin products, and by using fat-free cream cheese instead of whipped topping and cottage cheese.

Sweet Endings

EIGHTEEN CHOICES

If you think healthy eating means a prison sentence, especially when it comes to desserts, these recipes will quickly change your mind. Nearly all of them have fewer than 150 calories per serving and are low in fat and cholesterol. They rely on the natural sweetness of fruits, using only small amounts of honey or sugar. What is left is the flavor — and lots of it!

Dessert is sometimes just a sweet afterthought, particularly if you've devoted all your culinary energy to the dishes that precede it. But creating something fresh and delicious doesn't have to be an ordeal.

There are lots of simple ideas that can jazz up your post-meal possibilities. Along with your time-tested favorite desserts, like bread pudding, you will also find many new and enticing ideas. Try them — you (and your guests) will love them!

Quick Refreshing Desserts

- Puree cubed peeled mango with a touch of lime juice in the food processor and chill. Serve atop pineapple chunks and strawberries.
- Scoop nonfat frozen yogurt onto a wedge of ripe cantaloupe or sliced mango.

Pictured: Pumpkin Bread Pudding (pg. 158)

- Fold dried cherries, blueberries or cranberries into softened nonfat vanilla yogurt and refreeze.
- Top lemon sorbet with fresh raspberries and chunks of pineapple.
- Process 2 cans of undrained, unsweetened mixed fruit in a food processor till smooth. Freeze in a shallow pan, then return to processor until it's the consistency of sherbet.
- Pile fresh strawberries into large, stemmed balloon glasses, and add a generous splash of sparkling cider or champagne.
- Combine nonfat vanilla yogurt, all-fruit orange marmalade and a dash of cinnamon to make a dip for fresh peach slices.

On the following pages I offer eighteen more delicious dessert choices. From Chocolate Marble Cheesecake to Bavarian Cream, they prove that healthy desserts don't require sacrificing taste or pleasure.

Creamy Puddings

Health problems associated with sugar are controversial. The truth is this: Refined sugar has been shown to wreak havoc in the control of diabetes and hypoglycemia. It also raises triglycerides and the risk of dental cavities and obesity.

Sugar can cause a see-saw effect that can bring on the "more you have, the more you want" syndrome. It can lay the foundations for sugar dependency and abuse, and it sets a craving process in motion.

Pumpkin Bread Pudding

2 cups skim milk
1 cup honey
1 can (16 oz.) unsweetened pumpkin
1/2 tsp. ground ginger
1 1/2 tsp. cinnamon
2 egg whites, slightly beaten
2 tsp. vanilla
1/3 cup dates, soaked in water and coarsely chopped
1 large carrot, grated
1/2 loaf French bread, cubed
2 Tbsp. fat-free frozen yogurt, thawed, per serving
1 tsp. pourable fruit (purchased), per serving
sliced fruit for garnish

Preheat oven to 350 degrees.

Mix together milk, honey, pumpkin, spices, egg whites, vanilla, dates and grated carrot.

Place bread cubes in a 9 x 13-inch pan sprayed with cooking spray. Pour liquid mixture over bread cubes.

Cover pan with foil and bake for 35 minutes. Remove foil and bake an additional 10 minutes or until browned on top. Cut into 15 squares. To serve place a square on a plate or in a sundae glass. Spoon on 2 Tbsp. yogurt as sauce. Garnish with fruit and drizzle with 1 tsp. all-fruit syrup.

Serves 15.

Per Serving: 154 Calories	
Protein 3.5 gr.	Carb. 34 gr.
Fat 0 gr.	Cal. from fat 0%
Chol. 0 mg.	Sodium 130 mg.

Banana Pudding Soufflé

3/4 cup polenta or coarse ground cornmeal
2 cups skim milk
1 cup pureed bananas
2/3 cup egg whites
2 Tbsp. sugar
cornmeal (to dust mold)
1/3 cup fat-free frozen yogurt

Whisk polenta into skim milk and cook according to package directions. Refrigerate overnight.

Preheat oven to 400 degrees.

Mix polenta with banana puree. Whip egg whites with sugar to a medium peak meringue. Gently fold into polenta mixture.

Spray five individual soufflé molds with cooking spray. Lightly dust with cornmeal. Divide mixture into the five molds. Place molds in a 9 x 13-inch pan filled with water. Bake until soufflés rise but are still creamy in center (about 30 minutes).

Top each with 1 Tbsp. fat-free frozen yogurt and serve immediately.

Serves 5.

Per Serving: 108 Calories	
Protein 5 gr.	Carb. 22 gr.
Fat 0 gr.	Cal. from fat 0 %
Chol. 0 mg.	Sodium 56 mg.

Creamy Puddings (continued)

Rice Pudding

2 cups instant brown rice
1/4 cup sugar
1/2 tsp. cornstarch
1/8 tsp salt
3 1/4 cups skim milk
1/4 cup raisins, dark or golden
1 tsp. cinnamon
2 tsp. vanilla
sprinkle of nutmeg

In a medium-sized saucepan, mix together rice, sugar, cornstarch and salt. Gradually stir in milk and bring to a simmer over medium-high heat, stirring constantly. Reduce heat to low and simmer slightly, stirring often, until rice is tender and pudding is creamy, about 5 minutes. Remove from heat and stir in raisins, cinnamon and vanilla.

Cover and let stand for 5 minutes or until ready to serve.

Spoon into individual bowls and sprinkle with nutmeg. May serve with fresh sliced peaches or other fruit.

Serves 6.

Per Serving: 166 Calories	
Protein 6 gr.	Carb. 34 gr.
Fat 0 gr.	Cal. from fat 0%
Chol. 2 mg.	Sodium 116 mg.

Bavarian Cream

3/4 cup pure maple syrup
1 cup skim milk ricotta cheese
1 1/2 cups nonfat plain yogurt
1 tsp. vanilla
2 tsp. unflavored gelatin
4 tsp. water

Mix maple syrup, ricotta cheese, yogurt and vanilla in blender. Whip until smooth, then empty into a large bowl.

Gently stir gelatin into water. Heat water slowly to dissolve gelatin.

Stir 1 Tbsp. of cheese and yogurt mixture into the warmed gelatin mixture. Stir in the remaining cheese and yogurt mixture until smooth. Chill overnight. Serve as a wonderful topping for fruit and other desserts.

Makes 15 servings, 1/4 cup each.

Per Serving: 76 Calories	
Protein 3 gr.	Carb. 12 gr.
Fat 0 gr.	Cal. from fat 0 %
Chol. 6 mg.	Sodium 62 mg.

Phyllo Tower

A beautiful way to serve Bavarian Cream or frozen sorbet is in a pastry tower.

To make, wrap a strip of aluminum foil around an 8-oz. can of tomato juice. Spray foil lightly with cooking spray. Cut phyllo sheets into 2 1/2-inch widths and wrap sheets around foil, spraying each piece with more cooking spray. Take foil and dough off can and place on baking sheet. Repeat process to make 4 foil towers. Bake at 375 degrees for about 10 minutes or until browned. Let cool and remove foil.

Berry Banana Sundae

Cinnamon Tortilla Chips

2 burrito-sized, fat-free flour tortillas
2 tsp. cinnamon

Preheat oven to 400 degrees.

Cut tortillas into thin strips. Sprinkle the tortillas with cinnamon. Bake until crisp and lightly browned, about 3 minutes.

Makes 20 long strips; 2 strips per serving.

Berry Banana Sundae

3 oz. scoop (1/3 cup) fat-free frozen vanilla yogurt
3 oz. scoop (1/3 cup) orange sorbet
2 Tbsp. raspberry pourable fruit (purchased)
4 fresh berries
3 orange sections
1/2 banana, cut lengthwise and into quarters
2 Cinnamon Tortilla Chips

Put yogurt and sorbet scoops into sundae glass. Top with sauce and fruit. Stand bananas on end against sides of glass.

Garnish with fruit and tortilla chips.

Serves 1.

Per Serving: 153 Calories	
Protein 3 gr.	Carb. 35 gr.
Fat 0 gr.	Cal. from fat 0%
Chol. 0 mg.	Sodium 60 mg.

Freshly fruited desserts are a sweet treat, anytime of the year. To serve them with flair, use the serving bowls nature provides:

- *1/2 pineapple (sliced lengthwise, keeping the leaves intact)*
- *1/2 cantaloupe (scoop out the seeds and some melon)*
- *A large navel orange (slice off the top and scoop out the pulp)*
- *Bibb, green or red leaf lettuce leaves (serve as bed for fruit)*

Fruit Finales

Warm Pears in Raspberry Sauce

1/2 cup seedless raspberry all-fruit spread
1 cup apple juice
2 tsp. grated lemon peel
2 Tbsp. lemon juice
3 firm bosc pears, peeled and cut into quarters

Mix all ingredients except pears in a 10-inch skillet. Add pears. Heat to boiling; reduce heat to medium-low. Simmer, uncovered, 30 minutes, spooning juice mixture over pears, and turning every 10 minutes until pears are tender.

Serve warm or chilled.

Makes 6 servings.

Per Serving: 84 Calories	
Protein 0 gr.	Carb. 21 gr.
Fat 0 gr.	Cal. from fat 0%
Chol. 0 mg.	Sodium 16 mg.

Basket of Fresh Fruit

4 Wonton Cups
1 cup mixed fresh berries
4 oz. (or 1/2 cup) blueberries
2 kiwifruit, peeled and sliced
2 peaches, sliced
1 cup Strawberry Sauce (pg. 49)
1/4 cup peach pourable fruit (purchased)

Place baked Wonton Cup on its side on plate and fill with one-fourth of the mixed berries. Arrange one-fourth of the other fruits around plate. Drizzle with one-fourth of the remaining strawberry sauce. Dot side of plate with one-fourth of the peach syrup. Repeat for remaining Wonton Cups and fruit.

Serves 4.

Per Serving: 141 Calories	
Protein 1 gr.	Carb. 35 gr.
Fat 0 gr.	Cal. from fat 0 %
Chol. 0 mg.	Sodium 34 mg.

Wonton Cups

6 wonton skins (purchased)

Spray a muffin pan with cooking spray. Place a wonton skin inside each muffin well, making sure all sides are covered.

Bake on very low heat (225 degrees) for 4-6 minutes until lightly browned.

Serves 6.

Per Serving: 24 Calories	
Protein 1 gr.	Carb. 5 gr.
Fat 0 gr.	Cal. from fat 0 %
Chol. 0 mg.	Sodium 26 mg.

Bosc pears are perfect for poaching since they hold up well to heat. Firm Anjou pears can also be used. Remember — the sweeter and riper the pear, the sweeter the dessert.

Help pears ripen by placing them in a brown paper bag — with a banana. The banana releases a gas that naturally sweetens the fruit. Pears are ripe when slightly soft around stem end. Refrigerate and use them within 3 to 5 days.

Peach Crisp

Luscious peaches topped with a nutty, crunchy topping and vanilla bean yogurt speak to us of summer, yet warm us in the winter. It's a scrumptious end to any meal.

Peach Delights

Peach Crisp

10 medium peaches, sliced (or 4 cans, 15 1/2 oz. each, unsweetened sliced peaches)*
3/4 cup golden raisins
3 Tbsp. canola oil
3 Tbsp. honey
1 cup old-fashioned oats, uncooked
1/2 tsp. allspice
1 tsp. cinnamon
1/4 tsp. salt
1/3 cup whole wheat pastry flour
2 Tbsp. walnuts
1/2 cup unsweetened white grape juice
* ***may substitute sliced apples. Then bake for 40 to 45 minutes.***

Preheat oven to 375 degrees.

Spread half of peaches in a large rectangular pan; top with raisins. Heat together the oil and honey. Add oats, allspice, cinnamon, salt, flour and walnuts. Crumble half of this mixture onto the peaches in the pan. Cover with remaining peaches and the rest of topping. Pour grape juice over the top.

Bake uncovered for 25 minutes.

Makes 12 servings.

Per Serving: 158 Calories	
Protein 2.5 gr.	Carb. 28 gr.
Fat 4 gr.	Cal. from fat 23%
Chol. 0 mg.	Sodium 46 mg.

Gingered Peach Melba

1/2 cup all-fruit raspberry spread
2 Tbsp. orange juice
1/2 tsp. ground ginger
4 ripe peaches, cut in half and pitted (or canned, unsweetened)
4 gingersnaps, crushed

Preheat oven to 425 degrees.

In a small microwavable bowl, whisk together all-fruit spread, orange juice and ginger. Microwave for 2 to 3 minutes until thinned.

Place the peaches, cut side up, in a shallow 1-quart baking dish. Pour the gingered jam over the peaches and sprinkle with gingersnap crumbs. Bake for 15 to 20 minutes or until the peaches are tender when pierced with a knife and the syrup has thickened. Serve warm or at room temperature, with the sauce spooned over.

Serves 4.

Per Serving: 123 Calories	
Protein 1 gr.	Carb. 27 gr.
Fat 1 gr.	Cal. from fat 7%
Chol. 0 mg.	Sodium 54 mg.

If a recipe doesn't rely on sugar for texture (like certain cakes and cookies), I have tried to eliminate or replace sugar with concentrated fruit juices, applesauce, pureed bananas, prunes or apricots.

I also sometimes replace sugar with honey or maple syrup. These are not perfectly healthy substitutions — they are still forms of sugar. The benefit is that they have a higher sweetness concentration so a smaller quantity may be used. For example, 1/4 cup honey or maple syrup or 1/2 cup dried fruit puree will give the sweetness of 1 cup sugar; the addition of cinnamon or vanilla will enhance the sweetness of the dessert even more.

Sweet Endings

EIGHTEEN CHOICES

Withdraw from sweets long enough to allow your blood sugar levels to stabilize and your energy and proper appetite for good foods to return. Choose fruit and desserts that are sweetened without sugar, to satisfy your natural desire for a sweet taste.

Learning to enjoy foods with a lighter touch of sweetness and letting your taste buds change will transform your eating habits. Taste buds do change, but it takes time (about eight weeks). It's not easy, but it's worth it!

Beware of the tidal wave of sugar-free, fat-free desserts on the market. Usually the sugar has only been replaced with chemicals. These sweet treats will keep your taste buds from changing and leave you craving and desiring the "real thing."

Pleasing Pies

Strawberry Yogurt Pie

1 can (20 oz.) unsweetened, crushed pineapple
1 envelope unflavored gelatin
1 1/2 cups nonfat plain yogurt
3 Tbsp. honey
2 tsp. lemon juice
1 tsp. vanilla
1 cup fresh strawberries
1 cup ripe mashed bananas

Drain pineapple, reserving juice. Set fruit aside. If needed, add unsweetened apple or white grape juice to reserved juice to make 3/4 cup. Pour into saucepan. Add gelatin and heat, stirring to allow gelatin to dissolve. Remove from heat and chill until partially set (like the consistency of unbeaten egg whites). Whip partially set gelatin with electric mixture till fluffy.

Set aside 1/3 cup pineapple and 3 whole strawberries.

Slice remaining strawberries. Mix together yogurt, honey, lemon juice and vanilla. Fold in remaining pineapple, sliced strawberries and mashed banana. Fold into whipped gelatin mixture and pour into cooled Healthy Graham Crust. Chill until firm.

Cut remaining strawberries and use with reserved pineapple as garnish just before serving.

Makes 8 servings.

Per Serving: 165 Calories	
Protein 4 gr.	Carb. 36 gr.
Fat 1.5 gr.	Cal. from fat 8%
Chol. 3 mg.	Sodium 102 mg.

Healthy Graham Crust

2 Tbsp. reduced-calorie light butter
2 Tbsp. apricot all-fruit spread
3/4 cup fine graham cracker crumbs
1/3 cup Grape-Nuts cereal
1 tsp. cinnamon
1 Tbsp. brown sugar

Preheat oven to 375 degrees.

Spray a 9-inch pie plate with cooking spray. Set aside.

In a small saucepan, heat the butter and fruit spread just until melted.

In a medium bowl, stir together the cracker crumbs, cereal, cinnamon and sugar. Drizzle in the butter-fruit mixture. Using a fork, stir until well mixed.

Transfer the crumb mixture to the prepared pie plate. Using the back of a large spoon, press the crumb mixture firmly in the bottom and up the sides of the pie plate. Bake for 5 to 7 minutes or until the edges are lightly browned. Cool on a wire rack before filling.

Makes 1 pie crust; 8 servings.

Per Serving: 101 Calories	
Protein 1 gr.	Carb. 20 gr.
Fat 2 gr.	Cal. from fat 18%
Chol. 2 mg.	Sodium 52 mg.

Pleasing Pies (continued)

Raisin Pie

1 box (15½ oz.) raisins
2¼ cups water
2 Tbsp. cornstarch
2 tsp. grated orange rind
¼ tsp. salt
2 Tbsp. orange juice
3 Tbsp. finely chopped walnuts
Phyllo Pastry Shell

Preheat oven to 350 degrees.

Boil raisins in 2 cups water for 5 minutes. Mix cornstarch into remaining ¼ cup cold water and add to raisins. Boil 1 minute more until thickened. Add remaining ingredients and pour into prepared pastry shell. Bake for 30 minutes.

Makes 10 servings.

Per Serving: 137 Calories	
Protein 0 gr.	Carb. 32 gr.
Fat 1 gr.	Cal. from fat 6%
Chol. 0 mg.	Sodium 58 mg.

Phyllo Pastry Shell

1 package frozen phyllo dough

Preheat oven to 375 degrees.

Cut three sheets of phyllo dough in half to make 6 squares. Drape one square across a 9-inch pie plate. Press the phyllo into the plate and fold the overhanging edge toward the center, crumpling it slightly to fit. Lightly spray the dough with cooking spray. Repeat layering and spraying with the remaining squares. Bake for 4 to 6 minutes or until golden brown.

Makes 1 pastry shell, 8 servings.

Per Serving: 8 Calories	
Protein 0 gr.	Carb. 2 gr.
Fat 0 gr.	Cal. from fat 0%
Chol. 0 mg.	Sodium 26 mg.

Pumpkin Pie

Brown sugar topping:
¼ cup packed brown sugar
¼ cup quick-cooking oats
1 Tbsp. reduced-calorie light butter
1 can (16 oz.) pumpkin
1 can (12 oz.) evaporated skim milk
3 egg whites (or ½ cup egg substitute)
⅓ cup sugar
½ cup all-purpose flour
1½ tsp. pumpkin pie spice
¾ tsp. baking powder
⅛ tsp. salt
2 tsp. grated orange peel

Preheat oven to 350 degrees.

Prepare brown sugar topping by mixing the brown sugar, oats and butter together in a bowl. Set aside.

Spray 10-inch pie plate with cooking spray. Place remaining ingredients in blender or food processor in order listed. Cover and blend until smooth. Pour into pie plate. Sprinkle with topping.

Bake 50 to 55 minutes or until knife inserted in center comes out clean. Cool 15 minutes. Refrigerate about 4 hours or until chilled.

Makes 8 servings.

Per Serving: 157 Calories	
Protein 6 gr.	Carb. 32 gr.
Fat less than 1 gr.	Cal. from fat 3%
Chol. 3 mg.	Sodium 144 mg.

Phyllo (also known as filo) is tissue-thin pastry dough. It's found in boxes in the frozen foods section at most supermarkets. Once opened, use phyllo within a few days.

Phyllo can be kept frozen for up to one year. Thaw frozen dough overnight in the refrigerator, and do not refreeze — it will become dry and brittle. It will also become dry and brittle if you don't work quickly, so don't remove it from its wrapping until you're ready to go. And, keep those sheets you're not working on covered with wax paper topped by a damp cloth — it will keep it much more manageable. Just don't get the phyllo damp — it will become a soggy mess.

Pleasing Pies (continued)

A great dessert, to truly satisfy, must have a definite taste and texture, and it must be moist. With these criteria met, you can have one relatively small slice and be fulfilled. From a nourishment point of view, I also like the dessert to contain much more than empty sugar and white flour calories.

In making over a traditional dessert with healthy possibilities, I always attempt to replace at least a portion of the white flour with whole wheat pastry flour. This adds an extra boost of nutrients, yet is still low in gluten. I also try to replace butter or margarine for lesser amounts of canola oil, the heart-healthy monounsaturated fat.

Spiced Apple Cobbler Pie

2 tsp. fresh lemon juice
2 cups coarsely chopped apples
3 Tbsp. frozen apple juice concentrate, thawed
1/2 tsp. cinnamon
1 tsp. apple pie spice
1 cup whole wheat pastry flour
1/2 cup sugar
2 tsp. baking powder
4 egg whites, lightly beaten
1 tsp. vanilla
1/2 cup chopped walnuts

Preheat oven to 325 degrees.

Lightly spray a square baking pan with cooking spray; set aside. Sprinkle the lemon juice over the apples, then add frozen juice concentrate, cinnamon and apple pie spice and toss gently until coated. Set aside.

In a large bowl, stir together the flour, sugar and baking powder. Then stir in the egg whites and vanilla. Add the apple mixture and walnuts (the mixture will be thick).

Transfer the mixture to the prepared baking pan. Bake about 35 minutes or until golden brown.

Makes 8 servings.

Per Serving: 149 Calories	
Protein 4 gr.	Carb. 28 gr.
Fat 2.5 gr.	Cal. from fat 15%
Chol. 0 mg.	Sodium 113 mg.

Summertime Fruit Pizza

1 burrito-sized fat-free flour tortilla
cinnamon
4 oz. fat-free cream cheese
1/4 cup honey
1 tsp. vanilla
1/4 cup fat-free ricotta cheese
3 kiwi, peeled and sliced
1 cup strawberries, sliced
1 peach or nectarine, sliced
1/4 cup all-fruit apricot spread, warmed

Preheat oven to 375 degrees.

Spray a pizza pan with cooking spray. Place on tortilla; sprinkle lightly with cinnamon. Bake about 4 to 5 minutes until edges begin to lightly brown. Remove from oven and cool.

Beat together the cream cheese, honey and vanilla, then beat in the ricotta cheese till smooth. Spread the cheese mixture atop the cooled crust. Arrange the kiwi, strawberries and peaches on top, slightly overlapping. Chill in the refrigerator while preparing glaze.

Microwave the apricot spread in a small microwavable bowl on high for 1 minute. Using a clean pastry brush, brush the glaze over the fruit. Chill 1 hour before serving.

Makes 6 servings.

Per Serving: 124 Calories	
Protein 3 gr.	Carb. 28 gr.
Fat less than 1 gr.	Cal. from fat 3%
Chol. 0 mg.	Sodium 53 mg.

Delicious Cheesecake

Chocolate Marble Cheesecake

1 cup Yogurt Cheese (see right column)
$1^{1}/_{2}$ cups reduced-fat chocolate graham cracker crumbs
3 Tbsp. apricot all-fruit spread, melted
1 cup skim milk ricotta cheese
4 egg whites
1 pkg. (8 oz.) light cream cheese
1 Tbsp. unbleached flour
1 tsp. vanilla
$^{1}/_{2}$ cup sugar
$^{1}/_{4}$ cup unsweetened Dutch-process cocoa
1 tsp. almond extract

Preheat oven to 350 degrees.

Prepare yogurt cheese; set aside. Coat a 9-inch springform pan with cooking spray. In a bowl, mix graham cracker crumbs and all-fruit spread. Lightly press crumb mixture into bottom of pan. Bake for 8 minutes. Set aside. Increase oven temperature to 375 degrees.

Process ricotta cheese in a food processor until almost smooth. Add egg whites and process until smooth. Add Yogurt Cheese, cream cheese, flour, half of sugar and vanilla. Process until a smooth batter forms. Pour half of filling into a bowl. Add cocoa, remaining sugar and almond extract. Stir until well combined.

Alternately pour batters, half of each at a time, into crust. Gently swirl batters with a spatula.

Bake until a knife inserted in center comes out clean, 35 to 40 minutes. Cool on wire rack for 15 minutes. Run a knife blade around the edge of pan. Cool for 30 minutes. Remove side from pan. Cool completely. Chill for at least 4 hours.

Cut into 12 slices.

Per Serving: 100 Calories	
Protein 6 gr.	Carb. 17 gr.
Fat 1 gr.	Cal. from fat 9%
Chol. 1 mg.	Sodium 69 mg.

Orange-Blueberry Cheesecake

3 cups Yogurt Cheese (see right column)
5 gingersnaps, crushed
2 packages (8 oz. each) fat-free cream cheese
$^{1}/_{2}$ cup sugar
$^{1}/_{4}$ cup egg substitute (or 2 eggs)
4 egg whites
2 Tbsp. frozen orange juice concentrate, thawed
1 Tbsp. grated orange rind
1 tsp. orange extract
$^{1}/_{2}$ cup blueberry all-fruit spread

Preheat oven to 350 degrees.

Prepare Yogurt Cheese; set aside. Spray a 10-inch springform pan with cooking spray. Sprinkle crushed gingersnaps evenly over bottom of pan.

Blend cream cheese and sugar in food processor until light and fluffy. Add Yogurt Cheese and process until smooth. Add egg substitute, egg whites, orange juice concentrate, orange rind and orange extract. Process until mixture is well blended.

Spoon mixture over crushed gingersnaps. Bake for 35 minutes (center will be soft but firm when chilled). Remove from oven, and let cool to room temperature on a wire rack. Cover and chill 4 hours or until set.

Spread blueberry all-fruit spread evenly over top of cheesecake. Cover and chill 1 hour.

Makes 14 servings.

Per Serving: 117 Calories	
Protein 8 gr.	Carb. 19 gr.
Fat 0 gr.	Cal. from fat 0%
Chol. 2 mg.	Sodium 93 mg.

Yogurt Cheese

Low-fat yogurt cheese is easy to make and has a rich, creamy consistency that's just right for making cheesecakes, dips and spreads. To make yogurt cheese, simply line a strainer with cheesecloth and spoon in nonfat plain yogurt (with active cultures). Place the strainer over a deep bowl and refrigerate for 24 hours. Two cups of yogurt make $1^{1}/_{2}$ cups of cheese.

Angel Food Celebration

Sometimes dessert takes on a higher calling, the focus of the event itself. This festive offering of angel food cake filled and topped with tropical fruits and sorbets will bring oohs and aahs, as well as delight, whether it's topped with birthday candles or is simply a stand-up finish to a very special meal.

Angel Food Celebration Cake

1 10-inch Angel Food Cake*
1/2 pt. frozen mango sorbet
1/2 pt. frozen raspberry sorbet
1/2 pt. fat-free frozen vanilla yogurt
1 mango, peeled and sliced
1 cup raspberries
2 cups strawberries, halved
1/4 cup Strawberry Sauce (pg. 49)
* ***You may use your favorite recipe or buy a prepared mix and follow package directions.***

Cut cake horizontally to make 2 layers. (To split, mark side of cake with toothpicks and cut with long, thin serrated knife.)

Immediately before serving, top bottom layer with alternating scoops of half the sorbets and frozen yogurt. (Work quickly — it melts!) Sprinkle with half of the sliced fruits. Place top layer of cake firmly on the bottom layer, then top with rounded scoops of remaining frozen products and sprinkle with remaining fruit.

Drizzle sauce over all.

Makes 12 servings.

Per Serving: 143 Calories	
Protein 2 gr.	Carb. 25 gr.
Fat 1 gr.	Cal. from fat 1%
Chol. 0 mg.	Sodium 190 mg.

Brandied Pound Cake

1/2 cup strained apricot baby food (or 1/2 cup dried apricots, pureed with a little apple juice as needed until smooth)
1/2 cup canola oil
1 cup sugar
1 1/2 cups egg substitute (or 6 eggs)
8 oz. fat-free cream cheese, softened
1/2 cup apricot brandy or nectar
1 tsp. rum extract
2 tsp. vanilla
1 tsp. orange extract
1 Tbsp. freshly squeezed lemon juice
2 cups cake flour
1 cup whole wheat pastry flour
1 tsp. baking soda
1 tsp. baking powder
1/2 tsp. salt

Preheat oven to 325 degrees.

In a large mixing bowl, beat together apricot baby food and canola oil. Gradually add sugar, beating until creamy. Slowly add egg substitute while continuing to beat. Add softened cream cheese, brandy, extracts and lemon juice. Stir well.

In a separate bowl, combine flours, baking soda, baking powder and salt. Add the cream cheese mixture. Stir by hand until just blended. Pour batter into a 10-inch tube pan sprayed with cooking spray. Bake 1 hour and 20 minutes or until a toothpick inserted in the center comes out clean. Cool.

Serves 20.

Per Serving: 161 Calories	
Protein 4 gr.	Carb. 25 gr.
Fat 5 gr.	Cal. from fat 27%
Chol. 0 mg.	Sodium 130 mg.

In a traditional cake, oil and eggs are the major players that interact with baking powder and baking soda to provide the cake's texture.

These are the changes I make that allow healthy modifications without compromising the flavor or texture: I replace whole eggs with liquid egg substitute or egg whites; I cut the amount of fat in half and change it to a monounsaturated oil; and I replace the missing half of the fat with a fruit puree like bananas, apricots, prunes and apples. I double the spices and flavorings since there is less fat to distribute the flavors.

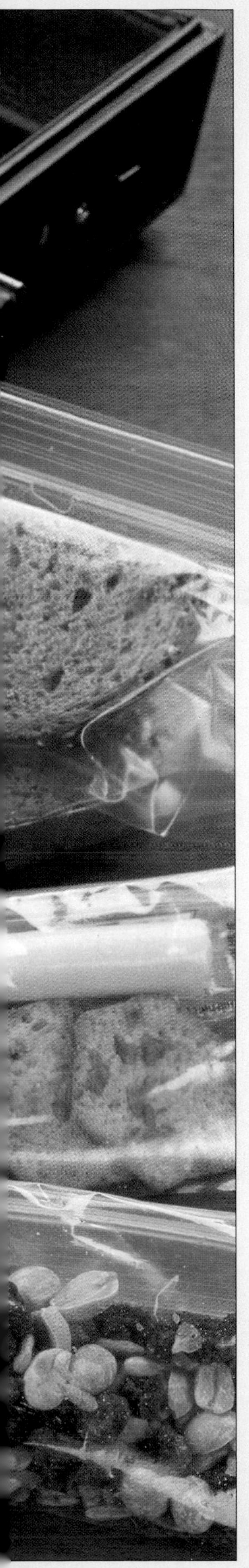

Making the Real Life the Good Life

PRACTICAL HELPS

Life in the nineties can be super — and super-stressful — all at the same time. We seem to be caught with too much to do and too little time in which to do it. We must make responsible choices in all the arenas of our lives — relationally, professionally, financially, politically — yet often we have little control over all of the factors or the outcome.

If this is the story of your life, you're a person who needs a continuous supply of nutritious food to meet those never-ceasing demands. You need the right foods at the right time in the right balance just to survive, let alone thrive, in the midst of stress.

The stresses of living life in the fast lane make your body respond as if your life were threatened. It reads your stress as a danger signal — and it sets off automatic chemical reactions within your body to prepare you to flee from or fight this present danger.

Pictured: Nonrefrigerated snacks (pg. 172)

These chemical reactions result in many of the maladies of life at the close of this century: fatigue, obesity, ulcers and gastrointestinal distress, high levels of cholesterol and triglycerides, raging hormones, migraines — even depression.

Couple these reactions with the reality that most of us are underfed and underfueled, that we push our bodies through the day without food much like pushing a car up a hill without gasoline, and it's not hard to understand why we are overcome with the stresses of life. More than likely we are too busy or too tired to do anything about it.

Making the Real Life the Good Life

PRACTICAL HELPS

The hope I want to give you is this: We all have bodies that are power plants, capable of producing more than enough energy to do just about anything that we want to do and then some. But certain aspects of our lifestyle block our ability to live better, and we're letting energy stores leak out unused.

Join with me as we navigate through these troubled waters of busy lives and learn how to answer the "what abouts" that get us off the course of wellness and often leave us shipwrecked. Learn how to make the real life the good life.

Alive and Well in the Fast Lane

Don't be caught without the fuel you need to go — learn the art of power snacking. I talked about the benefits of mini-meals on page 9. Take the word to heart: You need it!

Don't let your body go the distance without giving it the best; go for energy-boosting combos. Many don't need refrigeration (see chart), so even the road warrior can keep them available at all times — in a desk drawer, a briefcase, a suitcase or even a glove compartment.

Dining Out

New research shows that America spends 40 percent of its food dollars dining away from home; dining out is no longer just for special occasions. For the health-conscious, dining out presents a culinary challenge: to enjoy fine food without compromising health.

The health dangers of dining out lie mostly in the hidden fats; the typical restaurant meal will give the equivalent of twelve to fourteen pats of butter! Never be timid about ordering foods in a special style. You are paying (and paying well!) for the meal and the service, and you deserve to have foods prepared to your preference. Learn to be discriminating, not intimidated!

A Discriminating Guide

Plan ahead. When you're in charge, choose a restaurant that you know and trust for quality food and a willingness to prepare foods in a healthful way upon request. More and more restaurants recognize that this trend toward healthy eating is not a passing fad; many progressive and responsible restaurants have begun to offer healthy menu selections. Supporting these restaurants will help to establish this tremendous service to the discerning diner.

Read between the lines. Think before you order. Menus are filled with clues about what the selections contain. Avoid these words:

- à la mode (with ice cream)
- au fromage (with cheese)

NON-REFRIGERATED FOODS FOR SNACKS AND MINI-MEALS

Complex Carbohydrates

Whole wheat bread or pita rounds
Rice cakes or Wasa bread
Harvest Crisp crackers
Guiltless Gourmet No-Oil Tortilla Chips or Baked Tostitos
Whole grain cereals *(shredded wheat, muesli, Nutri-Grain, Raisin Squares)*

Proteins

Laughing Cow Light cheese *(doesn't need refrigeration)*
Weight Watchers skim milk in boxes *(also no refrigeration)*
Natural peanut butter
Trail mix *(pg. 10)*
Pop-top cans of tuna *(water-packed)* and chicken
Guiltless Gourmet or Jardine's fat-free bean dips

Simple Carbohydrates

Small boxes of raisins
Dried apricots
boxes of unsweetened juices *(no sugar added)*

- au gratin (in cheese sauce)
- au lait (with milk)
- basted (with extra fat)
- bisque (cream soup)
- buttered (with extra fat)
- casserole (in some type of cream sauce)
- creamed (in extra fat)
- crispy (fried)
- escalloped (with cream sauce)
- hash (with extra fat)
- hollandaise (with cream sauce)
- pan-fried (in fat)
- sautéed (fried with extra fat)

If you see these words in the description of an appealing entrée, be bold enough to ask for the entrée prepared in a special way. If the description says "buttered," ask for it without the added butter. If the description says "pan-fried," ask for it grilled or poached instead. Entrées poached in wine or lemon juice are good choices, as are those simmered in tomato sauce. A baked potato or a side of pasta with red sauce is often a better choice than rice pilaf, which is prepared in oil.

Ask questions. Remember — it's your health, your money and your waistline. If you have concerns about the way something will be prepared, discuss it kindly with the server. Don't be intimidated by the server or the people you are with.

Make special requests. Learn to say "on the side" and "no butter." Even though not stated on the menu, most foods will be prepared with fat, and more will be added before it is served to you. Ask for your salad dressing "on the side" (then apply sparingly; add extra lemon juice or vinegar for moistness). Order meats, fish or poultry broiled or grilled without butter and with sauces on the side. When fresh vegetables are available, ask for them steamed without butter. If you order a baked potato, ask for it without butter or with sour cream; request salsa, cottage cheese or mustard to the side.

Monitor extra fats. Watch for the pats of butter, the cream in coffee, and the whipped cream on desserts. If the restaurant brings bread and rolls to the table, ask them to remove the butter (if no one in your party objects!). It's too easy to find yourself spreading that roll liberally with butter. Good crusty rolls really don't need the extra fat, especially when they are heated. The heat brings out natural flavor and makes them more satisfying. When the dessert tray comes by, ask for fresh berries (a much healthier choice than mousse).

Controlling Portions

As an adult there are no rewards for cleaning your plate. Restaurant portions can be huge; yet we often eat them. Many restaurants are answering the cry of "too much" by offering luncheon options at dinnertime. You have other choices: Smaller appetizer selections are often just right and make a fine meal with an à la carte salad.

Try ordering one meal (and an extra plate) to share. And don't forget "take home." You can enjoy what's left as an elegant lunch the next day.

Never eat "all you can eat" at brunches, buffets or covered-dish dinners — affairs that can easily become feeding frenzies! Instead, revise your perspective from "I need to get my money's worth" to "Look at all I have to choose from."

Healthful Dining Strategies

Let's look at the good and bad qualities of various cuisines and restaurants. Think about this information as you consider the good life when eating out.

Breakfast Out:

If you buy breakfast later than usual, eat a snack when you first get up to gear up your metabolism and begin to stabilize your body.

Order unbuttered whole wheat toast, then add one teaspoon, if desired.

Grits may be substituted for a serving of bread, but be sure to order them unbuttered.

It's usually safer to order à la carte so you are not paying for, or being tempted by, the abundance of unhealthy food in the "breakfast specials" or buffets.

Be bold and creative. Rather than accepting French toast with syrup and bacon, ask for it prepared with whole wheat bread, no syrup and a side dish of fresh berries or fruit. Many restaurants will substitute cottage cheese or an egg for the breakfast meat.

Many restaurants serve oatmeal and cereal even though it's not on the menu. It's a nice whole grain carbohydrate. Don't forget to ask for low-fat milk or yogurt, and top it with fresh berries or a banana.

Always look for a protein and a carbohydrate — more than a Danish!

Healthy Choices:

- cereal with skim milk and fruit
- French toast (with whole wheat bread) and berries
- fresh fruit with cottage cheese or yogurt and whole wheat toast
- fresh vegetable egg-white omelet and toast
- scrambled egg substitute and unbuttered whole wheat toast

Dining Out:

Italian

Portion control is very important here. Although pasta with red sauce is a relatively low-fat choice, a plateful is five times too much! Order a side portion or an appetizer serving of pasta with steamed seafood or grilled chicken or fish.

Alfredo sauce is deadly, as is any white sauce. Ask for red sauce substitution.

Garlic bread sticks are rolled in butter, then garlic. Special order without butter, and you'll receive them straight from the oven!

Warning words: Alfredo, cheese sauce, cream sauce, fried, pancetta, parmigiana, prosciutto, saltimbocca, white sauce.

Healthy Choices:

- cioppino (seafood soup) or minestrone
- clams, mussels or scallops linguine with red sauce
- grilled chicken with pasta marinara
- grilled fresh fish with pasta marinara
- pasta e fagioli and salad

Mexican

Ask that your salad be brought in place of the chips. It will help stop the munch-a-bunch syndrome.

Beware of margaritas. They are loaded with salt and sugar — to say nothing of the alcohol.

Order à la carte; whole meal selections are laden with high-fat side dishes, such as refried beans (often made with pure lard).

Ask that the sour cream and cheese be omitted from your dish. The cheese is a high-fat cheese with ten grams of fat per ounce.

Ask for guacamole on the side; two tablespoons contain the fat of a pat of butter.

Never, never eat the fried tortilla shells that contain Mexican salads. Think of them as inedible, hard plastic bowls. They are sponges for the grease they are cooked in.

Warning words: chimichangas, chorizo, con queso, fried, guacamole, served in a tortilla shell, shredded cheese, sour cream, tortilla chips.

Healthy Choices:

- black bean soup or gazpacho
- chicken burrito or tostada
- chicken enchiladas
- chicken fajitas (without added fat)
- chili with salad
- soft chicken tacos

Oriental

Chinese, Korean, Thai or Vietnamese food is an excellent choice for dining out, as stir-frying is the main method of cooking. This terrific technique cooks the vegetables quickly, retaining the nutrients and using very little oil.

Order dishes lightly stir-fried (not deep-fried like egg rolls) and without heavy gravies or sweet-and-sour sauces.

Half a dinner portion is appropriate, with steamed brown or white rice. (Fried rice is just that — fried!)

Ask for food prepared *without* MSG and be careful with the soy sauce you add. (Both are loaded with sodium!)

Order sushi only at highly reputable restaurants that serve the freshest fish from the best sources.

Warning words: deep-fried, battered, fried, crispy, cashews, fried noodles, duck, bird's nest, tempura, tonkatsu (fried pork), torikatsu (fried chicken).

Healthy Choices:

- bamboo-steamed vegetables with scallops, chicken or whole steamed fish
- moo goo gai pan (no MSG, little oil)
- tofu with vegetables (no MSG, little oil)
- udon (noodles) served with meat and vegetables
- wonton, hot and sour, or miso soup
- yakitori (meats broiled on skewers)

Seafood

Order fresh seafood when possible — steamed, boiled, grilled or broiled without butter. For dipping, a small amount of cocktail sauce is a better choice than butter (two dips in butter = fifty calories). When fried, small seafood items such as shrimp and oysters are deadly in terms of fat and calories; the surface area is high, more breading adheres, absorbing more fat. All seafood can be low-fat and low-sodium if grilled *without butter* and served without sauces.

Healthy Choices:

- fresh fish of the day (grilled or poached, without butter, sauce to the side)
- lobster, crab meat, crab claws
- mesquite-grilled shrimp
- scallops (grilled or broiled without butter)
- seafood kabobs (grilled without butter)
- steamed clams, mussels, oysters or shrimp

Steak Houses

As with Italian restaurants, portion control is the key here. A 16-ounce steak or prime rib will give you five times more protein than needed. Order the smallest cut available (often a petite-cut fillet), and don't hesitate to take some home! You may do well to cut off an appropriate portion and separate it from the other on your plate. (Try this before you begin to eat, when control is at its highest!)

Remember always to have a complex carbohydrate and a protein source, never just meat and salad alone. Your carbohydrate may be a roll, a side of pasta or a baked potato.

Healthy Choices:

- charbroiled shrimp (grilled without butter)
- Hawaiian or marinated, grilled chicken breast
- petite-cut fillet
- shish-kabob or brochette (grilled without butter)
- slices of London broil (no sauces or gravies)

Fast-Food Restaurants

Just say no to sauces: It's the mayonnaise, special sauces and sour cream that triple the fat, sodium and calories in fast foods; always order your food without them! And undress your salad; a single packet of regular dressing can contain as much fat as a double cheeseburger.

Shun the cheese. The varieties commonly used by the fast-food chains are high in fat, cholesterol and calories.

Stuffed potatoes may seem a healthy addition to the fast-food menu, but not with the cheese sauces they hold — often the equivalent to nine pats of butter per potato! Try chili or broccoli and salsa instead.

Chicken is a lower-fat alternative to beef, but not when it's batter-fried. One serving of chicken nuggets has twice the fat of a regular hamburger. A chicken sandwich is no health package either. This greasy sandwich has enough fat to equal eleven pats of butter. The new grilled chicken sandwiches are much better, as long as you order them without the dressing and sauces.

Salad bars are a good way to add fiber and nutrients, but only the salad vegetables do so. Leave the mayonnaise-based salads, croutons and bacon bits on the bar. Add extra lemon juice or vinegar for moistness.

Croissant sandwiches aren't a whole lot more than breakfast on a grease bun. Most croissants have the fat equivalent of more than four and a half pats of butter, and the toppings add insult to injury!

Frozen yogurt, although lower in fat and cholesterol, contains more sugar than ice cream. It is not a perfectly healthy substitute.

Don't get discouraged and think you can't ever eat fast food and still be healthy. You can still have a healthy fast-food meal; the goal is to learn to make wise choices. Learn what and how to order fast food. Here is a guide to help you:

Burger King

Healthiest Choices:

- B.K. Broiler Chicken Sandwich (without ranch dressing or mayo)
- Hamburger Deluxe (no mayo) — for women
- Whopper (no mayo) — for men

You may order a side salad with any of the above meals (with the light Italian dressing). Some Burger King restaurants have also begun to offer fresh fruit.

Worst Choices:

- Breakfast or Burger Buddies
- Chicken Sandwich
- Croissan'wich With Sausage, Egg and Cheese
- Double Whopper With Cheese
- Scrambled Egg Platter With Sausage

Chick-Fil-A

Healthiest Choices:

- Hearty Breast of Chicken Soup
- Char-grilled Chicken Salad (no-oil salad dressing)
- Char-grilled Chicken Sandwich (no mayo)

Worst Choices:

- All else

McDonald's

Healthiest Choices:

- McGrilled Chicken Classic with BBQ sauce
- Chunky Chicken Salad (with your own crackers for carbohydrate)
- Hamburger (small)
- McLean Deluxe Sandwich (no mayo)

Worst Choices:

- Big Mac
- Chicken McNuggets
- Quarter Pounder With Cheese
- Sausage Biscuit With Egg
- Sausage McMuffin With Egg

Wendy's

Healthiest Choices:

- Baked Potato (plain, without cheese sauce, with a small chili)
- Grilled Chicken Sandwich (without honey mustard; it's in a fat base); try BBQ sauce for flavor
- Grilled Chicken Salad with reduced-fat Italian dressing
- Jr. Hamburger (without mayo)
- Salad Bar (use raw vegetables as desired; avoid potato salad, macaroni salad and the like; use garbanzo beans or chili for protein) with reduced-fat Italian dressing

Worst Choices:

- Big Classic
- Crispy Chicken Nuggets
- Fish Fillet Sandwich
- Hot Stuffed Baked Potato
- Jr. Swiss Deluxe
- Pasta With Alfredo Sauce

Hardee's

Healthiest Choices:

- Chicken 'n' Pasta Salad
- Grilled Chicken Sandwich (no mayo)
- Hamburger (no mayo)

Worst Choices:

- Bacon Cheeseburger
- Big Country Breakfast With Sausage or Ham
- Big Deluxe Burger
- Fisherman's Fillet
- The Lean 1 (18 grams of fat!)
- Mushroom 'n' Swiss Burger

Taco Bell

Healthiest Choices:

- Light Taco Salad (skip the nacho chips)
- Light Chicken Burrito
- Light Chicken Soft Taco Supreme
- Light Bean Burrito

Worst Choices:

- Mexican Pizza
- Nachos BellGrande, Nachos Supreme
- Soft Taco Supreme
- Taco BellGrande
- Regular Taco Salad (61 grams of fat — 905 calories!)

Arby's or Rax

Healthiest Choices:

- Arby's Grilled Chicken BBQ Sandwich (no mayo)
- Light Rax Turkey Delight (no mayo)
- Rax Turkey (no mayo)
- Roast Beef Sandwich (no sauce!)

Pizza Places

Healthiest Choices:

- personal-sized cheese pizza, with vegetables if desired (eat three-quarters and save the remaining quarter for a snack)
- thin-crust 13-inch (medium) cheese pizza, with vegetables (no sausage or pepperoni): two slices for women; three slices for men

Worst Choices:

- thick-crust or deep-dish pizza with sausage or pepperoni

Sub Shops or Delis

Healthiest Choices:

- mini-sub (turkey, roast beef; no oil or mayo)
- 6-inch sub (turkey, roast beef, cheese; no oil or mayo)
- veggie bar and turkey club

Worst Choices:

- tuna subs — loaded with fat

Deli and grocery stores will usually make you turkey, roast beef or Jarlsberg Lite sandwiches (ask for three ounces of meat on sandwich).

Boston Market

Healthiest Choices:

- Turkey Breast Sandwich and Fruit Salad

Worst Choices:

- all else

Health or Natural Food Restaurants

Although here you will have an opportunity to get whole grains and fresh vegetable salads, the fats and sodium can still sneak in quite deceptively. Beware of sauces and high-fat cheeses smothering the foods and high-fat dressings on salads and sandwiches. Many foods are prepared as they would be at a fast-food restaurant — but with healthier-sounding names. With judicious selections, you can do well here.

The salads and salad bars may be lovely, but follow the guideline of dressing to the side, used sparingly. Many salad bars have a protein source in cottage cheese, grated cheese or chopped eggs (aim for the egg whites, not the yolk).

If you have a cheese dish, use no other added fats; the cheese will contain enough for the day. Always ask if they can use mozzarella cheese (it is almost always partly skimmed of fat).

Healthiest Choices:

- bean soup with salad (dressing on side)
- chef-type salad with whole grain roll (no ham or cheese)
- fruit plate with nonfat plain yogurt or cottage cheese and whole grain roll
- pita stuffed with vegetables and meat or mozzarella cheese
- stir-fry dish (ask for "light on the soy sauce")

Survival Tips for the Road Warrior

Are you a road warrior — spending more time on the road than at home? For you, stress takes on a whole new meaning — it's a way of life. In order to stay alive and well, there are simple steps to take to ensure that you stay energized and strong. And you can come home feeling recharged rather than drained.

Getting There

How many times have you arrived at your destination exhausted, irritable and feeling swollen and bloated? Use these tips to arrive ready-to-go:

- Drink plenty of water, especially if you fly.

A dry airplane cabin is ten times more arid than the Sahara, causing you to lose fluids through your skin. This condition can easily lead to dehydration, which results in puffy hands and ankles and a generally bloated feeling. The key for preventing this is to drink eight to twelve ounces of replacement fluids each hour you are in the air. The best fluids: water, sparkling water or club soda, and fruit juices. The worst: caffeinated drinks (coffees, teas and sodas) and alcoholic beverages; they intensify the dehydration.

- Order a special meal.

Airline food is typically high in fat and salts, and certainly not a gourmet's delight! When booking your flight, request a diabetic meal. Just have your travel agent put it in your file as a standard order, or give the airline 24-hour notice if you are purchasing a ticket on your own (there is no added charge). Frequent fliers find that these special orders are prepared with fresher and more wholesome ingredients than the usual fare.

- Wear comfortable shoes and clothing.

Maintaining a cramped sitting position for two or more hours can wreak havoc on your circulation. When flying, choose an aisle seat when possible and attempt to get up and move every hour or so. If you are driving, short stretch breaks will yield a big payoff. (Drinking all the water you need will bring reminders as well!) While you are seated, do shoulder and head rolls and periodically point and flex your feet.

While You Are There

Keep your energy level high and even by minimizing the drag on your body systems. These tips will help:

- Stick to your normal routine.

Keeping a routine is difficult for many of us when we're at home — when traveling it's even more of a challenge. As much as possible, try to get the same number of hours of sleep as you usually get, and try to eat on an even schedule. Packing snacks will help you keep eating "on the move" more feasible and will keep your lagging metabolism burning high (see pg. 172).

- Stay in shape.

At the very least, plan on taking a brisk walk every morning or afternoon. Aside from offering terrific health benefits, walking can be a great way to see the sights. Also, attempt to choose a hotel with a swimming pool or exercise facility. By having such options conveniently located, you'll be more likely to use them. Exercise also appears to play a vital role in overcoming time zone change.

- Stepping out of jet lag.

When changing time zones, your body will be able to adapt more readily if you exercise within the first twelve hours of arriving at your destination. When you fly east, walk at least one half hour in the morning sun. When you fly west, walk at least one half hour in the late afternoon sun. You may not feel up to it, but it offers big payoffs the next day.

Soul Care

Whether your trip is for a day, a weekend or a week, look for (and grab!) an opportunity to get away from the normal distractions of life. Resist the temptation to schedule every moment of your trip with activities and people. Leave some time to make significant spiritual connections.

What About Weight Loss?

One out of nine people will go on a diet, get rid of excess weight and keep it off easily. The other eight get caught in a never-ending chain of disappointing diets that lead to despair and defeat. Statistics tell us that within one year, the remaining eight people will gain back the weight they've lost.

If you're one of the frustrated eight, take heart. There's good news on the dieting front: the secrets to successful weight loss aren't such a mystery any longer. Although diets never have prevailed — and never will — on a long-term basis, a new lifestyle of health does. Success is found in being set free from the dieting mind-set.

The right perspective will put you on the path to good health. You are not denying yourself when you eat well and live well; rather, you are giving yourself a precious gift. You need to understand your habit patterns and the way your body works. Good health is part of our genetic heritage; healing and repair have been scripted into every molecule of DNA in the body. The secret is to live so that you promote that healing and repair process rather than hinder it.

You who are card-carrying members of the *diet generation* must throw out the old belief systems and learn to separate fat from fiction! Use this blunder checklist to help you identify twenty ways of thinking that belong in the trash heap, right along with those old diet books:

Weight Loss Blunders

1. Binge eating before going on a diet.
2. Fasting, or cutting calories, to lose weight. Cutting too much will send the message to your body that you are starving, and your metabolism will slow down to preserve the very fat you are trying to eliminate.
3. Skipping meals, particularly breakfast, and hoping your stomach won't notice.
4. Skipping wisely chosen snacks. Smart snacking keeps your metabolism burning high and your appetite under control.
5. Substituting coffee, tea or diet soda for energy-producing meals or snacks and pure, wonderful water.
6. Going to a salad bar — and heaping on salad dressing, cheeses, meats and pasta mixed with mayonnaise or oil.
7. Keeping the on-a-diet/off-a-diet mentality, rather than eating moderately and wisely as the norm.
8. Thinking of any food as "bad" or "forbidden" rather than simply food; it's the power it has over us that is bad.
9. Expecting to lose more than one or two pounds a week. Any more than this results in the loss of body fluids and valuable muscle tissue.
10. Neglecting to exercise regularly (at least thirty nonstop minutes, three times a week). Regular exercise is a key to an activated metabolism. It allows the body to burst out of its cocoon — gearing up our calorie- and fat-burning potential by fanning the metabolic fire.
11. Losing weight to look good for someone else.
12. Losing weight with the mind-set that when you shed unwanted pounds, you'll become a wonderful person — forgetting that you already are a wonderful person.
13. Relying on diet pills or a shake or any product promising to do the work for you.
14. Thinking of weight loss as something you *have* to do, rather than what you're choosing to do.
15. Concentrating on which foods to avoid, rather than which ones to include. Cutting fat out of your eating long term is nearly impossible without adding fiber. Because fat in food leaves you feeling satisfied when you've eaten, you need to create that same feeling of fullness, without the fat, by increasing the amount of fiber in your meals. Grains, fruits and vegetables are excellent sources of fill-you-up nutrition and are low in fat — provided they aren't swimming in butter or sauces.
16. Buying groceries, preparing foods and eating meals on the run. A frantic life-style

prevents you from enjoying and feeling satisfied with the food you do eat.

17. Considering losing excess weight as an end in itself, rather than a means to an end — a healthier, happier, more energetic and productive life.
18. Believing that all calories are created equal. They aren't: It's fat that makes you fat. It's the kind of calories you eat, more than the sheer number, that has the most impact. Calories consumed as fat are converted into fat on the body more readily than the same number of calories consumed as protein or carbohydrate.
19. Falling into the trap of using many of the fat-free foods that are often nothing more than sugar bowls and chemical brews.
20. Failing to take charge the moment you discover you have gained two pounds over your desired weight.

What About You?

What about you? Do you fall into any of these belief systems and habit patterns?

What does your eating day look like? When do you eat? Where do you eat? What do you eat, and why?

If you're serious about changing your lifestyle of eating, you may find it helpful to keep a food diary for at least two weeks. Record everything you eat and drink, the time you eat, how you are feeling and any exercise you may do, like the sample provided. Make a copy of the blank diary on pages 185-186 and complete it for yourself. Your day may surprise you!

Compare your diary to the guides to good eating on pages 181-184. These are guides for minimum portions and proper balance to achieve your desired goals for healthy living. *The Good Life* meals are designed to go along with these meal plans. Portion sizes may need some adjustment to meet your individual body needs.

Get started with this way of eating and these amounts for two weeks and allow your body to stabilize. Then make needed adjustments. The next fourteen days are a well-worth-it investment in your new, healthy lifestyle!

What About Fasting?

As a nutritionist, I am asked as many questions about wise fasting as wise eating. These are the answers I give:

- Purify your fast.

Fasting is a *physical* act of great *spiritual* significance: It is a commitment and a decision not to look to the world for physical food, but instead to look to God for spiritual food. Don't let the power that comes through fasting and prayer be nibbled away by the wrong motives: to jump-start weight loss; to lose weight quickly; or to rid the body of poisons.

Actually, research shows that going without food for prolonged periods produces many more toxins than those that come through eating; plus, the metabolism slows drastically. Fasting for our own selfish motives is quite simply starvation, with all of its detriments.

- Prepare for your fast.

Eat smaller meals and snacks every two-and-a-half to three hours the day before the fast. To increase your body's store of energy, eat extra complex carbohydrates (bread, pasta or rice) at each of these meals and snacks along with low-fat proteins. Include a bedtime snack of cereal with milk or yogurt and fruit.

- Consider your type of fast.

I recommend a juice fast for busy people desiring to fast — not citrus juices (because of the citric acid), but "soft" juices like unsweetened apple juice, Mott's apple-cranberry or white grape juice. Drink twelve ounces of juice at meal times and six ounces of juice every two hours between meals, along with two to three quarts of water evenly throughout the day. Be careful with caffeine beverages and avoid strenuous exercise.

I recommend a water fast only if a person is

("What About Fasting?" continued on page 187.)

WEIGHT LOSS MEAL PLAN FOR WOMEN

BREAKFAST

(within 1/2 hour of arising)

Complex Carbohydrate
1 slice whole wheat bread
OR 1/2 whole wheat English muffin
OR 3/4 cup cereal with raw bran added *(begin with 1 teaspoon bran, gradually increasing to 2 tablespoons)*
Protein
1 ounce part-skim cheese
OR 1/2 cup nonfat plain yogurt
OR 3/4 cup skim milk for cereal
OR 1 egg *(limit whole eggs to 3 times per week)* or 1/4 cup egg substitute
Simple Carbohydrate
1 small piece fresh fruit

MORNING SNACK

Carbohydrate
3 whole grain crackers
OR 1 small piece fresh fruit
OR 1 rice cake or Wasa bread
Protein
1 ounce part-skim cheese or lean meat
OR 1/2 cup nonfat plain yogurt mixed with 1 teaspoon all-fruit spread

LUNCH

Complex Carbohydrate
2 slices whole wheat bread
OR 1 baked potato
OR 1 whole wheat pita bread
Protein
2 ounces part-skim cheese
OR 2 ounces cooked poultry, fish or lean roast beef
OR 1/2 cup cooked legumes
Simple Carbohydrate
1 small piece fresh fruit
OR 1 cup noncreamed soup
Healthy Munchie (optional)
raw vegetable salad with no-oil salad dressing
Added Fat (optional)
1 teaspoon mayonnaise (or 1 tablespoon light mayonnaise)
OR 1 teaspoon butter or margarine
OR 1 teaspoon olive oil or canola oil
OR 1 tablespoon salad dressing

AFTERNOON SNACK

Repeat earlier snack choices.

DINNER

Complex Carbohydrate
1/2 cup rice or pasta
OR 1/2 cup starchy vegetable
Protein
2 to 3 ounces cooked chicken, turkey, fish, seafood or lean roast beef
OR 1/2 cup cooked legumes
Simple Carbohydrate
1 cup nonstarchy vegetable
OR 1 small piece fresh fruit
Healthy Munchie (optional)
raw vegetable salad with no-oil salad dressing
Added Fat (optional)
1 teaspoon butter or margarine
OR 1 teaspoon olive oil
OR 1 tablespoon salad dressing

EVENING SNACK

1 small piece fresh fruit
OR 3 cups light microwave popcorn

FREE ITEMS

raw vegetables, mustard, vinegar, lemon juice, no-oil salad dressing

WEIGHT MAINTENANCE MEAL PLAN FOR WOMEN AND WEIGHT LOSS MEAL PLAN FOR MEN

BREAKFAST

(within 1/2 hour of arising)

Complex Carbohydrate
2 slices whole wheat bread
OR 1 whole wheat English muffin
OR 1 1/2 cups cereal with raw bran added *(begin with 1 teaspoon bran, gradually increasing to 2 tablespoons)*

Protein
2 ounces part-skim cheese
OR 1 cup skim milk for cereal
OR 2 eggs *(limit whole eggs to 2 times per week)* or 1/2 cup egg substitute

Simple Carbohydrate
1 piece fresh fruit

MORNING SNACK

Carbohydrate
5 whole grain crackers
OR 1 piece fresh fruit
OR 2 rice cakes or Wasa breads

Protein
2 ounces part-skim cheese or lean meat
OR 2 tablespoons natural peanut butter *(limit peanut butter to one time per day)*
OR 1 cup nonfat plain yogurt mixed with 1 teaspoon all-fruit spread

LUNCH

Complex Carbohydrate
2 slices whole wheat bread
OR 1 baked potato
OR 1 whole wheat pita bread

Protein
3 ounces part-skim cheese
OR 3 ounces cooked poultry, fish or lean roast beef
OR 3/4 cup cooked legumes

Simple Carbohydrate
1 piece fresh fruit
OR 1 cup noncreamed soup

Healthy Munchie (optional)
raw vegetable salad with no-oil salad dressing

Added Fat (optional)
1 teaspoon mayonnaise (or 1 tablespoon light mayonnaise)
OR 1 teaspoon butter or margarine
OR 1 teaspoon olive oil or canola oil
OR 1 tablespoon salad dressing

AFTERNOON SNACK

Repeat earlier snack choices
OR 1/2 cup Trail mix (pg. 10).

DINNER

Complex Carbohydrate
1 cup rice or pasta
OR 1 cup starchy vegetable

Protein
3 to 4 ounces cooked chicken, turkey, fish, seafood or lean roast beef
OR 1 cup cooked legumes

Simple Carbohydrate
1 cup nonstarchy vegetable
OR 1 piece fresh fruit

Healthy Munchie (optional)
raw vegetable salad with no-oil salad dressing

Added Fat (optional)
1 teaspoon butter or margarine
OR 1 teaspoon olive oil
OR 2 tablespoons sour cream
OR 1 tablespoon salad dressing

EVENING SNACK

Repeat earlier snack choices
OR 3/4 cup cereal with 1/2 cup skim milk

FREE ITEMS

raw vegetables, mustard, vinegar, lemon juice, no-oil salad dressing

WEIGHT MAINTENANCE MEAL PLAN FOR MEN

BREAKFAST

(within 1/2 hour of arising)

Complex Carbohydrate
2 slices whole wheat bread
OR 1 whole wheat English muffin
OR 1 1/2 cups cereal with raw bran added *(begin with 1 teaspoon bran, gradually increasing to 2 tablespoons)*

Protein
2 ounces part-skim cheese
OR 2 tablespoons natural peanut butter *(limit to one time per day)*
OR 1 cup skim milk for cereal
OR 2 eggs *(limit whole eggs to 2 times per week)* or 1/2 cup egg substitute

Simple Carbohydrate
1 piece fresh fruit

MORNING SNACK

Carbohydrate
5 whole grain crackers
OR 2 rice cakes or Wasa breads
AND 1 piece fresh fruit

Protein
2 ounces part-skim cheese or lean meat
OR 2 tablespoons natural peanut butter *(limit peanut butter to one time per day)*
OR 1 cup nonfat plain yogurt mixed with 1 teaspoon all-fruit spread

LUNCH

Complex Carbohydrate
2 slices whole wheat bread
OR 1 baked potato
OR 1 whole wheat pita bread

Protein
4 ounces part-skim cheese
OR 4 ounces cooked poultry, fish or lean roast beef
OR 1 cup cooked legumes

Simple Carbohydrate
1 piece fresh fruit
AND 1 cup noncreamed soup

Healthy Munchie (optional)
raw vegetable salad with no-oil salad dressing

Added Fat (optional)
1 teaspoon mayonnaise (or 1 tablespoon light mayonnaise)
OR 1 teaspoon butter or margarine
OR 1 teaspoon olive oil or canola oil
OR 1 tablespoon salad dressing

AFTERNOON SNACK

Repeat earlier snack choices
OR 1/2 cup Trail mix (pg. 10)

DINNER

Complex Carbohydrate
1 1/2 cups rice or pasta
OR 1 1/2 cups starchy vegetable

Protein
4 ounces cooked chicken, turkey, fish, seafood or lean roast beef
OR 1 cup cooked legumes

Simple Carbohydrate
1 cup nonstarchy vegetable
AND 1 piece fresh fruit

Healthy Munchie (optional)
raw vegetable salad with no-oil salad dressing

Added Fat (optional)
1 teaspoon butter or margarine
OR 1 teaspoon olive oil or canola oil
OR 2 tablespoons sour cream
OR 1 tablespoon salad dressing

EVENING SNACK

Repeat earlier snack choices
OR any power snack (pg. 10)
OR 1 cup cereal with 1 cup skim milk

FREE ITEMS

raw vegetables, mustard, vinegar, lemon juice, no-oil salad dressing

WEIGHT GAIN MEAL PLAN
(to build up, not fatten up)

UPON ARISING
12 ounces unsweetened juice (try apple, white grape OR Mott's apple-cranberry)

BREAKFAST
(within 1/2 hour of arising)

Complex Carbohydrate
4 slices of whole wheat toast OR 2 English muffins or bagels
AND 1 1/2 cups cereal with added bran

Protein
3 ounces low-fat cheese melted on toast
OR 3 egg whites OR 3/4 cup egg substitute
AND 12 ounces skim milk OR yogurt

Simple Carbohydrate
2 pieces of fresh fruit
OR 1/4 cup raisins
OR 8 apricots

MORNING SNACK
Begin with 12 ounces unsweetened juice,
AND

1) 1 cup Trail mix (pg. 10) OR
2) 1 power bar (purchased) OR
3) 2 slices bread or 1 bagel
   WITH 2 ounces cheese OR lean meat

LUNCH
Begin with 12 ounces unsweetened juice

Complex Carbohydrate
4 slices bread
OR 1 large sub roll
OR 2 wheat pitas

Protein
4 ounces skinless chicken, turkey, fish, seafood or lean meat
OR 1 1/2 cups cooked beans

Simple Carbohydrate
2 pieces of fruit

Healthy Munchie (optional)
raw vegetables as desired

AFTERNOON MINI-MEAL
Begin with 1 piece fresh fruit

Complex Carbohydrate
2 slices bread
OR 10 crackers
OR 1 bagel

Protein
2 ounces lean meat or low-fat cheese
OR 2/3 cup bean dip
OR 1 pop-top can of chicken/tuna

SECOND AFTERNOON SNACK
1 cup trail mix OR 1 power bar
OR 2 pieces fruit WITH 8 ounces yogurt or 2 ounces cheese

DINNER
Have 12 ounces juice as you begin dinner

Complex Carbohydrate
2 cups rice or pasta
OR 1 large baked potato
AND 2 rolls or 2 slices bread

Protein
3 ounces poultry, seafood, fish or lean meat
OR 1 1/2 cups cooked beans

Simple Carbohydrate
1 cup cooked nonstarchy vegetables
AND 2 pieces fruit or 1 cup cut fruit

Healthy Munchie (optional)
raw veggies (up to 2 cups) as desired with lemon juice, vinegar, no-oil dressing

Added Fat (optional)
May use 1 teaspoon olive oil or butter
OR 1 tablespoon dressing

EVENING SNACK
1 1/2 cups cereal with 1 cup skim milk
AND 1 piece fruit

FOOD DIARY

Name : ______________________ Week Beginning: ______________________

DAY	BREAKFAST	LUNCH	DINNER	COMMENTS & EXERCISE
MONDAY	Protein: Simple Carb: Complex Carb: Added Fat: Snack (Protein & Carb):	Protein: Simple Carb: Complex Carb: Added Fat: Snack (Protein & Carb):	Protein: Simple Carb: Complex Carb: Added Fat: Snack (Protein & Carb):	
TUESDAY	Protein: Simple Carb: Complex Carb: Added Fat: Snack (Protein & Carb):	Protein: Simple Carb: Complex Carb: Added Fat: Snack (Protein & Carb):	Protein: Simple Carb: Complex Carb: Added Fat: Snack (Protein & Carb):	
WEDNESDAY	Protein: Simple Carb: Complex Carb: Added Fat: Snack (Protein & Carb):	Protein: Simple Carb: Complex Carb: Added Fat: Snack (Protein & Carb):	Protein: Simple Carb: Complex Carb: Added Fat: Snack (Protein & Carb):	

DAY	BREAKFAST	LUNCH	DINNER	COMMENTS & EXERCISE
THURSDAY	Protein: Simple Carb: Complex Carb: Added Fat: Snack (Protein & Carb):	Protein: Simple Carb: Complex Carb: Added Fat: Snack (Protein & Carb):	Protein: Simple Carb: Complex Carb: Added Fat: Snack (Protein & Carb):	
FRIDAY	Protein: Simple Carb: Complex Carb: Added Fat: Snack (Protein & Carb):	Protein: Simple Carb: Complex Carb: Added Fat: Snack (Protein & Carb):	Protein: Simple Carb: Complex Carb: Added Fat: Snack (Protein & Carb):	
SATURDAY	Protein: Simple Carb: Complex Carb: Added Fat: Snack (Protein & Carb):	Protein: Simple Carb: Complex Carb: Added Fat: Snack (Protein & Carb):	Protein: Simple Carb: Complex Carb: Added Fat: Snack (Protein & Carb):	
SUNDAY	Protein: Simple Carb: Complex Carb: Added Fat: Snack (Protein & Carb):	Protein: Simple Carb: Complex Carb: Added Fat: Snack (Protein & Carb):	Protein: Simple Carb: Complex Carb: Added Fat: Snack (Protein & Carb):	

going into a retreat-type status, withdrawing totally from the physical demands of daily life. Drink lukewarm or cool water throughout the day and exercise moderately.

Some people should never fast, not even for a day: 1) women who are pregnant or breast-feeding; 2) anyone who is diabetic or hypoglycemic; 3) those with liver or kidney problems; 4) anyone who is malnourished. A better choice for these people is to sacrifice eating a particular favorite food.

- Break the fast wisely.

Don't break your fast with a huge meal or a feeding frenzy but with a small snack, then your first meal two hours later. Your metabolism has slowed down in response to no food, and it will quickly store away large amounts of food taken in after the fast. This is why any weight lost in fasting is quickly regained. Guard against "fasting" breakfast, working through lunch, then going out for a huge meal.

By following sound guidelines your fast can be a wise and meaningful one.

What About Exercise?

As you are learning, what and how you eat is vital for proper, long-lasting weight loss. But what is also important for most overweight, out-of-shape Americans is how we exercise.

Healthy eating is not an alternative to exercise but should be its companion.

Actually, you know that! Everyone seems to know that fitness is a vital part of healthful living. And most of us know that exercising does a lot more than burn calories. It helps to right the wrongs of overstressed bodies — gearing up slowed metabolisms, thereby providing help for cholesterol and weight control, improving one's muscle tone, helping to reduce blood pressure and putting the brakes on simple depression and stress. It also keeps us well. One study found that those who walked forty-five minutes a day, five days a week, were half as likely to be sick with colds or flus as those who were not exercising.

But knowing the benefits of exercise isn't enough. More people *don't* exercise than *do*.

What's the problem? It comes down to a three-letter word called "fun." For a lot of us, exercise is not fun — and it's hard to do something everyday that we don't enjoy.

To "Just Do It," as the advertisements say, and to keep on doing it, we have to find an exercise routine that matches our lifestyle, our fitness needs and our own definition of enjoyment.

Do you want to put the fun into fitness? Try these tips:

- Know yourself. The exercises you'll find most enjoyable will probably be those you can accomplish best. If you have difficulty with eye-hand coordination, you may be frustrated by a sport like tennis but would do well with walking or swimming. If you are not naturally flexible, you may be happier with bicycling than you would be with ballet.
- Consider the shape you presently are in. If you are overweight, you may stress your joints with an activity that involves pounding on your feet, such as running or aerobic dance. Try riding a stationary bike or swimming instead, at least to start. If you're over thirty-five, most exercise experts encourage you to see a health professional for an all-points check before beginning an exercise program.
- Vary your exercise. It's a lot more fun if you do a variety of exercises so you aren't bored, particularly exercises that give you fitness without trying for it, like ballroom dancing or swimming.
- Exercise with a friend. Besides having a chance to socialize, you'll be more motivated to show up and keep your commitment. Sometimes other people's enthusiasm and energy can inspire you.
- Take up a sport that allows you to get exercise while working on skills and having fun. Volleyball, racquetball, in-line skating and even badminton are activities that provide terrific fitness benefits but don't feel as

if you're exercising. Pick activities that reduce stress — not those that add to it! If risk-taking isn't your idea of fun — leave skydiving to someone else!

- Distract yourself. If your exercise of choice isn't particularly interesting, combine it with something that is — for example, doing the stairstepper while listening to books on tape, or singing to praise music while walking on the treadmill.
- Focus on how good you'll feel after you exercise! Remind yourself of the long-term benefits you're getting: better energy, better health, better stress-handling and a better, leaner body.

Three types of exercise are needed to provide the best workout and to work all the muscles of your body: warm-up, conditioning and aerobic exercise. Use warm-up exercises such as light side-to-side movements to limber muscles and to prevent injuries from other types of exercise.

Conditioning or strengthening exercises are those that tone muscles through repetitive movements. Either handheld weights or a weight machine can be used to shape and define the muscles — and even help the body to burn calories at a higher rate.

Experts agree that we get the most benefit from aerobic exercises — those that work the heart and the circulatory systems — such as walking, running, jumping rope, swimming and aerobic dancing. Aerobics work the major muscle groups, burn fat and keep your body performing efficiently. You can choose one or a combination of several, but you're most apt to stick with the ones you find the most fun.

Fitness walking works the best for me. When our schedule permits, my husband and I walk together, often in silence, just enjoying exercising and the time together. I also enjoy walking alone; it is my time to be outside, seeing and experiencing the world God has created. It is my time to "divert daily" from the demands and stresses of life.

Plan on getting some fitness in every day or at least four days a week. Within a few weeks your exercise program will be a habit, and you'll feel uncomfortable if you have to miss a day. You'll see and feel the benefits of more energy, better moods, more resiliency against stress and more restful sleep each night.

Let fitness be something you choose to do — for fun — and for life!

What Does Exercise Do for You?

- Exercise increases metabolism and decreases appetite.
- Aerobic exercise increases your protection against heart disease by improving your heart's condition (making it more efficient) and increasing your HDL (high-density lipoproteins) cholesterol, the heart-protective form of cholesterol. Any exercise that raises your pulse to a training rate or, more simply, gets you breathing hard is an aerobic exercise. The benefits occur from achieving that increased pulse rate and maintaining it for at least twenty straight minutes three times a week. It is recommended that you gradually increase your exercise time up to an hour every other day.
- Exercise breaks the plateaus or set points of weight loss. It is an external way of boosting metabolism that has been naturally lowered in the body's attempt to maintain a certain weight.
- Exercise is nature's best tranquilizer. Exercising every day is one of the best ways of releasing tension. Exercise is *the* healthy outlet for stress — certainly an acceptable alternative to eating, drinking or smoking!
- Recent studies have shown that exercise seems to be a vital factor in promoting excellent bone growth and lifelong maintenance. A well-planned exercise routine may stimulate the development of strong bone mass and later slow down any bone loss resulting from osteoporosis. Exercise increases the circulation and flow of nutrients to the bone, encouraging new bone growth and repair. Without routine exer-

cise, bones may shrink, weaken and become porous.

The best exercises to build strong bones are the weight-bearing type, such as brisk walking, jumping rope and bicycling. As bones are stressed from these activities, they become stronger and denser. Swimming, although an excellent aerobic exercise, is not as effective in strengthening bones. To prevent and reduce the effects of osteoporosis, a person should exercise at least every other day for a minimum of twenty-five to thirty minutes.

What About Feeding Athletes?

As a nutritionist working with athletes (professional as well as potential), I am often asked how best to "eat to win." The advice I give is based on the principle of getting the body operative from a point of physical strength, allowing natural gifts and learned skills to flow freely.

My goal is to get an athlete's body strong and stable. The body has a chance to work at its best, energized and ready to go for the gold, by optimal boosting of the metabolism, undergirding the blood sugars and getting (and keeping) the body well-hydrated.

Stabilizing the blood sugars and stress-rushes of adrenaline will produce better concentration and energy, even when the heat of the competition is on. More lean body tissue and proper fuel provide more strength and muscle control. Proper fluid balance keeps fatigue down, protection from energy loss up, and helps prevent injury.

For the elite athlete, fueling the power means eating the right foods at the right time in the right balance, with lots of water — the beverage of champions. To win consistently, the body has to stay properly fit and fueled. These are the tips I give:

Fuel with power meals and power snacks.

- Eat every two and a half to three hours to keep energy and concentration high and focused.
- Meals and snacks should include energy-filled carbohydrates, power-building lean proteins and brightly colored fruits and/or vegetables.
- Pre-event carbo-loading (three hours before an event): a very large serving of pasta, rice or potatoes with a serving of fish, seafood, chicken or veal, prepared without added fat.

Within twenty minutes of competition, replenish with:

- Lots of water
- Nonacid juice (apple, grape, cranberry)
- Fresh fruits

Choose foods low in fat.

- Fat slows down the metabolism.
- Fat increases stomach acids and stomach upsets.
- Fat makes you fat!

Drink plenty of cool water.

- Drink at least eight 8-ounce glasses of water every day and an additional six to eight ounces for every twenty minutes of exercise, training or competition.
- Avoid carbonated, high-sugar drinks. Water is best and more quickly absorbed, providing optimal hydration to the muscles.

Keep your iron and calcium intake high.

- At least 20 percent of Americans have severely low iron stores and may be suffering from iron deficiency anemia. Because iron carries oxygen through the body, keeping iron stores high is critical for meeting the athlete's energy demand. Balancing whole grains, lean proteins and dark green, leafy vegetables will assure a higher intake of iron.

- Calcium intake is critical for prevention of muscle cramping and, in the future, osteoporosis. Calcium is found in milk products, dark green leafy vegetables, canned salmon and legumes.

Don't be fooled by fads.

- Quick weight loss and fasting diets cause a dangerous type of weight loss, that of muscle and fluids — not fat!
- Never use sauna suits or dehydrators.
- Megadoses of nutrition supplements or drinks can make you very sick. Natural doesn't mean safe!

If you gain weight, do it the right way.

- The goal is not to "fatten up," but to build up. This is best accomplished with eating every two hours and eating a balance of carbohydrates and lean proteins (see meal plan for weight gain on pg. 184).

Be an overcomer.

- Pace yourself with your activities.
- Don't burn the candle at both ends. Get uninterrupted sleep. A body under constant demand needs to be treated well and given rest.

Choosing to eat well, day by day, meal by meal, supplies the fuel and the reserves to stay strong and resilient in the midst of stress — be it for sports or for life itself. Remember this: You don't need to learn how to diet, you need to learn how to eat! Choosing to eat the right foods at the right time empowers your body to fulfill your natural gifts. Although we cannot always control the situations of our lives, the people in our lives or how the game is played, we can control what food goes into our bodies, our energy levels and our own well-beings.

Wellness Is an Inside-Out Job

You are what you eat. This cliché is an oft-neglected but sobering thought for us — that what we are feeding our bodies affects what we are. The fuel we put in determines whether we thrive or just survive.

This realization is even more sobering when applied to our emotional and spiritual health. Are our responses to life's joys and heartaches a reflection of what is inside us?

I have found through years of counseling others that the good life is more than just eating well — and that eating well is not enough to make us well. The good life is best accomplished through caring for and feeding our souls, as well as our physical beings, with the right kind of soul food.

To care for your whole being requires a choice. It requires believing the truth about who you are and why you were created. Knowing the truth of who you are is critical to your emotional well-being. It determines how you live, what you accomplish and how you treat — and are treated by — others.

The truth is that you are not a mistake, nor have you been created by chance. You are a unique and valuable individual — deserving of being treated well.

I believe that if you don't feel valuable, taking care of yourself will seem unimportant. It will be easy to get caught in destructive patterns of eating. If you think you are junk, you will eat junk food.

Once you see yourself as valuable, you will take care of yourself. You are worth it! You deserve to live happy and healthy.

You deserve the good life.

Pamela M. Smith, R.D., L.D.N.

Pamela Smith is a nationally known nutritionist, best-selling author and culinary consultant. She has been featured on *The Today Show,* CNN news, the TV Food Network and Focus on the Family. Her radio feature, "Tips for Living Well," may be heard daily across the nation.

Pamela is the founder of Nutritional Counseling Services in Orlando, Florida, one of the original private practices of dietetics in America. She is the nutritionist for NBA basketball teams as well as individual players, among whom is superstar Shaquille O'Neal. Pamela has also served as the nutrition consultant to industry giants such as Walt Disney World, Hyatt Hotels and Resorts, and Darden Restaurants.

Pamela counsels her clients on an interactive basis, helping them to identify and alter eating and behavioral habits for disease prevention, peak performance in sports, child and family nutrition, weight loss, dining-out strategies and, very importantly, stress and emotional wellness.

Pamela's books include *Eat Well – Live Well,* a best-selling nutrition guide and cookbook; *Alive and Well in the Fast Lane,* a lighthearted book with the ten commandments of healthy eating; *Perfectly Pregnant,* a nutrition book for the expectant mother; *Come Cook With Me,* an extraordinary children's cookbook; *Food for Life,* an in-depth look at the physical, emotional and spiritual aspects of food dependencies in America; and *The Food Trap*, which explores our relationship with food.

Pamela received her degree in nutrition from Florida State University and completed her ADA internship at Miami-Valley Hospital in Dayton, Ohio. She has completed continuing education at the Cooper Clinic in Dallas, Texas, as well as Harvard Medical School. Pamela has also been the nutrition instructor at the University of Central Florida Department of Nursing.

Pamela received the Recognized Young Dietitian award for the state of Florida as well as the Award for Excellence in medical journalism by the Florida AMA. She has done radio and TV talk and news shows since 1980 and is in demand for corporate management programs, seminars, conventions and corporate wellness programs.

Metric Conversion

METRIC SYMBOLS

Celsius: C	gram: g
liter: L	centimeter: cm
milliliter: mL	millimeter: mm
kilogram: kg	

COMMON CAN/PACKAGE SIZES

VOLUME		MASS	
4 oz.	114 mL	4 oz.	113 g
10 oz.	284 mL	5 oz.	142 g
14 oz.	398 mL	6 oz.	170 g
10 oz.	540 mL	7 3/4 oz.	220 g
28 oz.	796 mL	15 oz.	425 g

OVEN TEMPERATURE CONVERSIONS

IMPERIAL	METRIC
250°F	120°C
275°F	140°C
300°F	150°C
325°F	160°C
350°F	180°C
375°F	190°C
400°F	200°C
425°F	220°C
450°F	230°C
500°F	260°C

LENGTH

IMPERIAL	METRIC
1/4 inch	5 mm
1/3 inch	8 mm
1/2 inch	1 cm
3/4 inch	2 cm
1 inch	2.5 cm
2 inches	5 cm
4 inches	10 cm

VOLUME

IMPERIAL	METRIC
1/4 tsp.	1 mL
1/2 tsp.	2 mL
3/4 tsp.	4 mL
1 tsp.	5 mL
2 tsp.	10 mL
1 Tbsp.	15 mL
2 Tbsp.	25 mL
1/4 cup	50 mL
1/3 cup	75 mL
1/2 cup	125 mL
2/3 cup	150 mL
3/4 cup	175 mL
1 cup	250 mL
4 cups	1 L
5 cups	1.25 L

MASS (WEIGHT)

IMPERIAL	METRIC
1 oz.	25 g
2 oz.	50 g
1/4 lb.	125 g
1/2 lb. (8 oz.)	250 g
1 lb.	500 g
2 lb.	1 kg
3 lb.	1.5 kg
5 lb.	2.2 kg
8 lb.	3.5 kg
10 lb.	4.5 kg
11 lb.	5 kg

This chart was developed by the Canadian Home Economics Association and the American Home Economics Committee. These guidelines were developed to simplify the conversion from Imperial measures to metric. The numbers have been rounded for convenience. When cooking from a recipe, work in the same system throughout the recipe; do not use a combination of the two.

List of Charts and Tables

RECIPE INDEX

D

E

F

G

Q

R

S

T

V

W

Y

Z

SUBJECT INDEX

OTHER BOOKS AND TAPES BY PAMELA M. SMITH

EAT WELL — LIVE WELL

The nutrition guide and cookbook for healthy, productive people. This large, hardback edition presents "The Ten Commandments of Good Nutrition" in detail, cooking tips, menu planning, grocery shopping, a dining-out guide and a large cookbook section of innovative recipes that can be prepared in a time-saving manner. Meal plans are also included.

FOOD FOR LIFE

This is a beautiful, hardback book on how to: choose the best foods, eat for physical stamina and energy, deal with stress, and nourish your body physically, emotionally and spiritually. The seven Body Secrets for staying fit, fueled and free are presented along with exercise tips and perspectives for exploring our behavior patterns. Meal plans and recipes are included.

ALIVE AND WELL IN THE FAST LANE

A lighthearted and informative nutritional guide book for the whole family. This book presents "The Ten Commandments of Good Nutrition" in a fun, handwritten and illustrated format. Includes menus for perfect breakfasts, lunches and dinners for the busy family. Meal plans are also included.

PERFECTLY PREGNANT

This expectant mother's handbook contains the latest information to nourish mother and baby properly. Included is a wonderful, proven solution for morning sickness. Handwritten and tasty recipes, too. Meal plans are included.

COME COOK WITH ME

This is the kid's cookbook! It's a wonderful way to teach children nutrition by teaching them how to cook. Great for picky eaters. Includes kid-proven recipes, how to set a table and some great manners. Featured nationally on cable and network television. Handwritten and fun.

THE FOOD TRAP

This book explores our relationship with food. Pamela Smith asks, "Is the refrigerator light the light of your life?" Informative and enlightening, this book reveals case studies and personal insights into the physical, emotional and spiritual aspects of food dependencies. Learn how to break free in all areas.

THE FOOD TRAP SEMINAR

This is an audio tape album. Hear Pamela Smith present a live seminar covering the physical, emotional and spiritual needs that we have, and how to properly meet and nourish those needs. A nutritional strategy for dealing with stress is also presented. Very practical and informative.

AUDIO TAPES

These are available on a variety of topics related to nutrition and health.

FOR MORE INFORMATION

To find out more about books, tapes
and seminars, please write or call:

PAMELA M. SMITH, R.D.
P.O. Box 541009
Orlando, FL 32854
1-800-896-4010 (orders)
(407) 896-1179 (information)

or

CREATION HOUSE
600 Rinehart Road
Lake Mary, FL 32746
1-800-283-8494
Fax (407) 333-7100

SPECIAL FREE OFFER FROM PAM SMITH

Thank you for reading — and using — this book. I would like to give you something to help you live the good life every day. Please check below if you would like to receive these items. Then send a copy of this coupon to the address below.

❏ Please send me a free pad with 25 copies of Pam Smith's Good Life Grocery List. I have enclosed U.S. $2 to cover postage and handling (Canada, enclose U.S. $3.50).

❏ Please send me a Recipe for Soul Food — Pam's perspective on spiritual wellness.

Name ____

Address _______________________________________

City ______________ State ________ Zip ______________

Send a copy of this coupon and a check to:

Pamela M. Smith, R.D. — P.O. Box 541009 — Orlando, FL 32854

RECIPE NOTES

RECIPE NOTES

RECIPE NOTES